The Books Of Magic

JOHN NEY RIEBER
WRITER

GARY AMARO
PENCILS
PAGES 10–37, 39–62, 64–87,
90–94, 101–103, 108–111

**SHERILYN VAN
VALKENBURGH**
COLORS

JOHN COSTANZA
LETTERS

INTRODUCTION

TIMOTHY HUNTER AND THE BOOKS OF MAGIC CREATED BY NEIL GAIMAN AND JOHN BOLTON

PETER GROSS
PENCILS
PAGES 89, 95–100, 104–107

PETER GROSS
INKS

INGS

CHARLES VESS
COVERS

NEIL GAIMAN
CONSULTANT

BY JANE YOLEN

DEATH CREATED BY NEIL GAIMAN AND MIKE DRINGENBERG

THE BOOKS OF MAGIC: BINDINGS

Published by DC Comics. Cover and
compilation copyright © 1995 DC Comics.
All Rights Reserved.

Originally published in single magazine
form as THE BOOKS OF MAGIC 1-4.
Copyright © 1994 DC Comics.
All Rights Reserved.

DC Comics, 1700 Broadway,
New York, NY 10019
A division of Warner Bros. -
A Time Warner Entertainment Company

Printed in Canada. Third Printing.

ISBN: 1-56389-187-5

Cover illustration by Charles Vess

Publication design by
Richard Bruning

Introduction

BY JANE YOLEN

*T*he world's glue is story.

Picture this: The skald, whose grandfather was a berserker and a werewolf, sits by the side of his chief. The skald is a big man, big as a troll, and as ugly, with wolf-grey hair. His teeth are sharp. He is halfway through a story that has taken all night and into the rind of the day. No one moves, except to drink a cup of mead. To move is to miss a part of the tale.

Picture this: A Goddess emerges from a thatched dressing room, a mask of flowers and fresh leaves over her face. Her skirt is made of palm leaves and her entrance is lit by coconut oil torches. She is called Bhagavati and she tells her story as if in a trance until dawn. No one moves, except the musicians with their horns and drums. To move is to miss a part of the tale.

Picture this: Prayers are over and the men gather on the porch while the rabbi tells stories into the gathering dark. Cross-legged on a bench, the bearded old man speaks, his voice never rising above a hoarse whisper. No one moves except to sip a glass of tea, except to take a long, slow pull on a cigarette. To move is to miss one of the tales.

The world's glue is story.

The story's adhesive is magic. The skald tells stories about dwarves and trolls. Bhagavati tells stories about demons and monkey kings. The rabbi tells of angels and dybbuks.

Everyone believes them.

Picture this: A fifty-five-year-old writer sits in her musician-son's living room. His fiancée, an Alzheimer's nurse, is lying on the couch. She is recovering from a neck injury. One of her patients had attacked her. They are passing around comic books scripted by Neil Gaiman, the first of the BOOKS OF MAGIC. No one moves except to reach for another comic. To get up, to stretch, to go to the kitchen for a drink or to the bathroom for some pain medication, is to miss the next installment of the story.

Story does that to us.

Storytellers do that to us.

Like the skald, the goddess, the rabbi; like the shanaachies and griots; like the troubadours, meistersingers, bards; like all the storytellers before them, the makers of the BOOKS OF MAGIC glue us to our seats.

In this new series of four books, called BINDINGS and comprising "Tearing Down," "Lost Causes," "A Book of Leaves," and "Closing Circles," the writer and artists have mixed their metaphors magically. (Say that nine times fast.) Tamlin and Titania come from two linked fairy traditions, balladry and folk tale. Tamlin's mentor, Merlin, (say that seven times fast), arises from the Arthurian mythos. The unicorn and manticore travel from a fourth and fifth mythic dimension. The unicorn reaches us from the Greeks, by way of the Continent's millefleur tapestries, to dwell ever after in the Scottish kingdom as its emblem. The manticore is a nasty Persian invention, with threefold row of teeth. Its name in Persian means – literally – "Man eater" and it savors human flesh. The Bestiaries say it is so powerful a leaper, neither the "most extensive space nor the most lofty obstacle" can contain it.

And Death?

Like her horrible sister Taxes – whom no one ever mentions in magic books – she has been with us for always.

Now this new mix of magics, this run of four comics scripted by John Ney Rieber from Neil Gaiman's brilliant concept, is a hearty stew, a potpourri. It has not been thrown together without thought. We are not talking Dungeons-and-You-Knows(TM) here. This is a well-planned meal, seasoned and simmered.

What I mean is: BOOKS OF MAGIC is about something. It is a by-gosh story with a beginning, a middle and an end. (Though the end always leaves us with some tantalizing piece...in this case, of paper...to make us want more.) This is a classic tale of a boy's search for himself. It is a Quest, as Death tells Tim in an aside. In fact, a lot of what the story is really about – like all good stories — comes in asides or besides or to the side of the tale. If you blink, if you skim, if you do not listen carefully, if you move...

you will miss it.

So sit still.

Read.

Then read again.

The magic will touch you.

Touch magic, as some wiseacre once said, then pass it on. But as the world's glue is story, some of it is bound to stick to you.

—Jane Yolen

Jane Yolen is known as the Hans Christian Andersen of America because of her many original fairie tales. She has published over 150 award-winning books for children, young adults and adults and is a past president of the Science Fiction and Fantasy Writers of America (SFWA). Some of her most recent books are **Here There Be Unicorns**, **Briar Rose**, **The Girl in the Golden Bower** and, coming in the spring of 1995, **The Wild Hunt**.

BINDINGS

Book One

Tearing Down

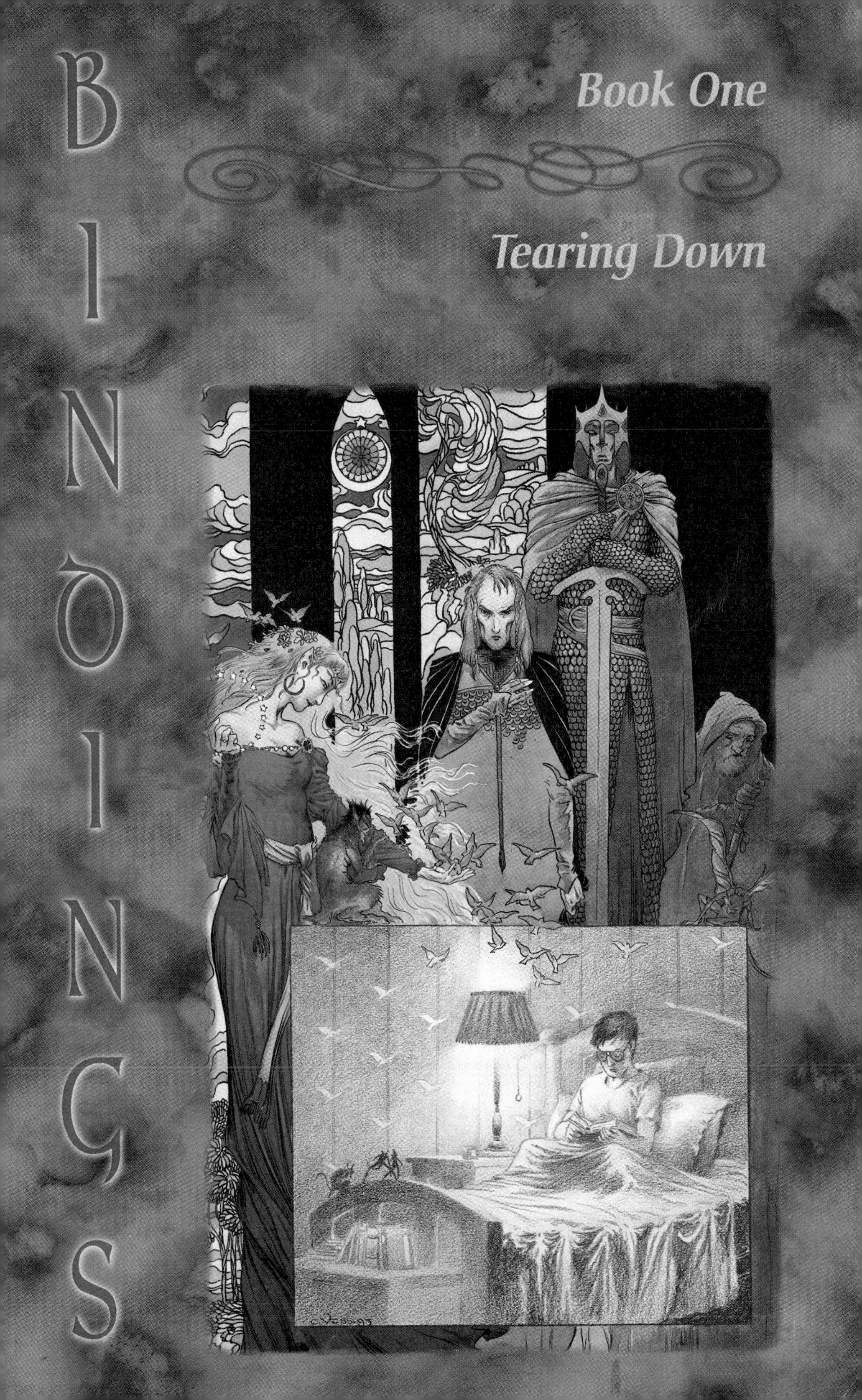

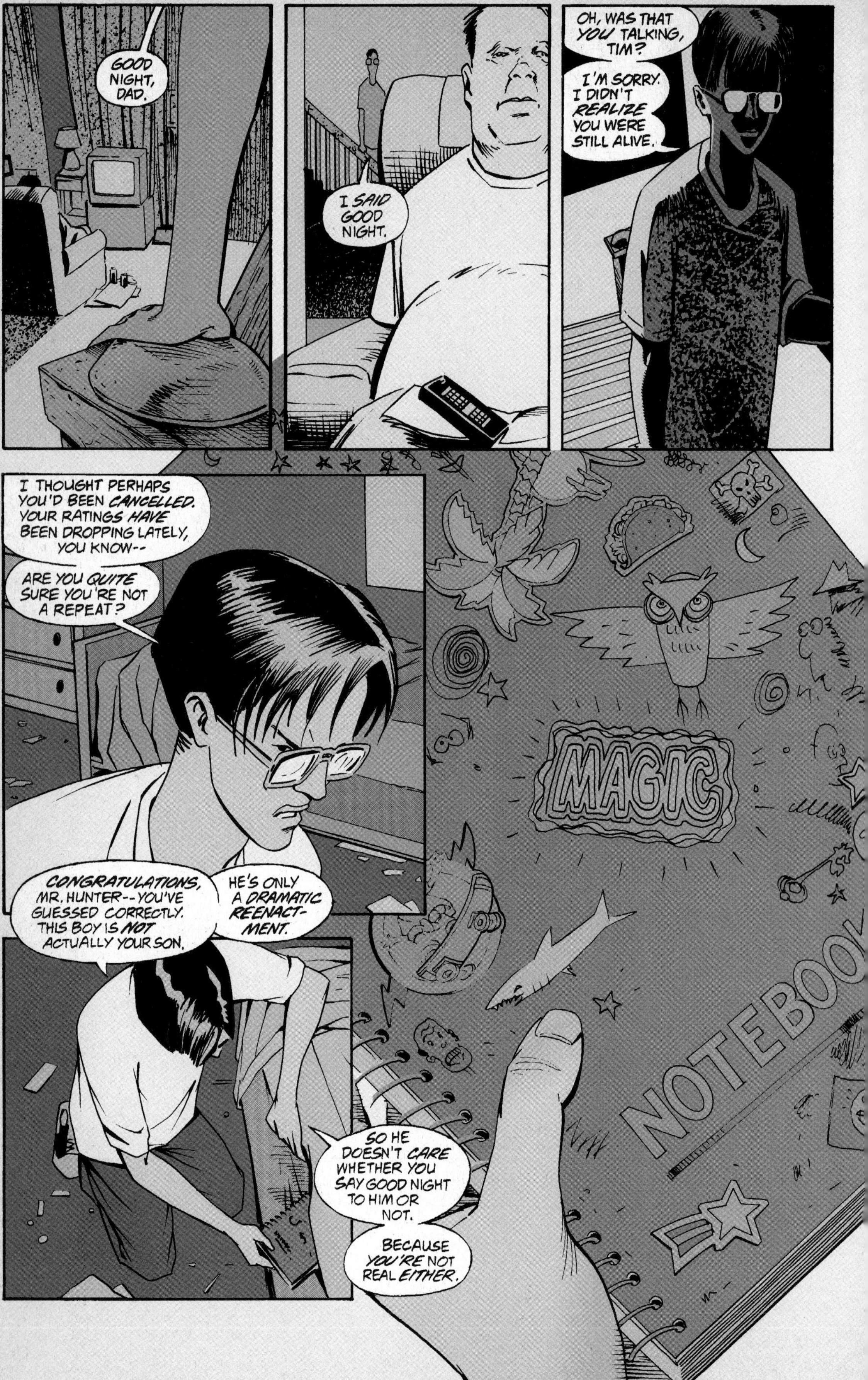
GOOD NIGHT, DAD.
I SAID GOOD NIGHT.
OH, WAS THAT YOU TALKING, TIM?
I'M SORRY. I DIDN'T REALIZE YOU WERE STILL ALIVE.
I THOUGHT PERHAPS YOU'D BEEN CANCELLED. YOUR RATINGS HAVE BEEN DROPPING LATELY, YOU KNOW--
ARE YOU QUITE SURE YOU'RE NOT A REPEAT?
MAGIC
CONGRATULATIONS, MR. HUNTER--YOU'VE GUESSED CORRECTLY. THIS BOY IS NOT ACTUALLY YOUR SON.
HE'S ONLY A DRAMATIC REENACT-MENT.
NOTEBOOK
SO HE DOESN'T CARE WHETHER YOU SAY GOOD NIGHT TO HIM OR NOT.
BECAUSE YOU'RE NOT REAL EITHER.

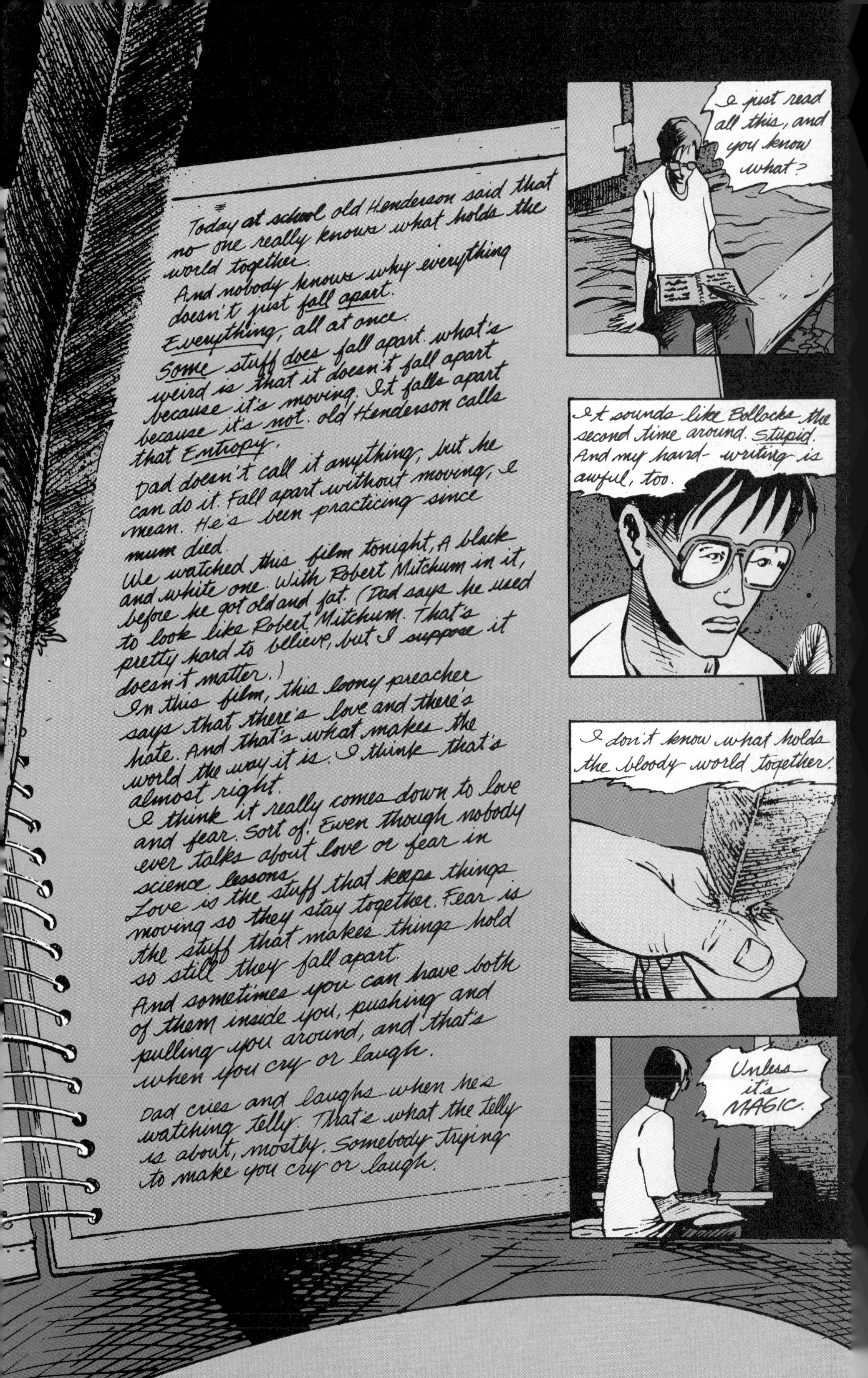
Today at school old Henderson said that
no one really knows what holds the
world together.
And nobody knows why everything
doesn't just fall apart.
Everything, all at once.
Some stuff does fall apart. what's
weird is that it doesn't fall apart
because it's moving. It falls apart
because it's not. old Henderson calls
that Entropy.
Dad doesn't call it anything, but he
can do it. Fall apart without moving, I
mean. He's been practicing since
mum died.
We watched this film tonight, A black
and white one. With Robert Mitchum in it,
before he got old and fat. (Dad says he used
to look like Robert Mitchum. That's
pretty hard to believe, but I suppose it
doesn't matter.)
In this film, this loony preacher
says that there's love and there's
hate. And that's what makes the
world the way it is. I think that's
almost right.
I think it really comes down to love
and fear. Sort of. Even though nobody
ever talks about love or fear in
science lessons.
Love is the stuff that keeps things
moving so they stay together. Fear is
the stuff that makes things hold
so still they fall apart.
And sometimes you can have both
of them inside you, pushing and
pulling you around, and that's
when you cry or laugh.
Dad cries and laughs when he's
watching telly. That's what the telly
is about, mostly. Somebody trying
to make you cry or laugh.
I just read all this, and you know what?
It sounds like Bollocks the second time around. Stupid. And my hand-writing is awful, too.
I don't know what holds the bloody world together.
Unless it's MAGIC.

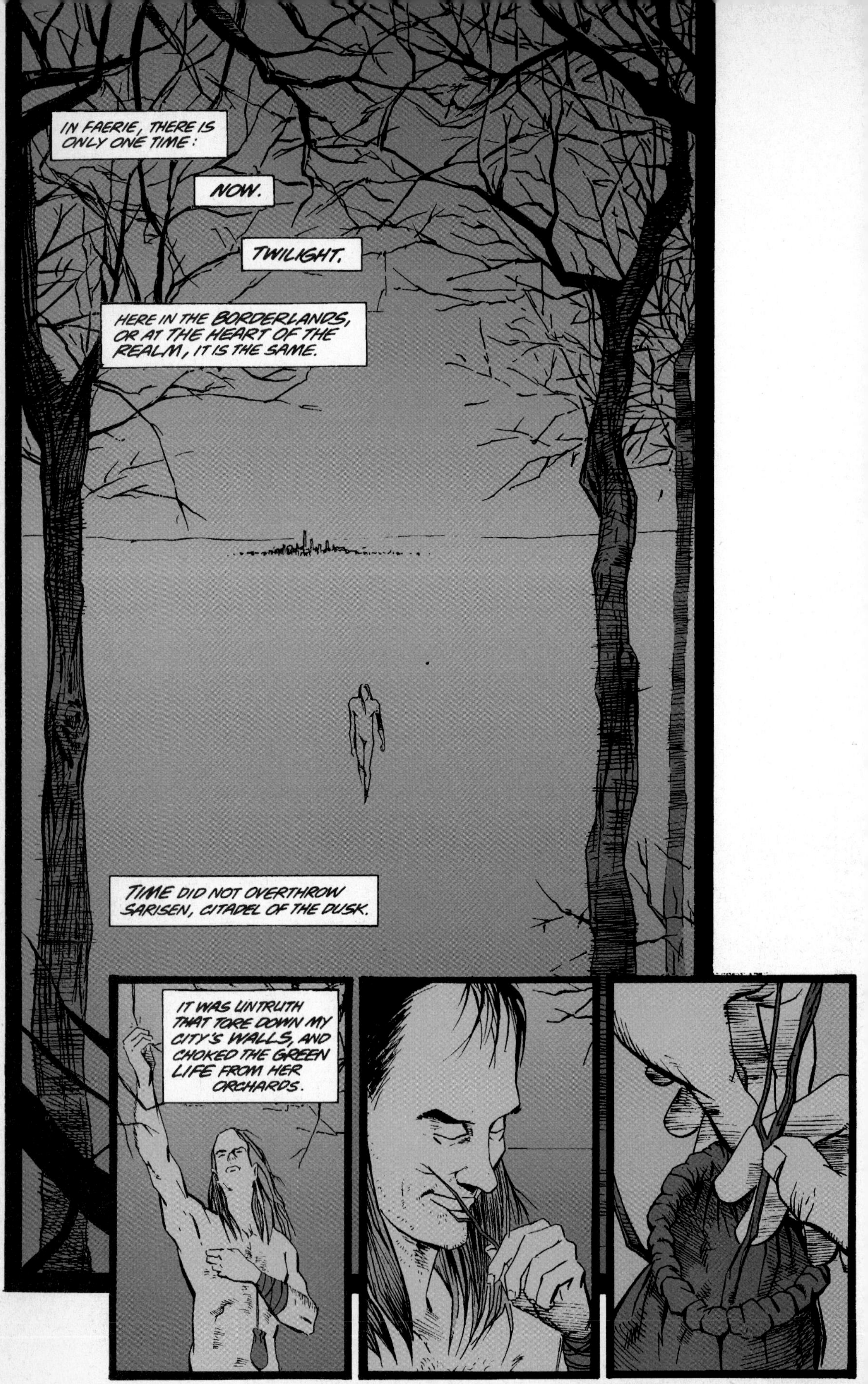
IN FAERIE, THERE IS ONLY ONE TIME:
NOW.
TWILIGHT.
HERE IN THE BORDERLANDS, OR AT THE HEART OF THE REALM, IT IS THE SAME.
TIME DID NOT OVERTHROW SARISEN, CITADEL OF THE DUSK.
IT WAS UNTRUTH THAT TORE DOWN MY CITY'S WALLS, AND CHOKED THE GREEN LIFE FROM HER ORCHARDS.

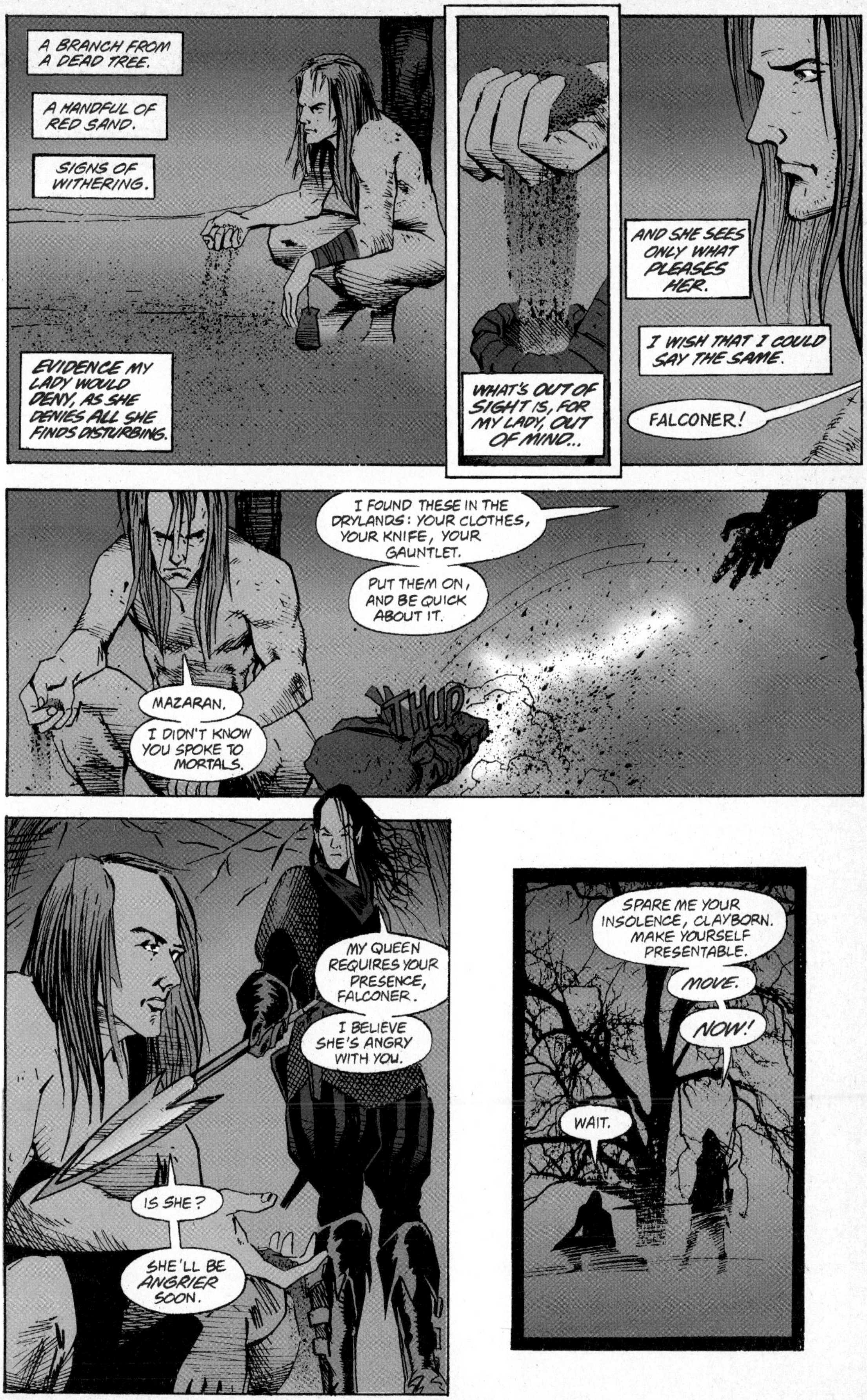
A BRANCH FROM A DEAD TREE.
A HANDFUL OF RED SAND.
SIGNS OF WITHERING.
EVIDENCE MY LADY WOULD DENY, AS SHE DENIES ALL SHE FINDS DISTURBING.
WHAT'S OUT OF SIGHT IS, FOR MY LADY, OUT OF MIND...
AND SHE SEES ONLY WHAT PLEASES HER.
I WISH THAT I COULD SAY THE SAME.
FALCONER!
I FOUND THESE IN THE DRYLANDS: YOUR CLOTHES, YOUR KNIFE, YOUR GAUNTLET.
PUT THEM ON, AND BE QUICK ABOUT IT.
THUD
MAZARAN.
I DIDN'T KNOW YOU SPOKE TO MORTALS.
MY QUEEN REQUIRES YOUR PRESENCE, FALCONER.
I BELIEVE SHE'S ANGRY WITH YOU.
IS SHE?
SHE'LL BE ANGRIER SOON.
SPARE ME YOUR INSOLENCE, CLAYBORN. MAKE YOURSELF PRESENTABLE.
MOVE.
NOW!
WAIT.

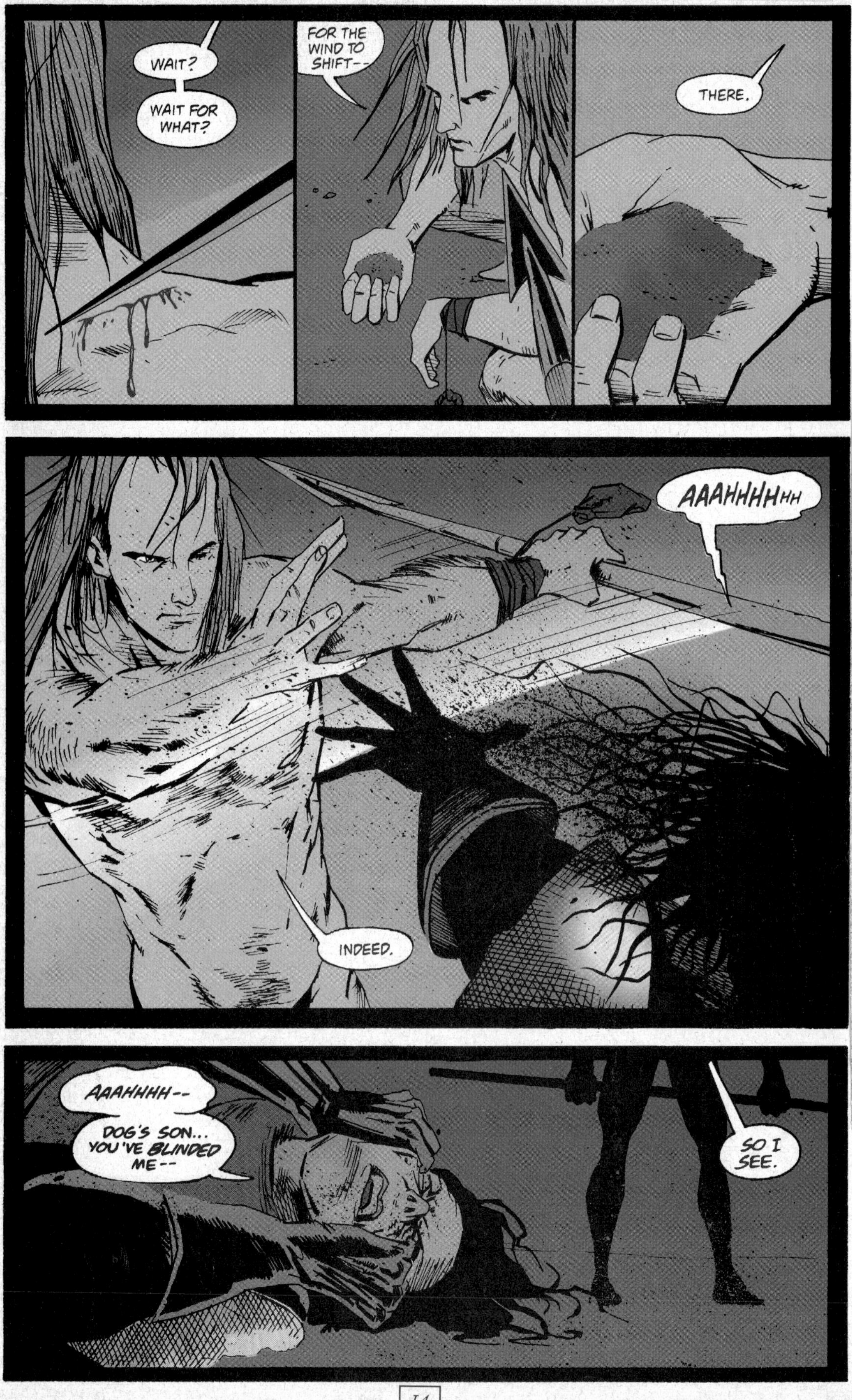
WAIT?
WAIT FOR WHAT?
FOR THE WIND TO SHIFT--
THERE.
AAAHHHHHH
INDEED.
AAAHHHH--
DOG'S SON... YOU'VE BLINDED ME--
SO I SEE.

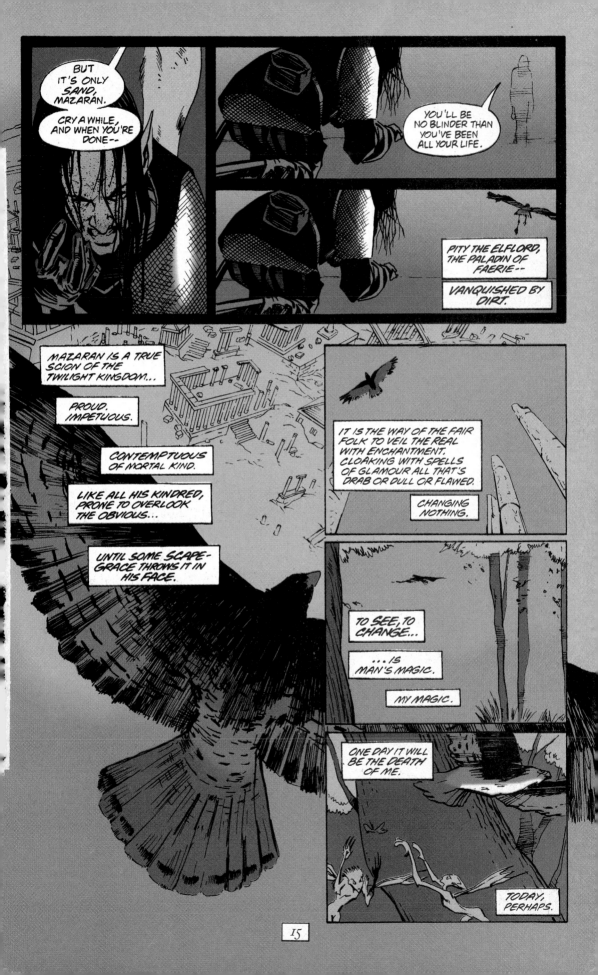

BUT IT'S ONLY SAND, MAZARAN.

CRY A WHILE, AND WHEN YOU'RE DONE--

YOU'LL BE NO BLINDER THAN YOU'VE BEEN ALL YOUR LIFE.

PITY THE ELFLORD, THE PALADIN OF FAERIE--

VANQUISHED BY DIRT.

MAZARAN IS A TRUE SCION OF THE TWILIGHT KINGDOM...

PROUD. IMPETUOUS.

CONTEMPTUOUS OF MORTAL KIND.

LIKE ALL HIS KINDRED, PRONE TO OVERLOOK THE OBVIOUS...

UNTIL SOME SCAPE-GRACE THROWS IT IN HIS FACE.

IT IS THE WAY OF THE FAIR FOLK TO VEIL THE REAL WITH ENCHANTMENT. CLOAKING WITH SPELLS OF GLAMOUR ALL THAT'S DRAB OR DULL OR FLAWED.

CHANGING NOTHING.

TO SEE, TO CHANGE...

...IS MAN'S MAGIC.

MY MAGIC.

ONE DAY IT WILL BE THE DEATH OF ME.

TODAY, PERHAPS.

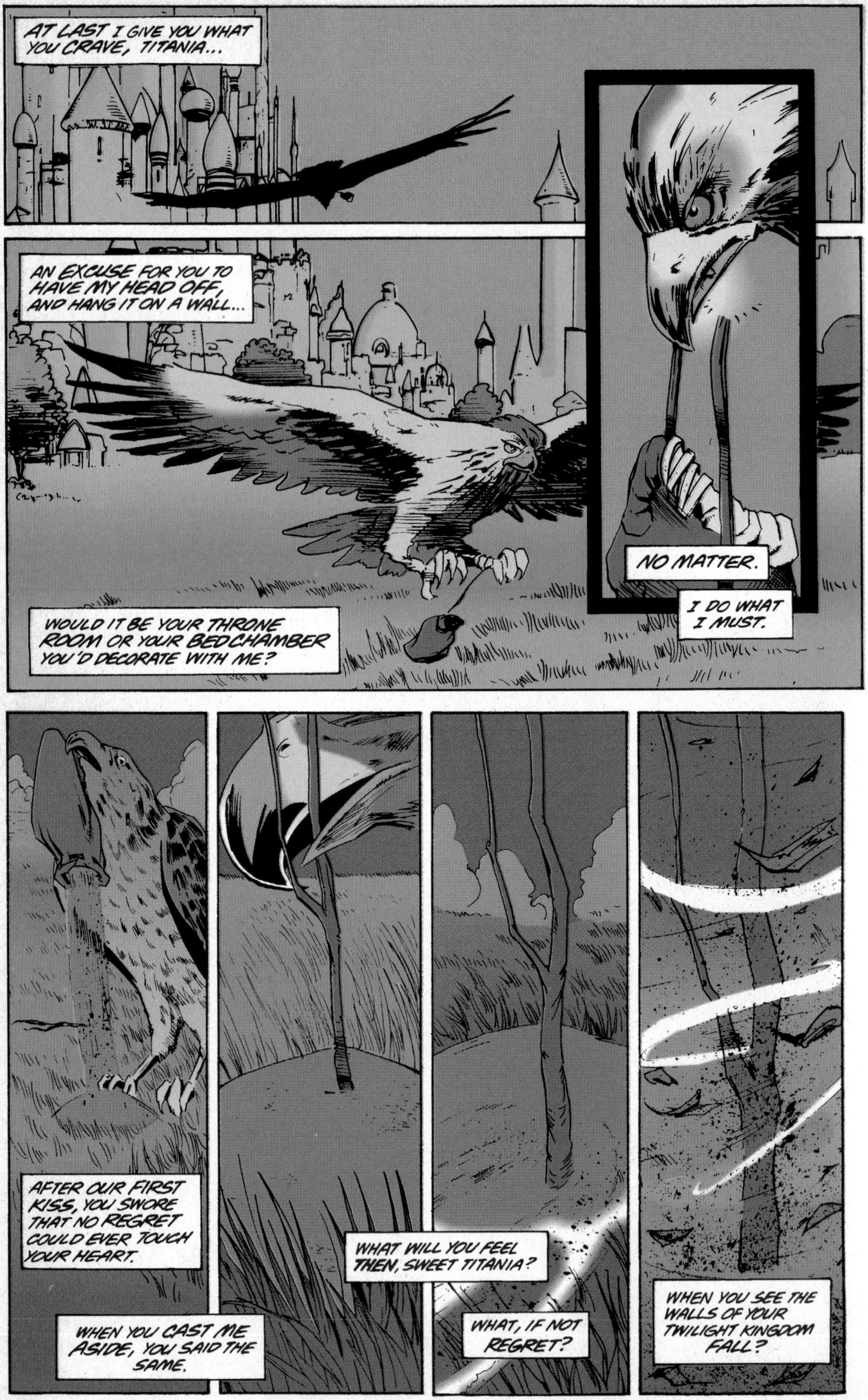
AT LAST I GIVE YOU WHAT YOU CRAVE, TITANIA...
AN EXCUSE FOR YOU TO HAVE MY HEAD OFF, AND HANG IT ON A WALL...
WOULD IT BE YOUR THRONE ROOM OR YOUR BEDCHAMBER YOU'D DECORATE WITH ME?
NO MATTER.
I DO WHAT I MUST.
AFTER OUR FIRST KISS, YOU SWORE THAT NO REGRET COULD EVER TOUCH YOUR HEART.
WHEN YOU CAST ME ASIDE, YOU SAID THE SAME.
WHAT WILL YOU FEEL THEN, SWEET TITANIA?
WHAT, IF NOT REGRET?
WHEN YOU SEE THE WALLS OF YOUR TWILIGHT KINGDOM FALL?

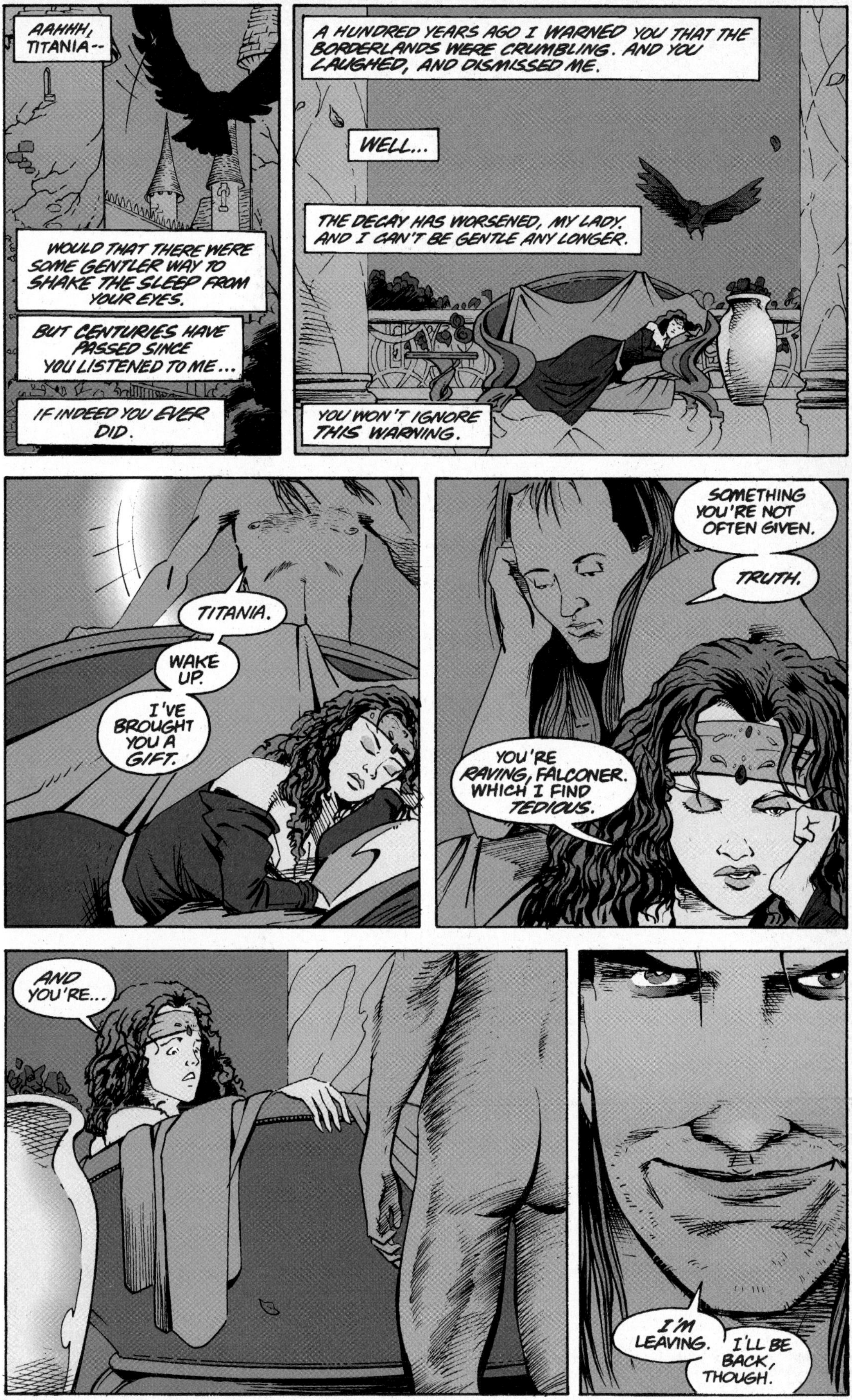
AAHHH, TITANIA--
WOULD THAT THERE WERE SOME GENTLER WAY TO SHAKE THE SLEEP FROM YOUR EYES.
BUT CENTURIES HAVE PASSED SINCE YOU LISTENED TO ME...
IF INDEED YOU EVER DID.
A HUNDRED YEARS AGO I WARNED YOU THAT THE BORDERLANDS WERE CRUMBLING. AND YOU LAUGHED, AND DISMISSED ME.
WELL...
THE DECAY HAS WORSENED, MY LADY. AND I CAN'T BE GENTLE ANY LONGER.
YOU WON'T IGNORE THIS WARNING.
TITANIA.
WAKE UP.
I'VE BROUGHT YOU A GIFT.
SOMETHING YOU'RE NOT OFTEN GIVEN.
TRUTH.
YOU'RE RAVING, FALCONER. WHICH I FIND TEDIOUS.
AND YOU'RE...
I'M LEAVING.
I'LL BE BACK, THOUGH.

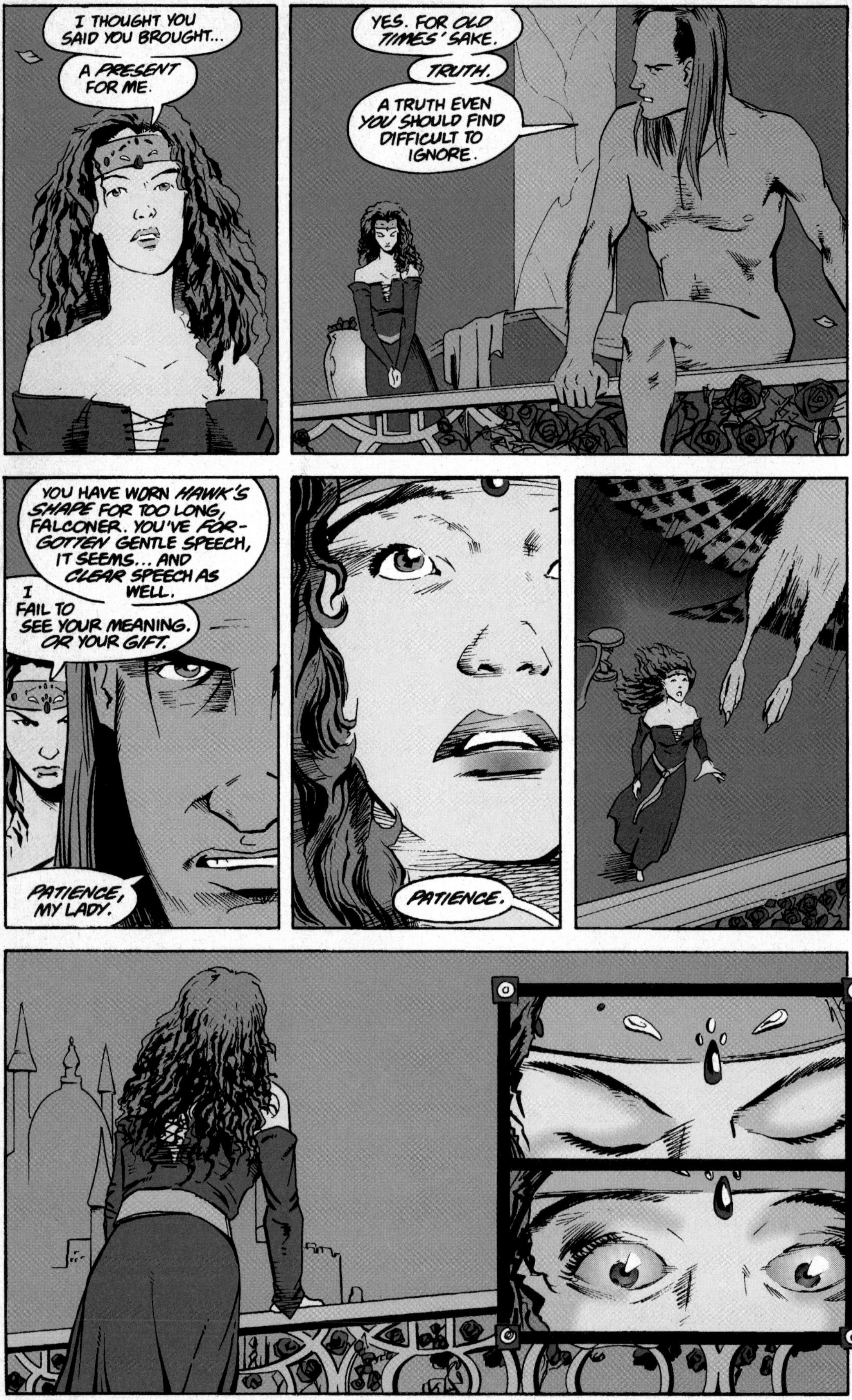

I THOUGHT YOU SAID YOU BROUGHT...
A PRESENT FOR ME.
YES. FOR OLD TIMES' SAKE.
TRUTH.
A TRUTH EVEN YOU SHOULD FIND DIFFICULT TO IGNORE.
YOU HAVE WORN HAWK'S SHAPE FOR TOO LONG, FALCONER. YOU'VE FORGOTTEN GENTLE SPEECH, IT SEEMS... AND CLEAR SPEECH AS WELL.
I FAIL TO SEE YOUR MEANING. OR YOUR GIFT.
PATIENCE, MY LADY.
PATIENCE.

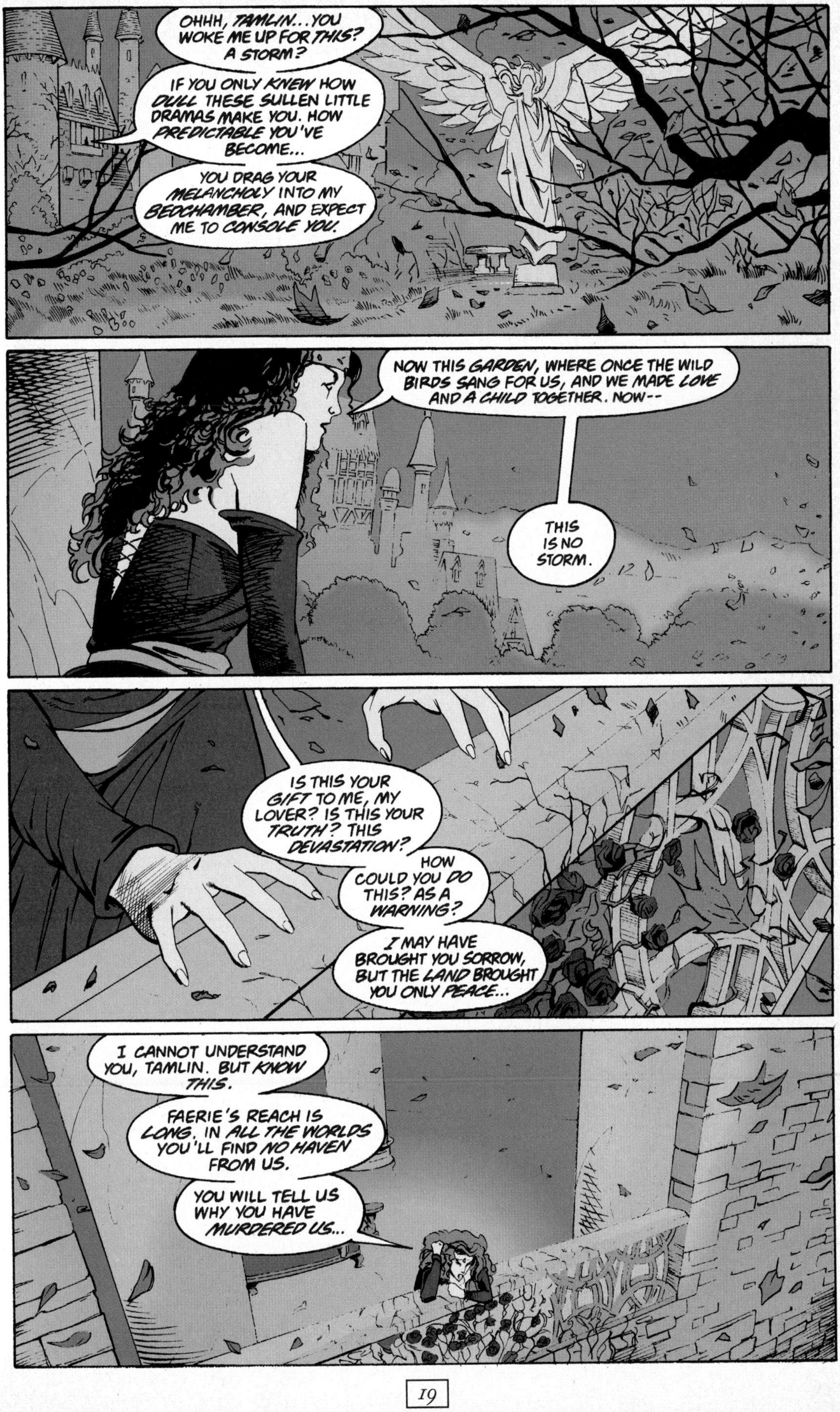
OHHH, TAMLIN...YOU WOKE ME UP FOR THIS? A STORM?
IF YOU ONLY KNEW HOW DULL THESE SULLEN LITTLE DRAMAS MAKE YOU. HOW PREDICTABLE YOU'VE BECOME...
YOU DRAG YOUR MELANCHOLY INTO MY BEDCHAMBER, AND EXPECT ME TO CONSOLE YOU.
NOW THIS GARDEN, WHERE ONCE THE WILD BIRDS SANG FOR US, AND WE MADE LOVE AND A CHILD TOGETHER. NOW--
THIS IS NO STORM.
IS THIS YOUR GIFT TO ME, MY LOVER? IS THIS YOUR TRUTH? THIS DEVASTATION?
HOW COULD YOU DO THIS? AS A WARNING?
I MAY HAVE BROUGHT YOU SORROW, BUT THE LAND BROUGHT YOU ONLY PEACE...
I CANNOT UNDERSTAND YOU, TAMLIN. BUT KNOW THIS.
FAERIE'S REACH IS LONG. IN ALL THE WORLDS YOU'LL FIND NO HAVEN FROM US.
YOU WILL TELL US WHY YOU HAVE MURDERED US...

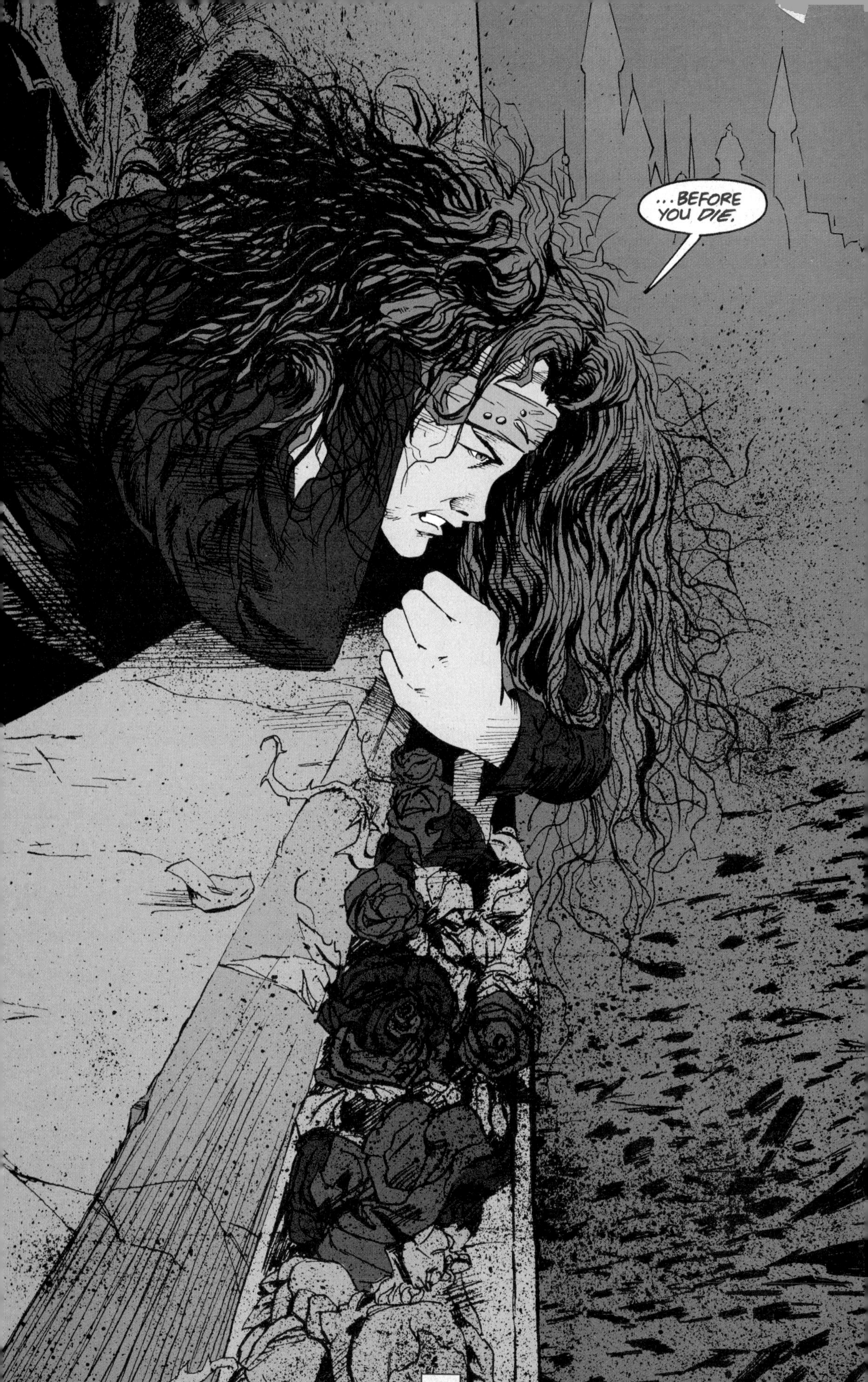
...BEFORE YOU DIE.

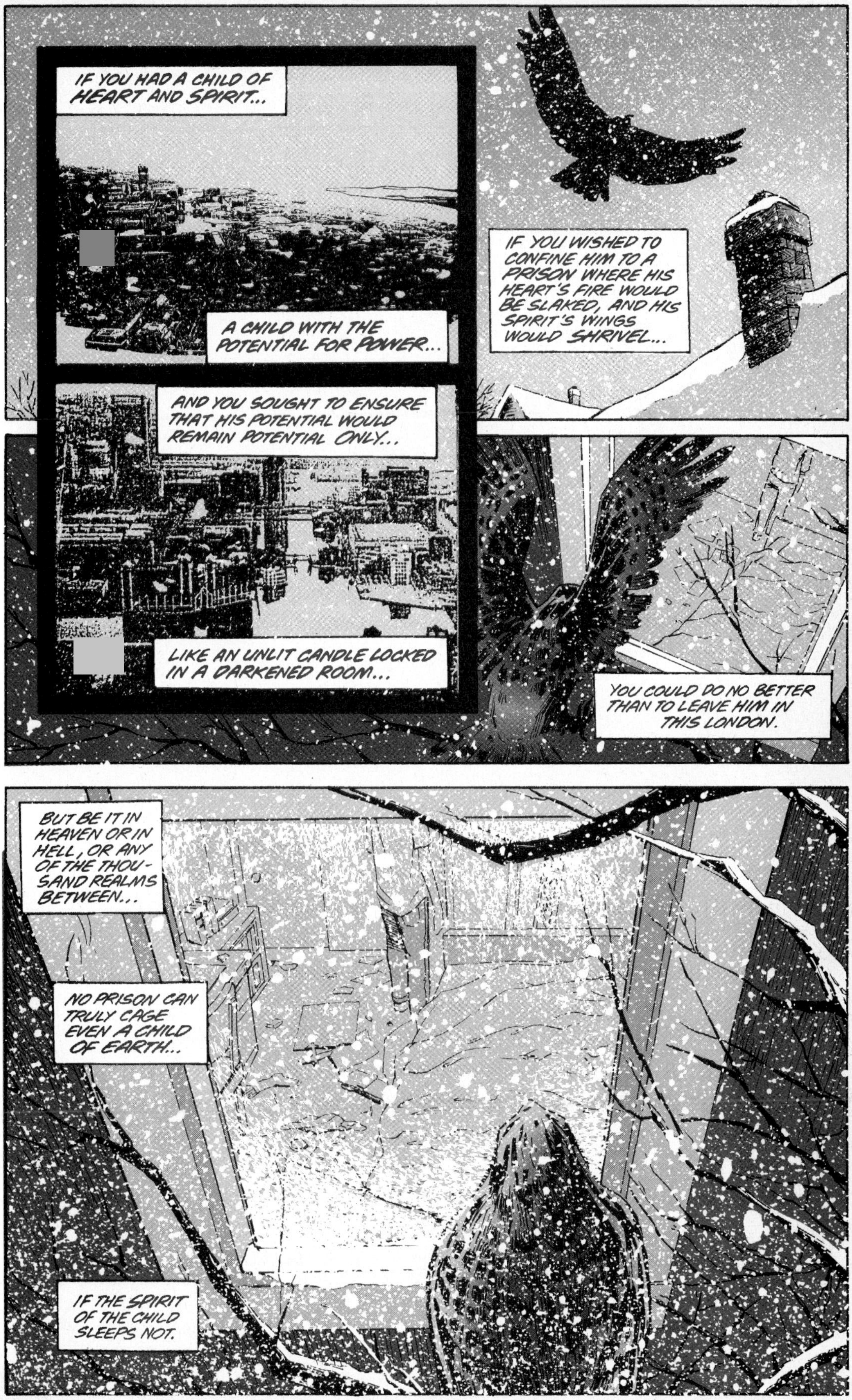
IF YOU HAD A CHILD OF HEART AND SPIRIT...
A CHILD WITH THE POTENTIAL FOR POWER...
IF YOU WISHED TO CONFINE HIM TO A PRISON WHERE HIS HEART'S FIRE WOULD BE SLAKED, AND HIS SPIRIT'S WINGS WOULD SHRIVEL...
AND YOU SOUGHT TO ENSURE THAT HIS POTENTIAL WOULD REMAIN POTENTIAL ONLY...
LIKE AN UNLIT CANDLE LOCKED IN A DARKENED ROOM...
YOU COULD DO NO BETTER THAN TO LEAVE HIM IN THIS LONDON.
BUT BE IT IN HEAVEN OR IN HELL, OR ANY OF THE THOUSAND REALMS BETWEEN...
NO PRISON CAN TRULY CAGE EVEN A CHILD OF EARTH...
IF THE SPIRIT OF THE CHILD SLEEPS NOT.

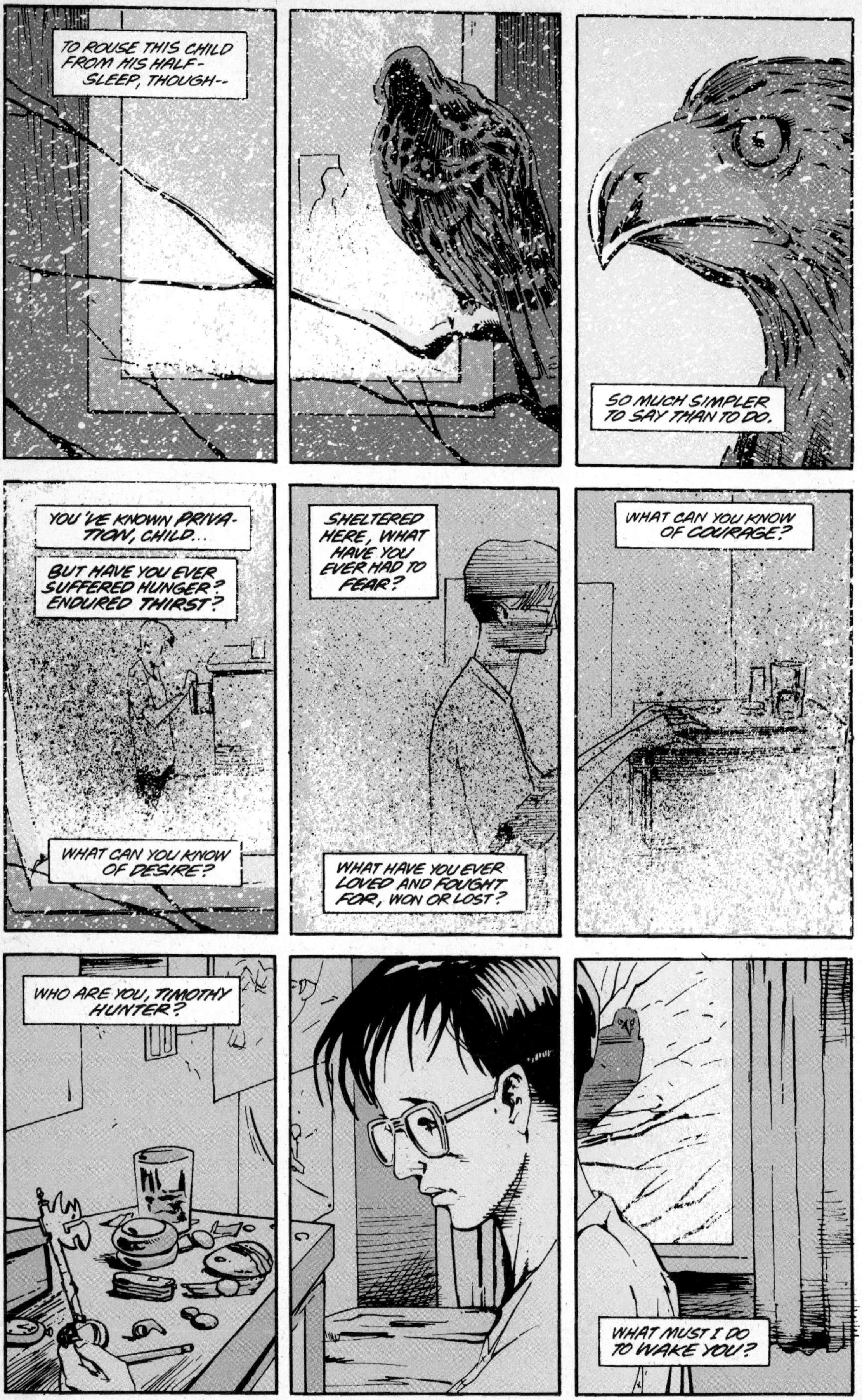
TO ROUSE THIS CHILD FROM HIS HALF-SLEEP, THOUGH--
SO MUCH SIMPLER TO SAY THAN TO DO.
YOU'VE KNOWN PRIVATION, CHILD...
BUT HAVE YOU EVER SUFFERED HUNGER? ENDURED THIRST?
WHAT CAN YOU KNOW OF DESIRE?
SHELTERED HERE, WHAT HAVE YOU EVER HAD TO FEAR?
WHAT HAVE YOU EVER LOVED AND FOUGHT FOR, WON OR LOST?
WHAT CAN YOU KNOW OF COURAGE?
WHO ARE YOU, TIMOTHY HUNTER?
WHAT MUST I DO TO WAKE YOU?

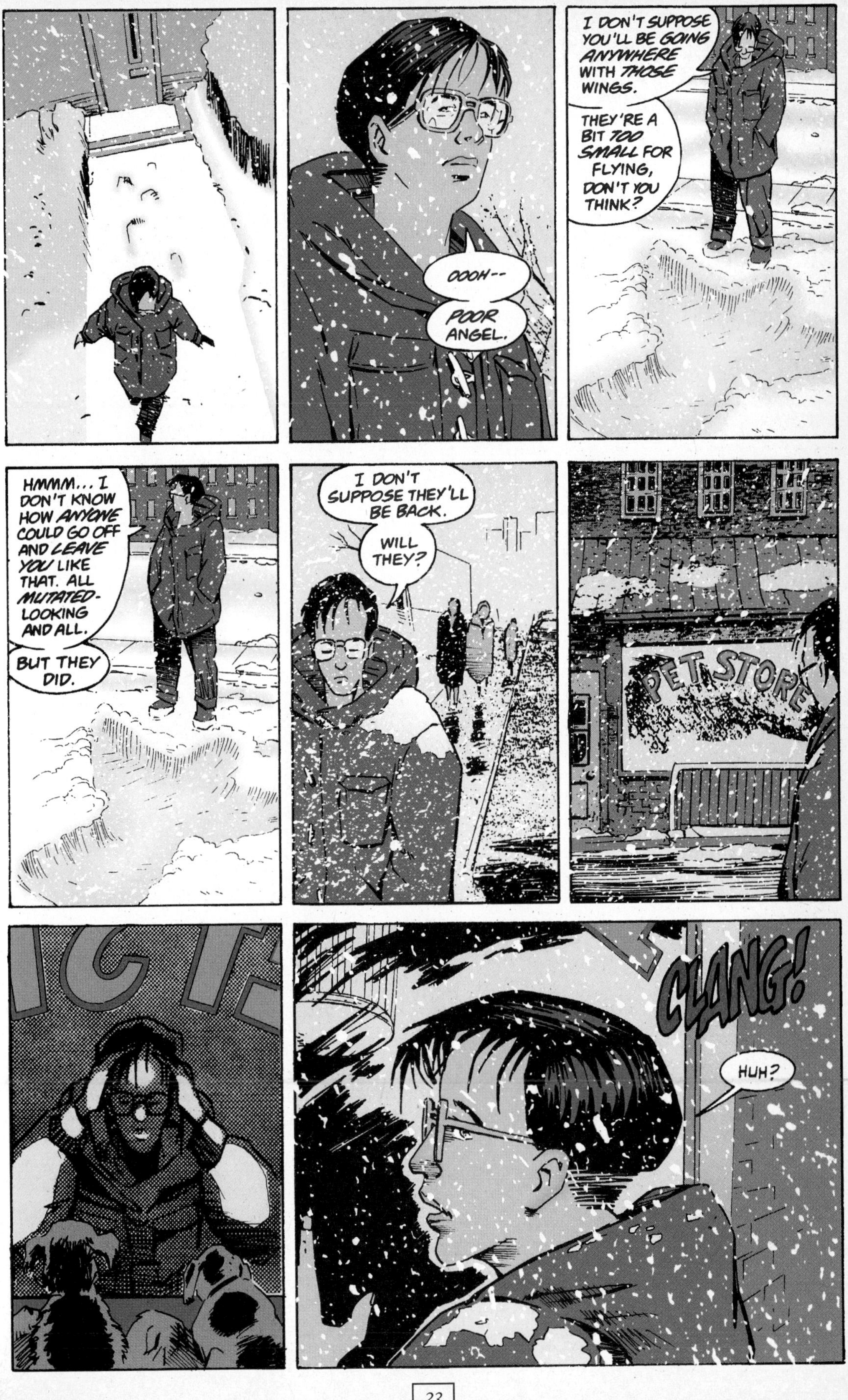
OOOH--
POOR ANGEL.
I DON'T SUPPOSE YOU'LL BE GOING ANYWHERE WITH THOSE WINGS.
THEY'RE A BIT TOO SMALL FOR FLYING, DON'T YOU THINK?
HMMM... I DON'T KNOW HOW ANYONE COULD GO OFF AND LEAVE YOU LIKE THAT. ALL MUTATED-LOOKING AND ALL.
BUT THEY DID.
I DON'T SUPPOSE THEY'LL BE BACK.
WILL THEY?
PET STORE
CLANG!
HUH?

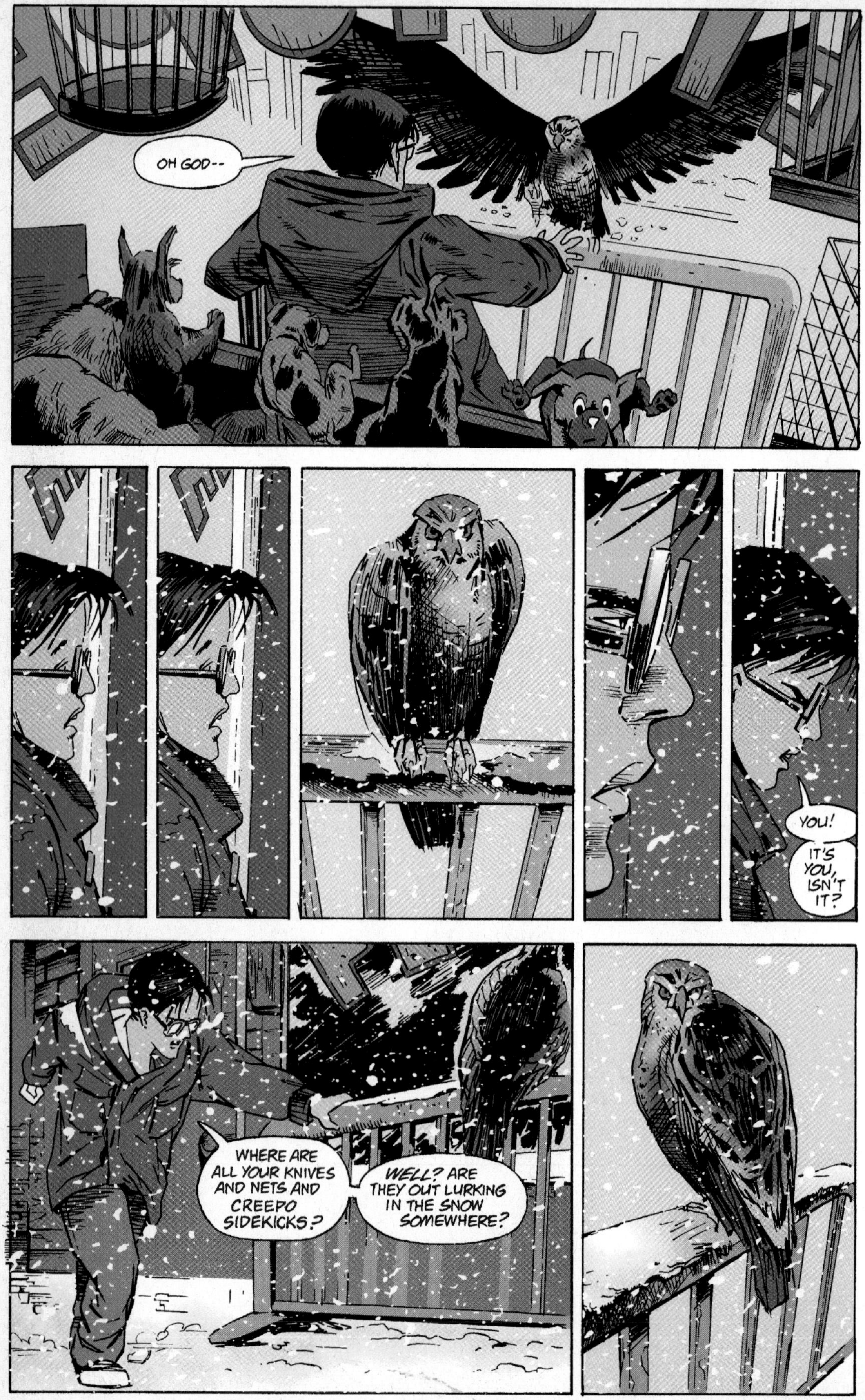
OH GOD--
YOU!
IT'S YOU, ISN'T IT?
WHERE ARE ALL YOUR KNIVES AND NETS AND CREEPO SIDEKICKS?
WELL? ARE THEY OUT LURKING IN THE SNOW SOMEWHERE?

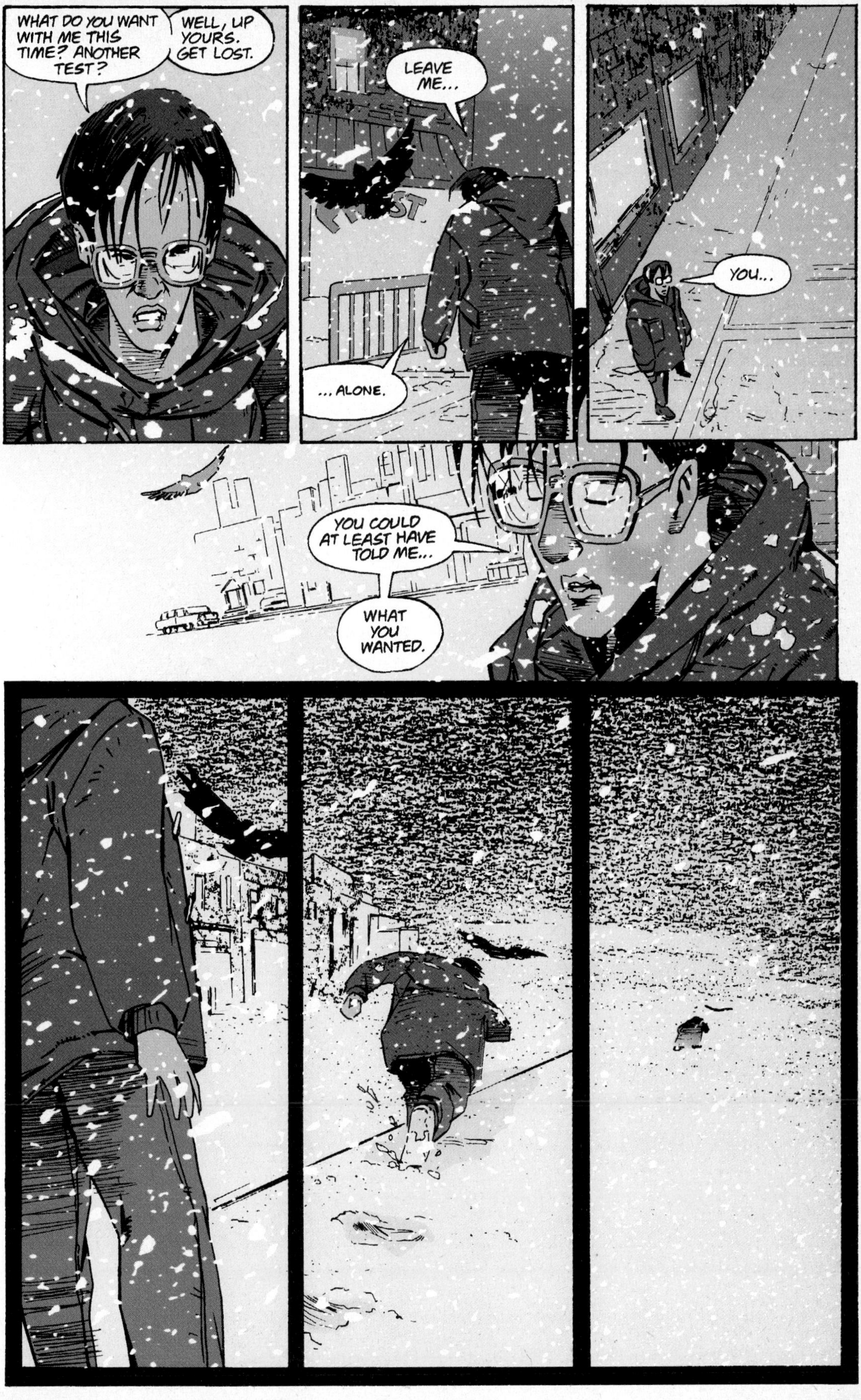
WHAT DO YOU WANT WITH ME THIS TIME? ANOTHER TEST?
WELL, UP YOURS. GET LOST.
LEAVE ME...
...ALONE.
YOU...
YOU COULD AT LEAST HAVE TOLD ME...
WHAT YOU WANTED.

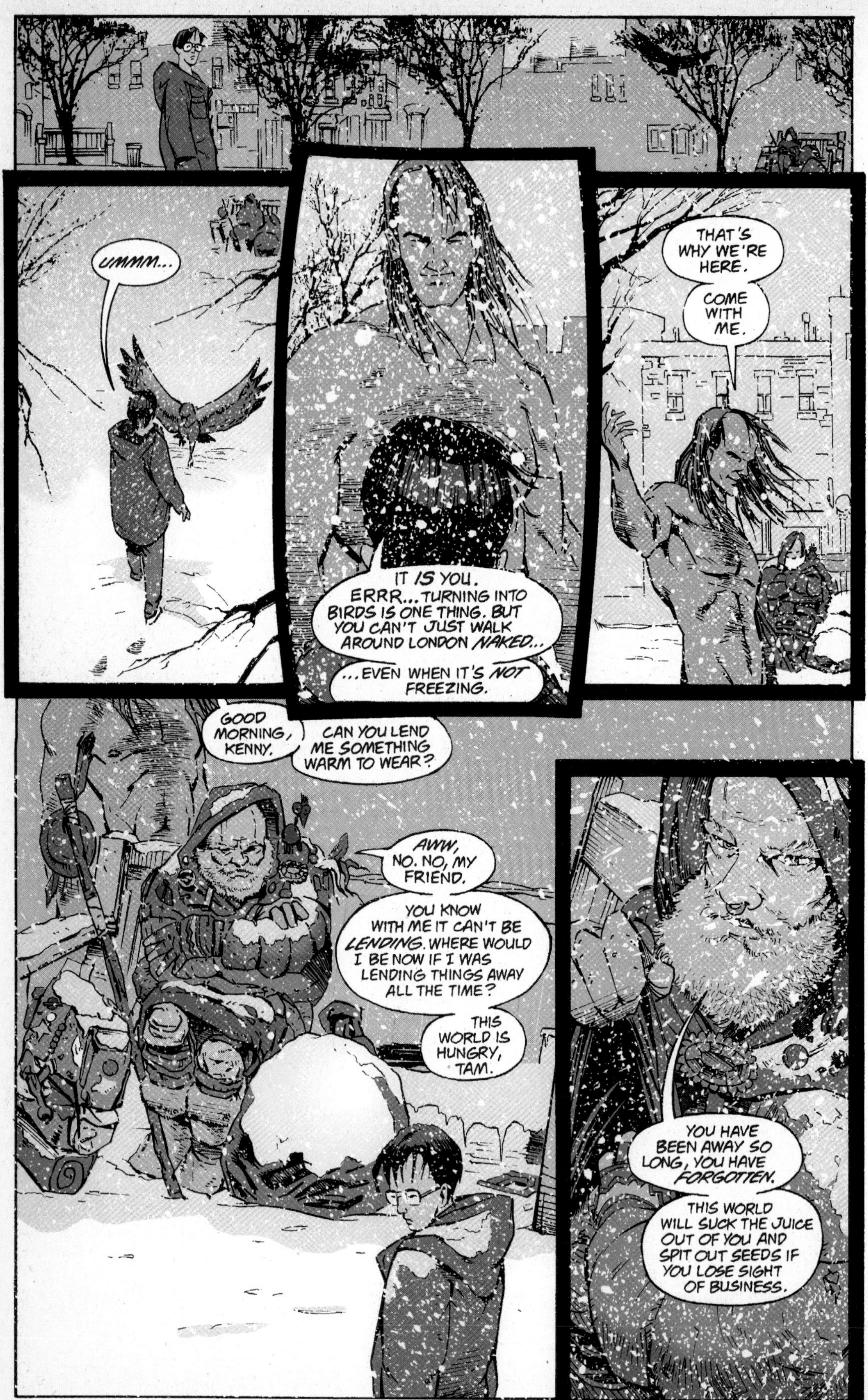
UMMM...
IT *IS* YOU.
ERRR... TURNING INTO BIRDS IS ONE THING. BUT YOU CAN'T JUST WALK AROUND LONDON *NAKED*...
...EVEN WHEN IT'S *NOT* FREEZING.
THAT'S WHY WE'RE HERE.
COME WITH ME.
GOOD MORNING, KENNY.
CAN YOU LEND ME SOMETHING WARM TO WEAR?
AWW, NO. NO, MY FRIEND.
YOU KNOW WITH ME IT CAN'T BE *LENDING*. WHERE WOULD I BE NOW IF I WAS LENDING THINGS AWAY ALL THE TIME?
THIS WORLD IS HUNGRY, TAM.
YOU HAVE BEEN AWAY SO LONG, YOU HAVE *FORGOTTEN*.
THIS WORLD WILL SUCK THE JUICE OUT OF YOU AND SPIT OUT SEEDS IF YOU LOSE SIGHT OF BUSINESS.

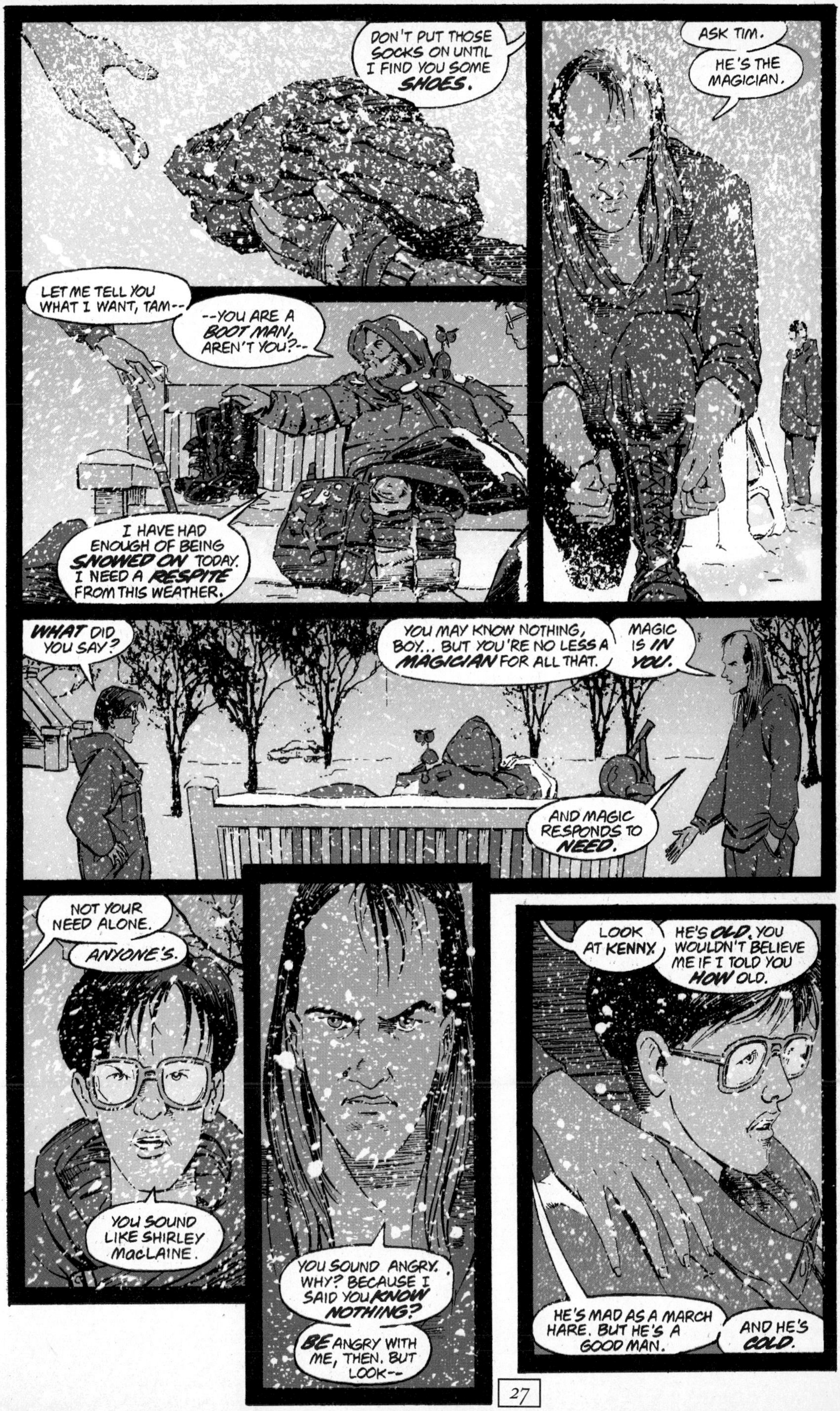
DON'T PUT THOSE SOCKS ON UNTIL I FIND YOU SOME SHOES.
ASK TIM.
HE'S THE MAGICIAN.
LET ME TELL YOU WHAT I WANT, TAM--
--YOU ARE A BOOT MAN, AREN'T YOU?--
I HAVE HAD ENOUGH OF BEING SNOWED ON TODAY. I NEED A RESPITE FROM THIS WEATHER.
WHAT DID YOU SAY?
YOU MAY KNOW NOTHING, BOY... BUT YOU'RE NO LESS A MAGICIAN FOR ALL THAT.
MAGIC IS IN YOU.
AND MAGIC RESPONDS TO NEED.
NOT YOUR NEED ALONE.
ANYONE'S.
YOU SOUND LIKE SHIRLEY MacLAINE.
YOU SOUND ANGRY. WHY? BECAUSE I SAID YOU KNOW NOTHING?
BE ANGRY WITH ME, THEN. BUT LOOK--
LOOK AT KENNY.
HE'S OLD. YOU WOULDN'T BELIEVE ME IF I TOLD YOU HOW OLD.
HE'S MAD AS A MARCH HARE. BUT HE'S A GOOD MAN.
AND HE'S COLD.

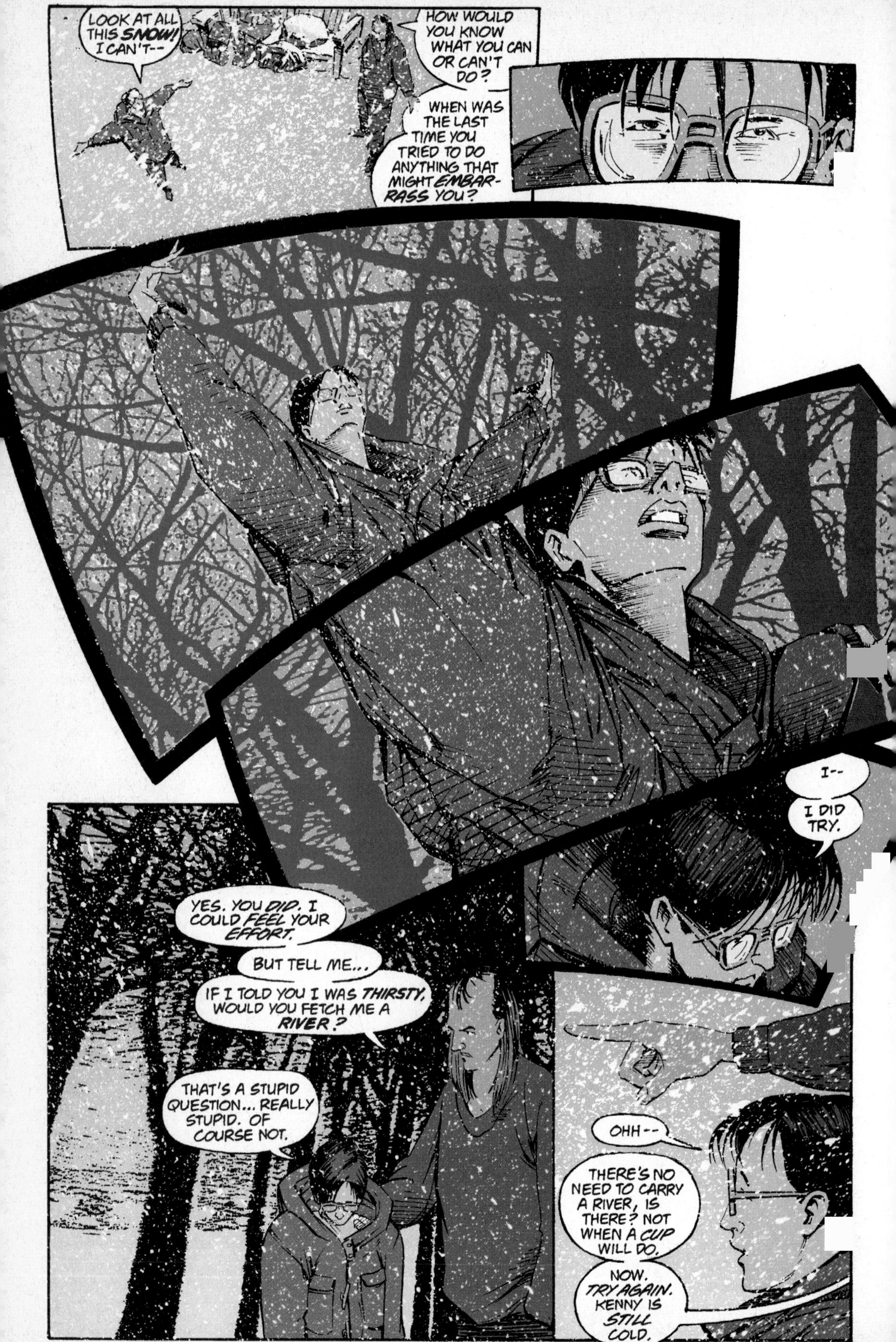
LOOK AT ALL THIS SNOW! I CAN'T--
HOW WOULD YOU KNOW WHAT YOU CAN OR CAN'T DO?
WHEN WAS THE LAST TIME YOU TRIED TO DO ANYTHING THAT MIGHT EMBARRASS YOU?
I--
I DID TRY.
YES. YOU DID. I COULD FEEL YOUR EFFORT.
BUT TELL ME...
IF I TOLD YOU I WAS THIRSTY, WOULD YOU FETCH ME A RIVER?
THAT'S A STUPID QUESTION... REALLY STUPID. OF COURSE NOT.
OHH--
THERE'S NO NEED TO CARRY A RIVER, IS THERE? NOT WHEN A CUP WILL DO.
NOW. TRY AGAIN. KENNY IS STILL COLD.

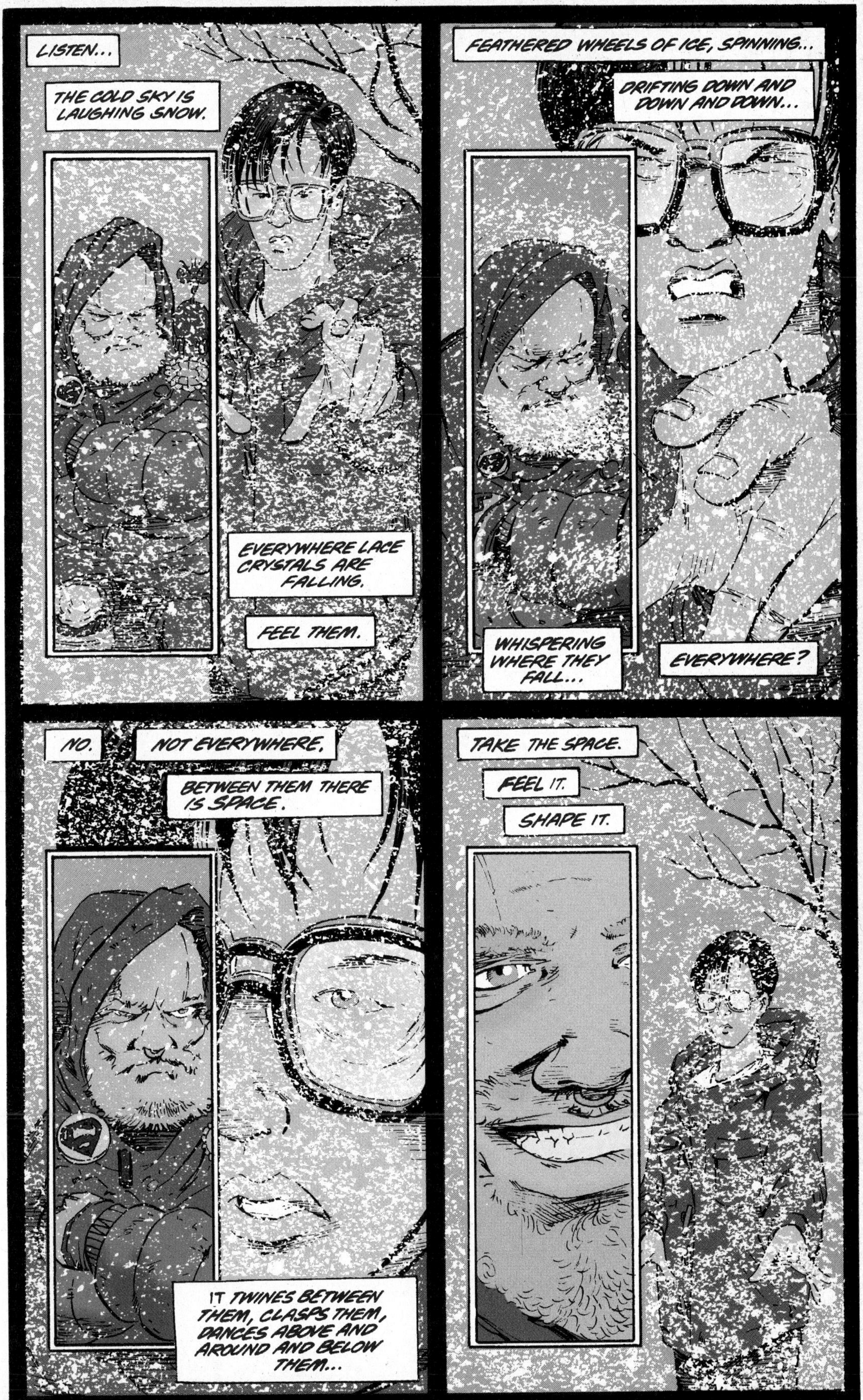
LISTEN...
THE COLD SKY IS LAUGHING SNOW.
EVERYWHERE LACE CRYSTALS ARE FALLING.
FEEL THEM.
FEATHERED WHEELS OF ICE, SPINNING...
DRIFTING DOWN AND DOWN AND DOWN...
WHISPERING WHERE THEY FALL...
EVERYWHERE?
NO.
NOT EVERYWHERE.
BETWEEN THEM THERE IS SPACE.
IT TWINES BETWEEN THEM, CLASPS THEM, DANCES ABOVE AND AROUND AND BELOW THEM...
TAKE THE SPACE.
FEEL IT.
SHAPE IT.

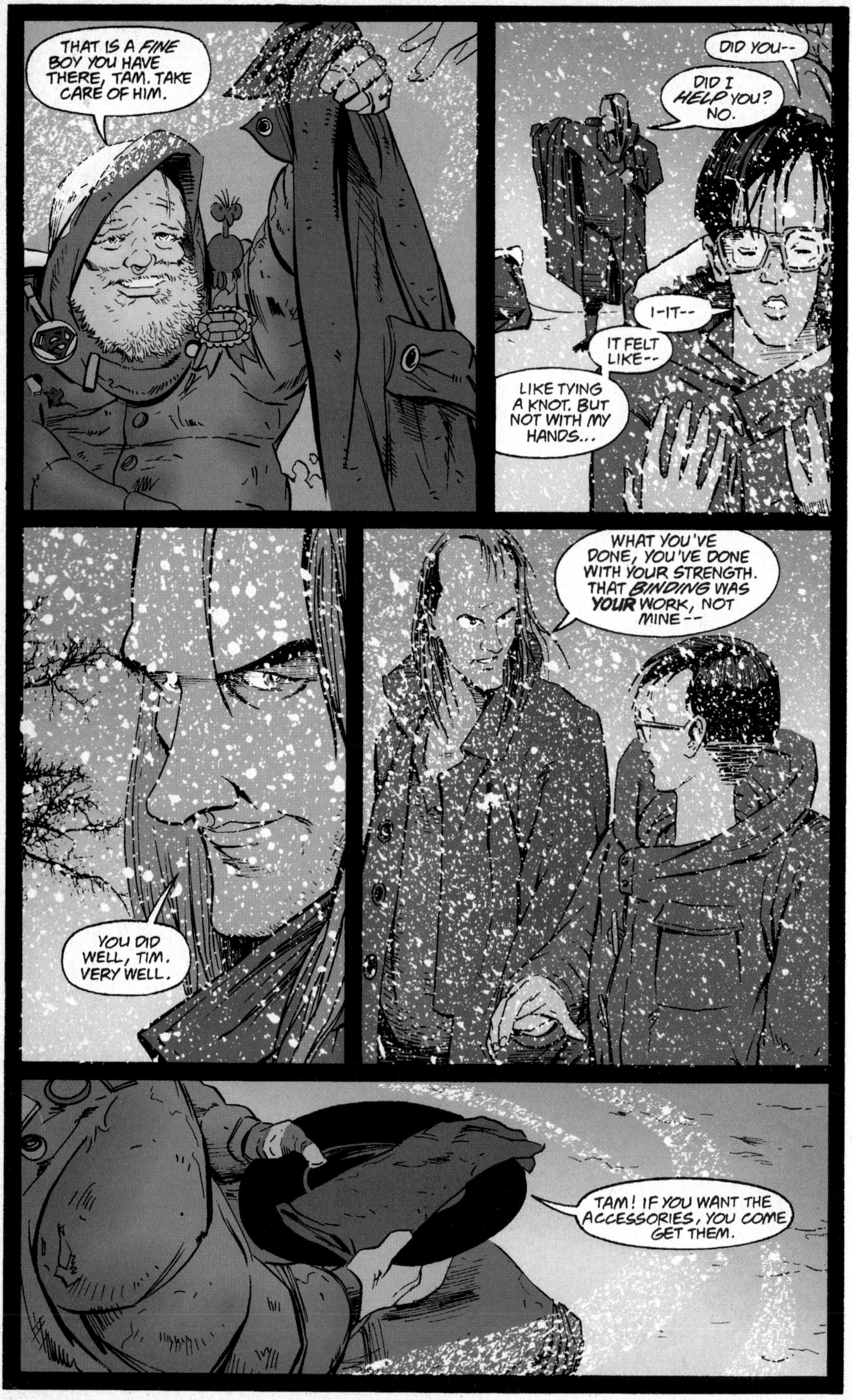
THAT IS A FINE BOY YOU HAVE THERE, TAM. TAKE CARE OF HIM.
DID YOU--
DID I HELP YOU? NO.
I-IT--
IT FELT LIKE--
LIKE TYING A KNOT. BUT NOT WITH MY HANDS...
YOU DID WELL, TIM. VERY WELL.
WHAT YOU'VE DONE, YOU'VE DONE WITH YOUR STRENGTH. THAT BINDING WAS YOUR WORK, NOT MINE--
TAM! IF YOU WANT THE ACCESSORIES, YOU COME GET THEM.

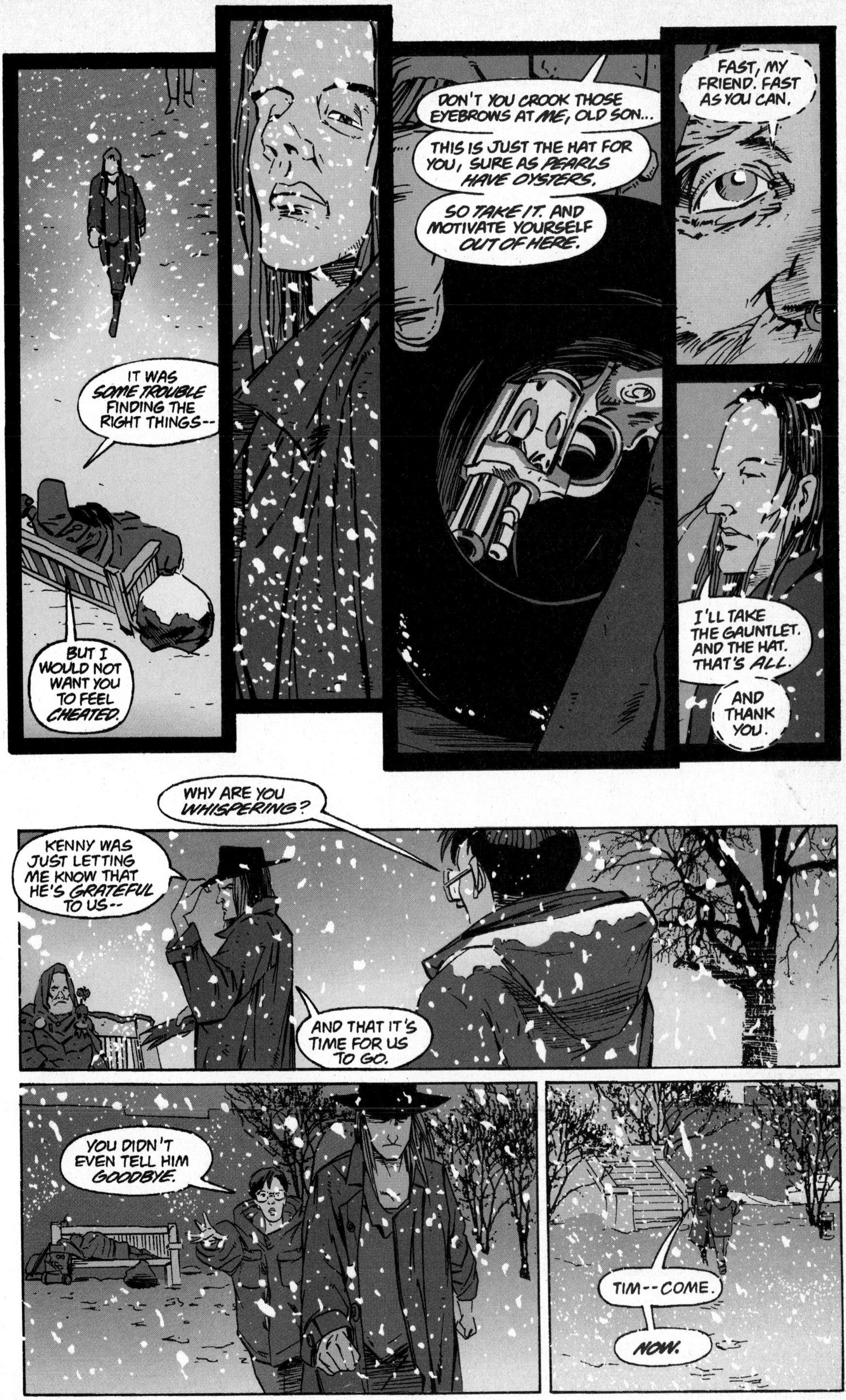
IT WAS SOME TROUBLE FINDING THE RIGHT THINGS--
BUT I WOULD NOT WANT YOU TO FEEL CHEATED.
DON'T YOU CROOK THOSE EYEBROWS AT ME, OLD SON...
THIS IS JUST THE HAT FOR YOU, SURE AS PEARLS HAVE OYSTERS.
SO TAKE IT. AND MOTIVATE YOURSELF OUT OF HERE.
FAST, MY FRIEND. FAST AS YOU CAN.
I'LL TAKE THE GAUNTLET. AND THE HAT. THAT'S ALL.
AND THANK YOU.
WHY ARE YOU WHISPERING?
KENNY WAS JUST LETTING ME KNOW THAT HE'S GRATEFUL TO US--
AND THAT IT'S TIME FOR US TO GO.
YOU DIDN'T EVEN TELL HIM GOODBYE.
TIM--COME.
NOW.

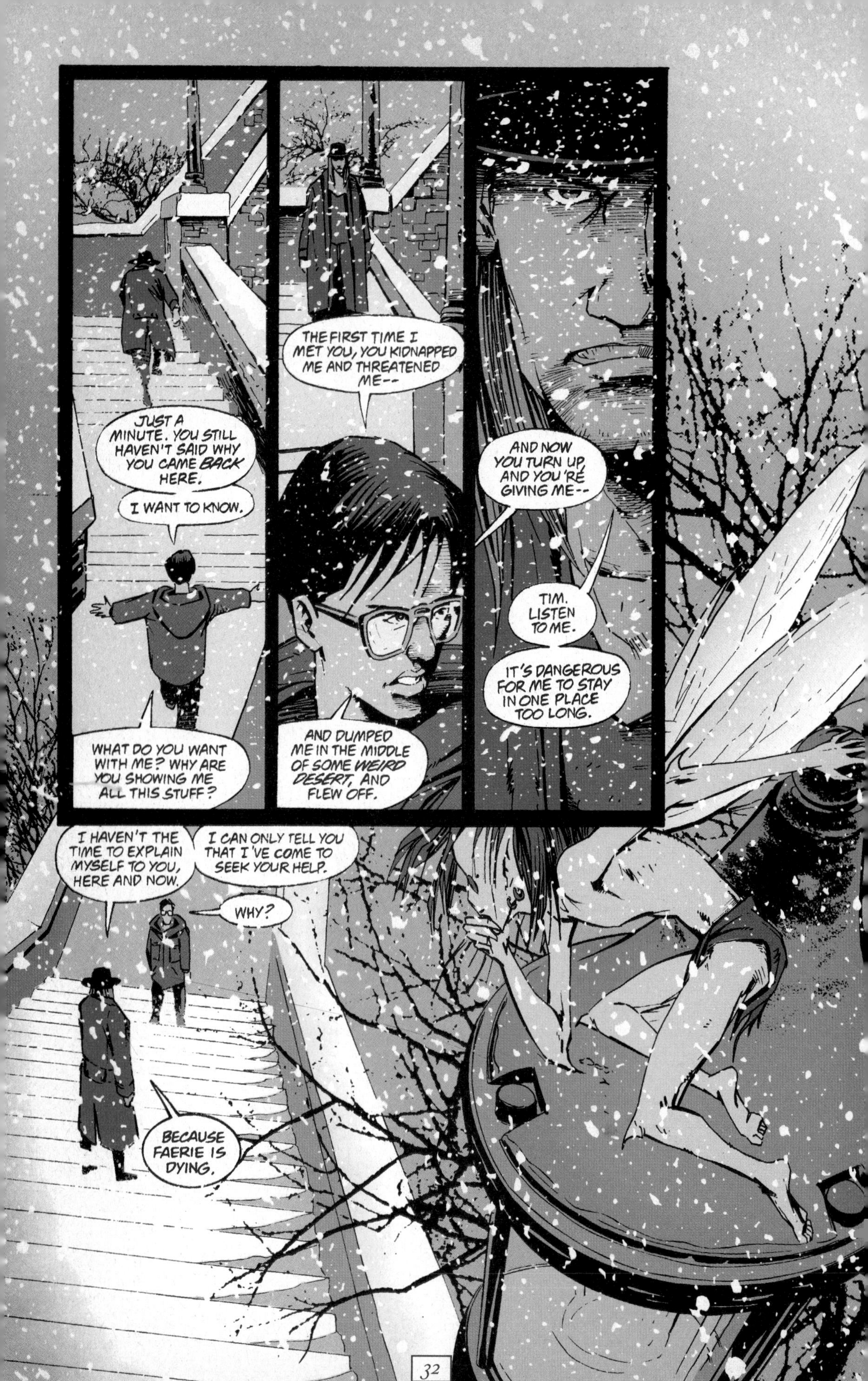
JUST A MINUTE. YOU STILL HAVEN'T SAID WHY YOU CAME BACK HERE.
I WANT TO KNOW.
WHAT DO YOU WANT WITH ME? WHY ARE YOU SHOWING ME ALL THIS STUFF?
THE FIRST TIME I MET YOU, YOU KIDNAPPED ME AND THREATENED ME--
AND DUMPED ME IN THE MIDDLE OF SOME WEIRD DESERT, AND FLEW OFF.
AND NOW YOU TURN UP, AND YOU'RE GIVING ME--
TIM. LISTEN TO ME.
IT'S DANGEROUS FOR ME TO STAY IN ONE PLACE TOO LONG.
I HAVEN'T THE TIME TO EXPLAIN MYSELF TO YOU, HERE AND NOW.
I CAN ONLY TELL YOU THAT I'VE COME TO SEEK YOUR HELP.
WHY?
BECAUSE FAERIE IS DYING.

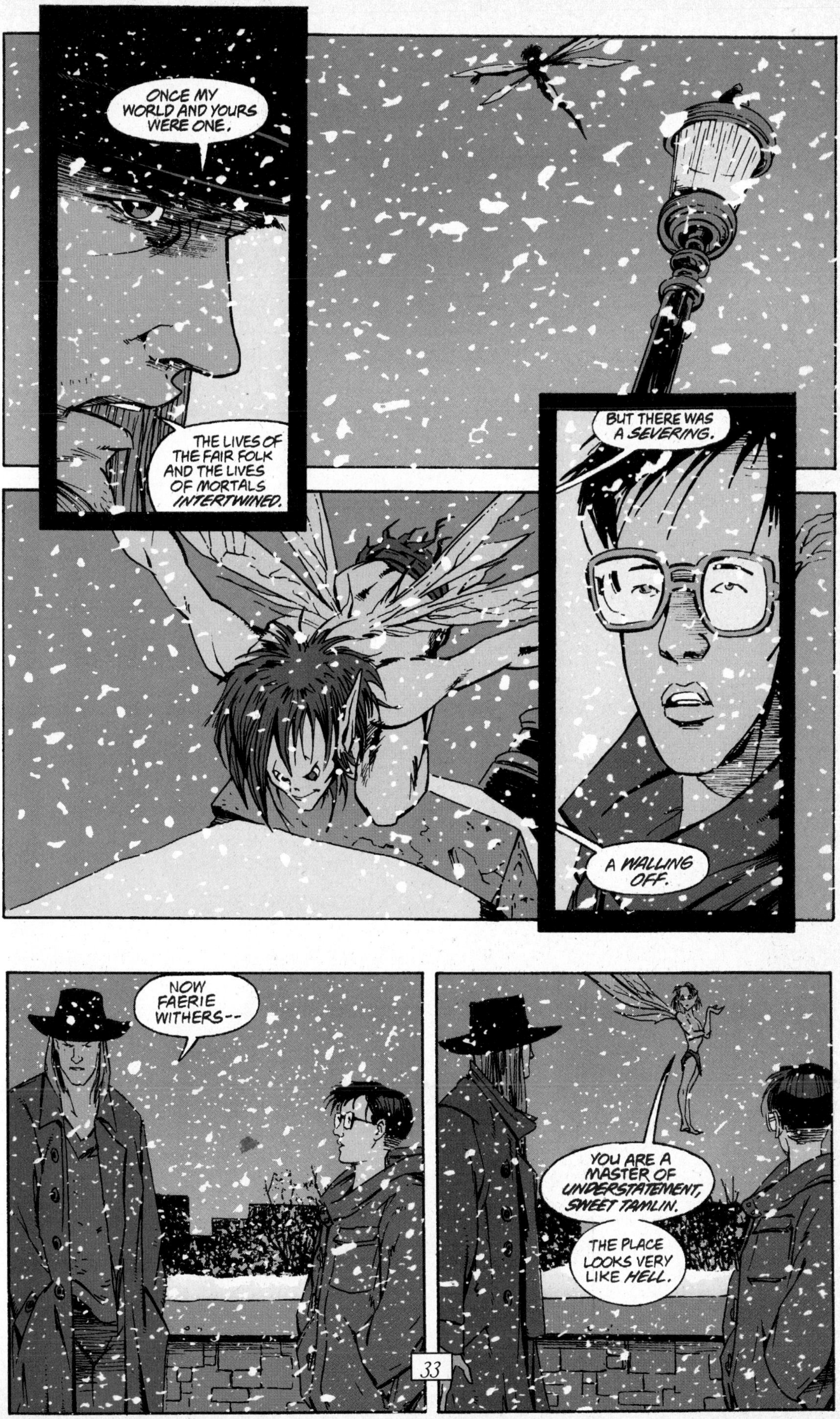
ONCE MY WORLD AND YOURS WERE ONE.
THE LIVES OF THE FAIR FOLK AND THE LIVES OF MORTALS INTERTWINED.
BUT THERE WAS A SEVERING.
A WALLING OFF.
NOW FAERIE WITHERS--
YOU ARE A MASTER OF UNDERSTATEMENT, SWEET TAMLIN.
THE PLACE LOOKS VERY LIKE HELL.

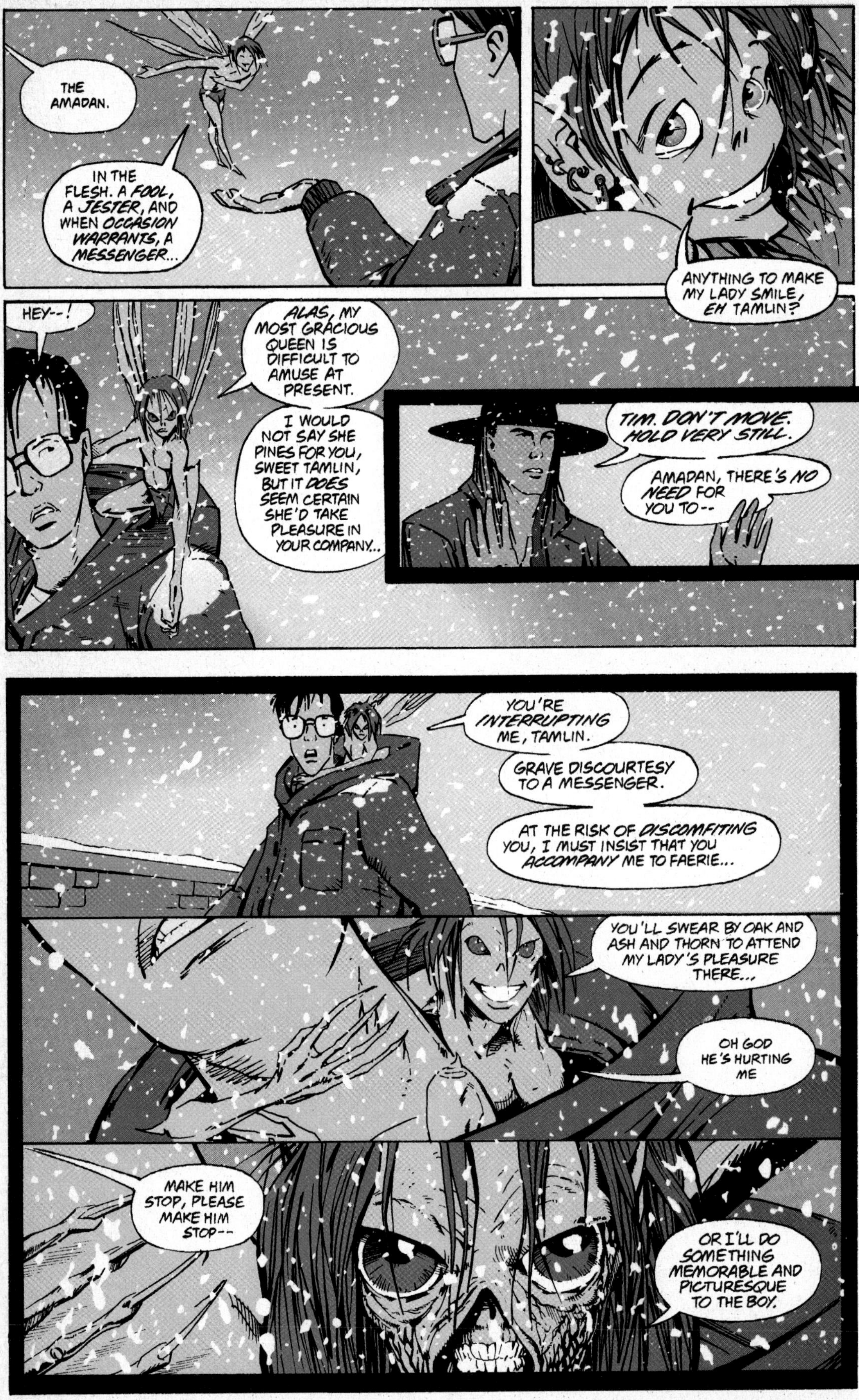
THE AMADAN.
IN THE FLESH. A FOOL, A JESTER, AND WHEN OCCASION WARRANTS, A MESSENGER...
ANYTHING TO MAKE MY LADY SMILE, EH TAMLIN?
HEY--!
ALAS, MY MOST GRACIOUS QUEEN IS DIFFICULT TO AMUSE AT PRESENT.
I WOULD NOT SAY SHE PINES FOR YOU, SWEET TAMLIN, BUT IT DOES SEEM CERTAIN SHE'D TAKE PLEASURE IN YOUR COMPANY...
TIM. DON'T MOVE. HOLD VERY STILL.
AMADAN, THERE'S NO NEED FOR YOU TO--
YOU'RE INTERRUPTING ME, TAMLIN.
GRAVE DISCOURTESY TO A MESSENGER.
AT THE RISK OF DISCOMFITING YOU, I MUST INSIST THAT YOU ACCOMPANY ME TO FAERIE...
YOU'LL SWEAR BY OAK AND ASH AND THORN TO ATTEND MY LADY'S PLEASURE THERE...
OH GOD HE'S HURTING ME
MAKE HIM STOP, PLEASE MAKE HIM STOP--
OR I'LL DO SOMETHING MEMORABLE AND PICTURESQUE TO THE BOY.

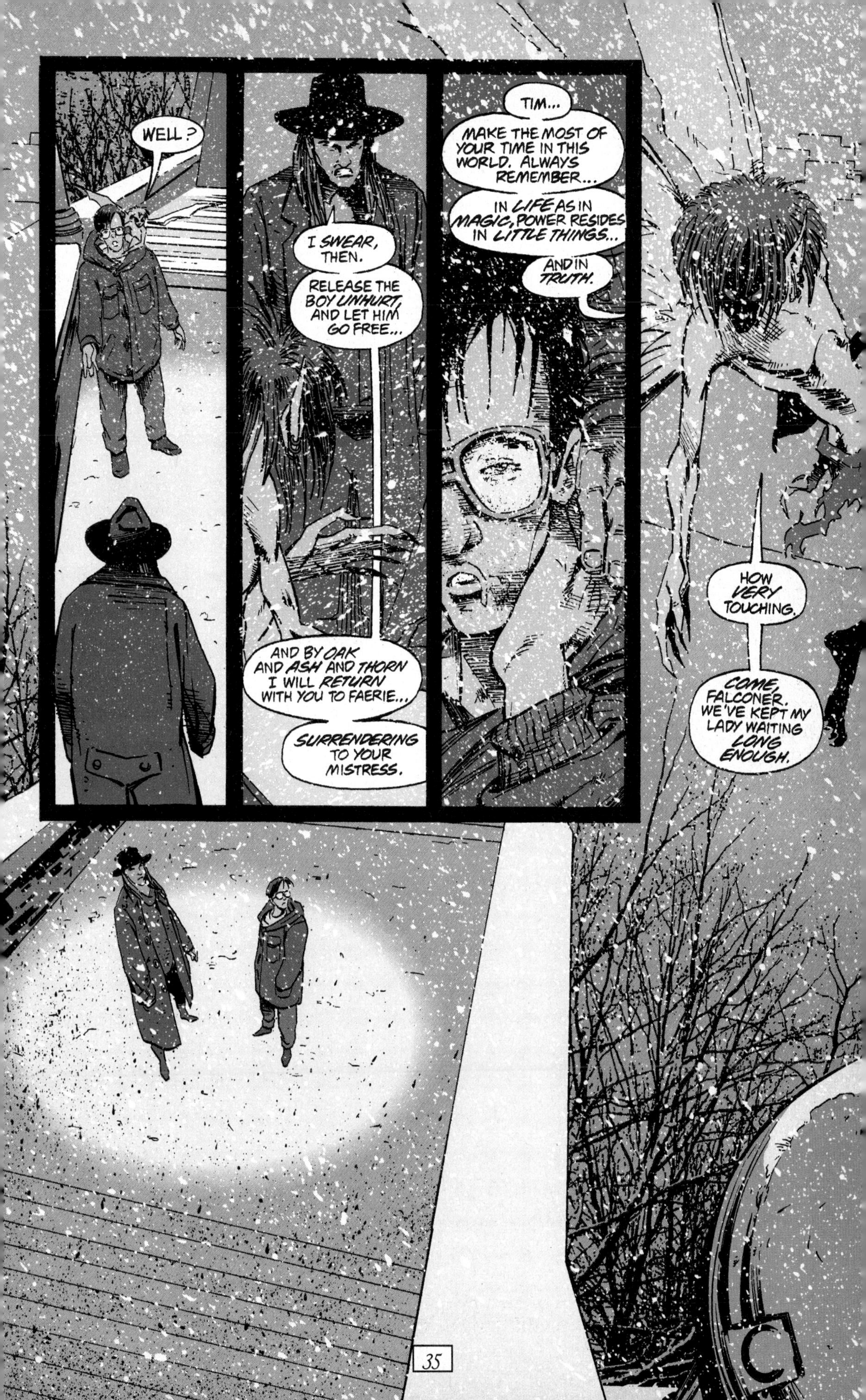
WELL?
I SWEAR, THEN.
RELEASE THE BOY UNHURT, AND LET HIM GO FREE...
AND BY OAK AND ASH AND THORN I WILL RETURN WITH YOU TO FAERIE...
SURRENDERING TO YOUR MISTRESS.
TIM...
MAKE THE MOST OF YOUR TIME IN THIS WORLD. ALWAYS REMEMBER...
IN LIFE AS IN MAGIC, POWER RESIDES IN LITTLE THINGS...
AND IN TRUTH.
HOW VERY TOUCHING.
COME, FALCONER. WE'VE KEPT MY LADY WAITING LONG ENOUGH.

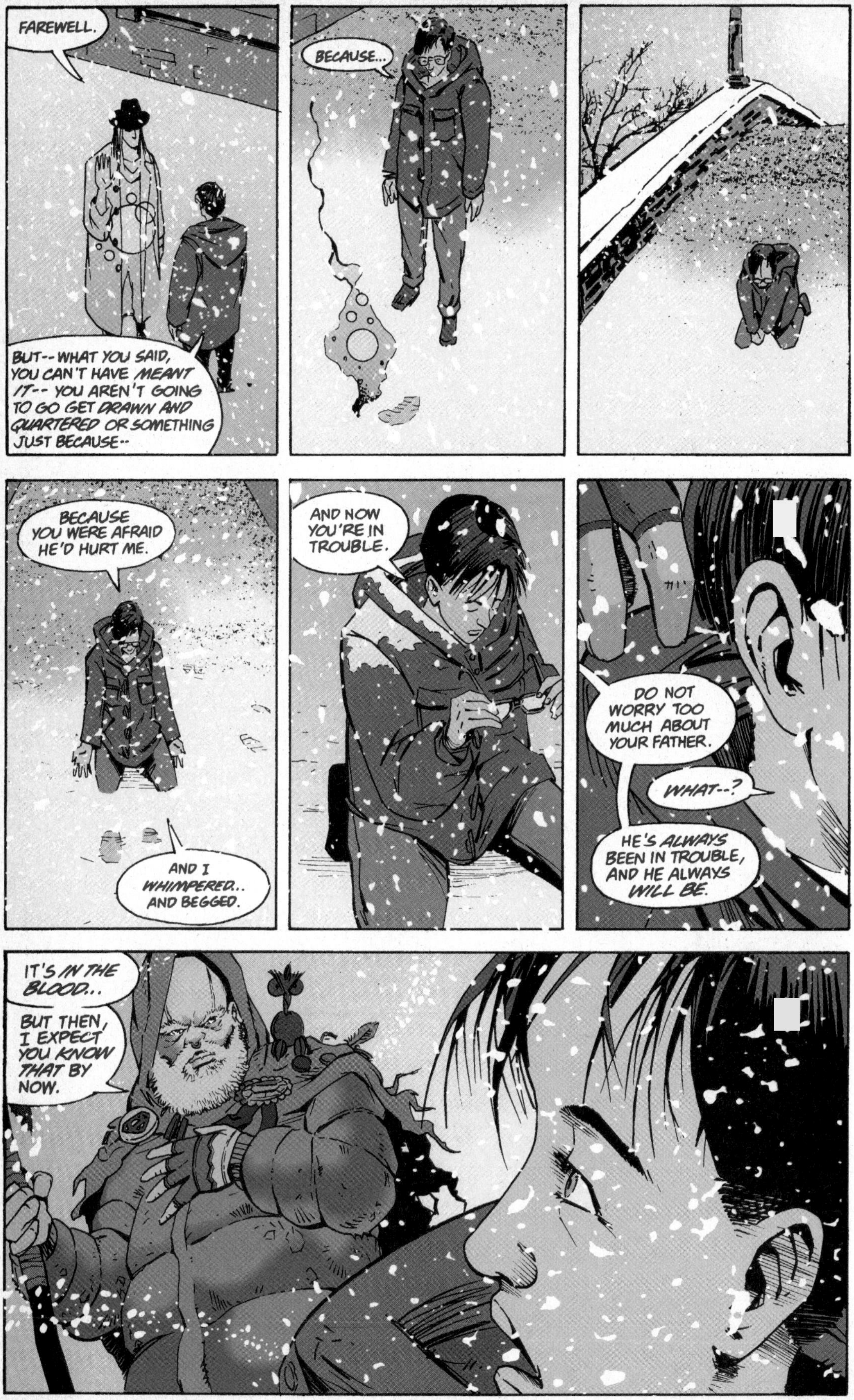
FAREWELL.
BUT--WHAT YOU SAID, YOU CAN'T HAVE MEANT IT-- YOU AREN'T GOING TO GO GET DRAWN AND QUARTERED OR SOMETHING JUST BECAUSE--
BECAUSE...
BECAUSE YOU WERE AFRAID HE'D HURT ME.
AND I WHIMPERED... AND BEGGED.
AND NOW YOU'RE IN TROUBLE.
DO NOT WORRY TOO MUCH ABOUT YOUR FATHER.
WHAT--?
HE'S ALWAYS BEEN IN TROUBLE, AND HE ALWAYS WILL BE.
IT'S IN THE BLOOD...
BUT THEN, I EXPECT YOU KNOW THAT BY NOW.

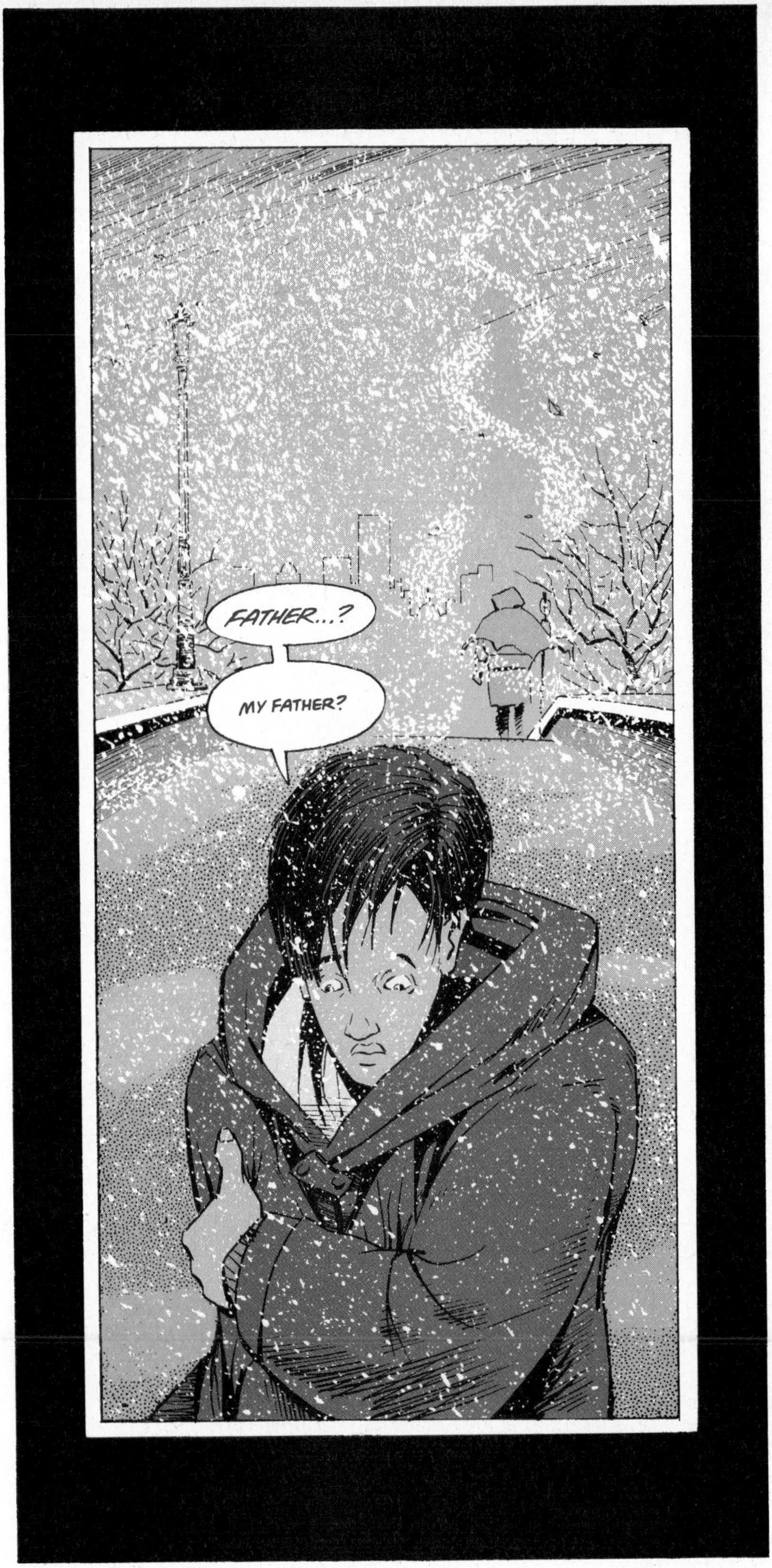
FATHER...?
MY FATHER?

BINDINGS

Book Two

A Book of Leaves

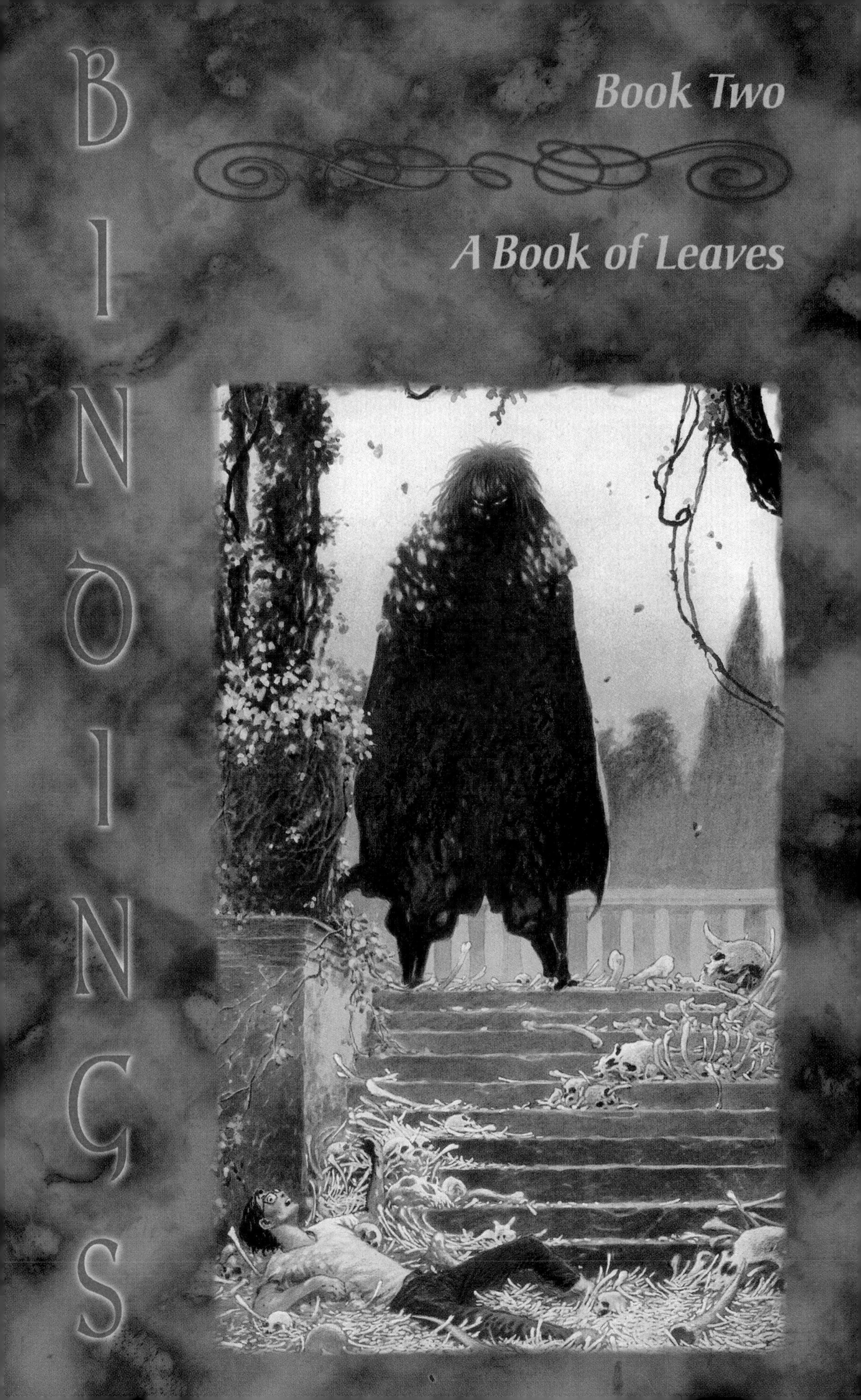

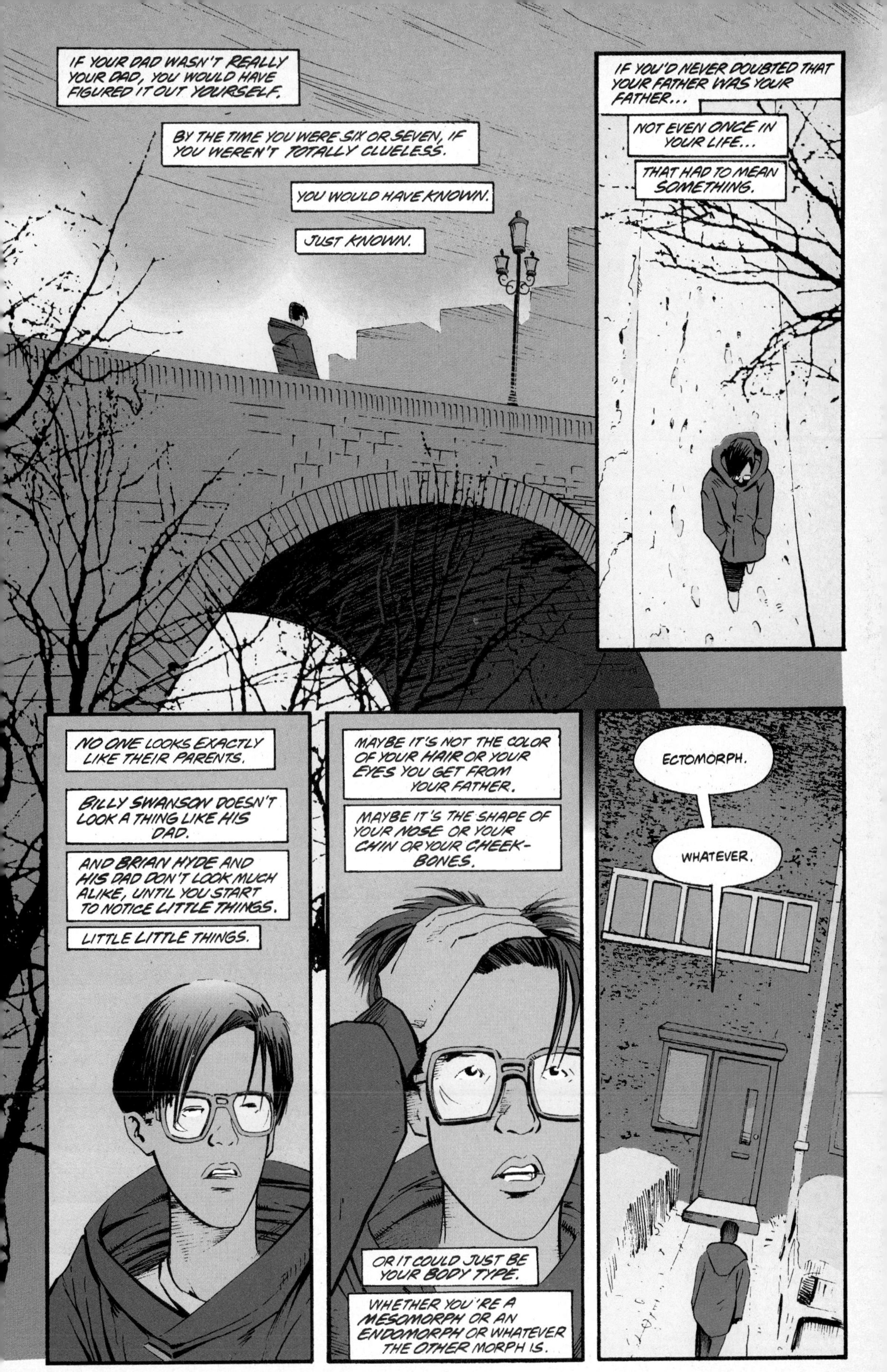
IF YOUR DAD WASN'T REALLY YOUR DAD, YOU WOULD HAVE FIGURED IT OUT YOURSELF.
BY THE TIME YOU WERE SIX OR SEVEN, IF YOU WEREN'T TOTALLY CLUELESS.
YOU WOULD HAVE KNOWN.
JUST KNOWN.
IF YOU'D NEVER DOUBTED THAT YOUR FATHER WAS YOUR FATHER...
NOT EVEN ONCE IN YOUR LIFE...
THAT HAD TO MEAN SOMETHING.
NO ONE LOOKS EXACTLY LIKE THEIR PARENTS.
BILLY SWANSON DOESN'T LOOK A THING LIKE HIS DAD.
AND BRIAN HYDE AND HIS DAD DON'T LOOK MUCH ALIKE, UNTIL YOU START TO NOTICE LITTLE THINGS.
LITTLE LITTLE THINGS.
MAYBE IT'S NOT THE COLOR OF YOUR HAIR OR YOUR EYES YOU GET FROM YOUR FATHER.
MAYBE IT'S THE SHAPE OF YOUR NOSE OR YOUR CHIN OR YOUR CHEEK-BONES.
OR IT COULD JUST BE YOUR BODY TYPE.
WHETHER YOU'RE A MESOMORPH OR AN ENDOMORPH OR WHATEVER THE OTHER MORPH IS.
ECTOMORPH.
WHATEVER.

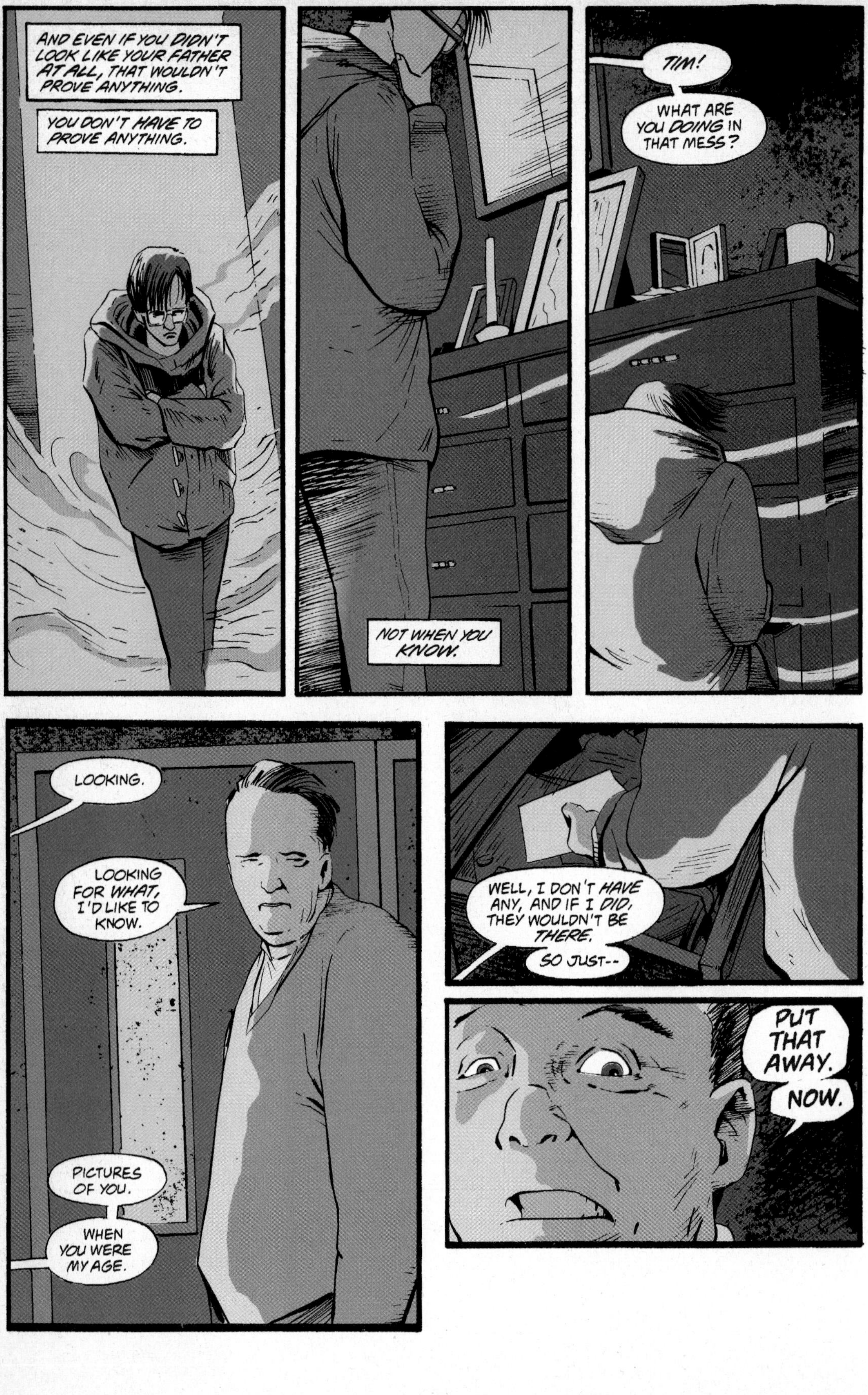
AND EVEN IF YOU DIDN'T LOOK LIKE YOUR FATHER AT ALL, THAT WOULDN'T PROVE ANYTHING.
YOU DON'T HAVE TO PROVE ANYTHING.
NOT WHEN YOU KNOW.
TIM!
WHAT ARE YOU DOING IN THAT MESS?
LOOKING.
LOOKING FOR WHAT, I'D LIKE TO KNOW.
PICTURES OF YOU.
WHEN YOU WERE MY AGE.
WELL, I DON'T HAVE ANY, AND IF I DID, THEY WOULDN'T BE THERE.
SO JUST--
PUT THAT AWAY.
NOW.

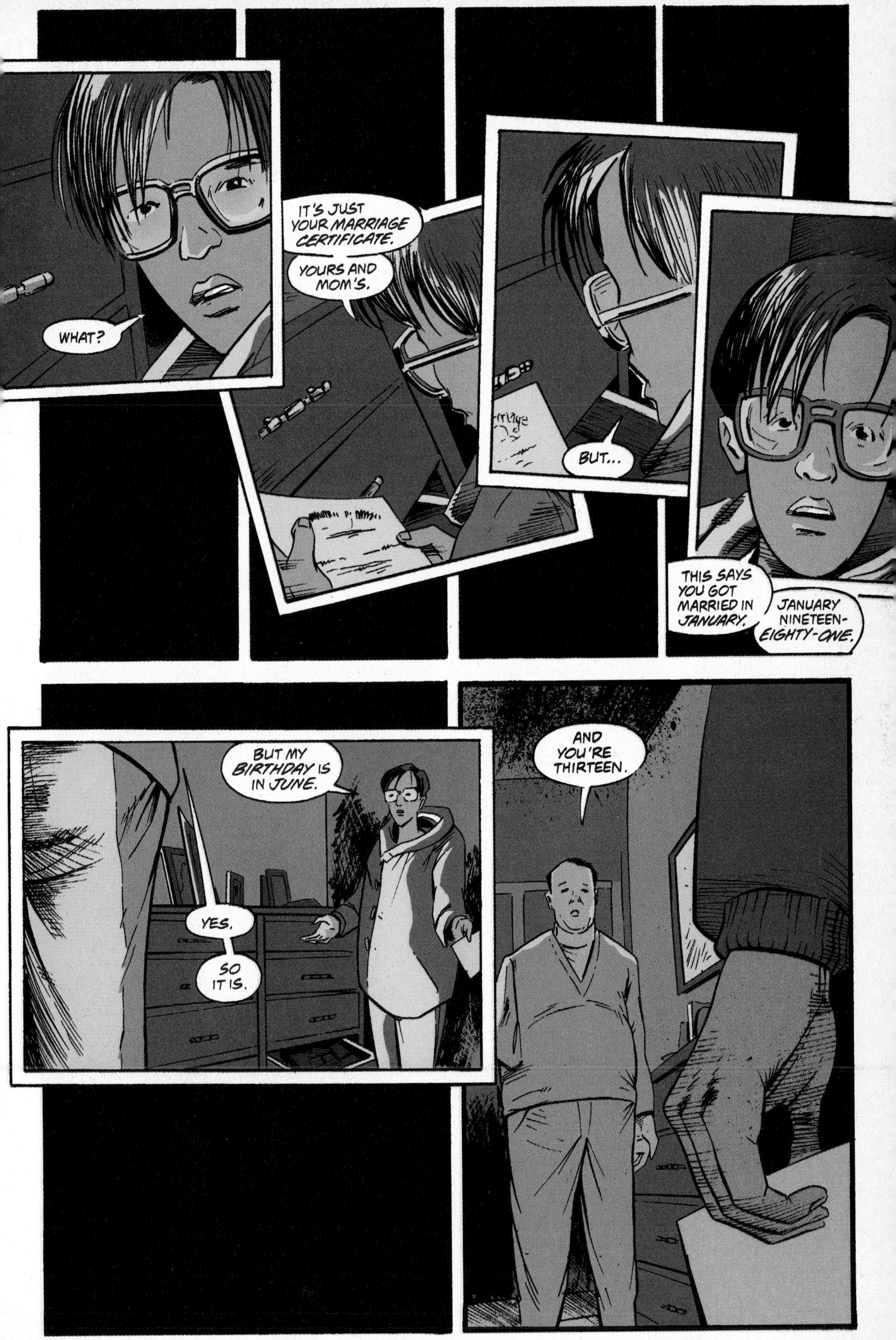
WHAT?
IT'S JUST YOUR MARRIAGE CERTIFICATE.
YOURS AND MOM'S.
BUT...
THIS SAYS YOU GOT MARRIED IN JANUARY.
JANUARY NINETEEN-EIGHTY-ONE.
BUT MY BIRTHDAY IS IN JUNE.
YES.
SO IT IS.
AND YOU'RE THIRTEEN.

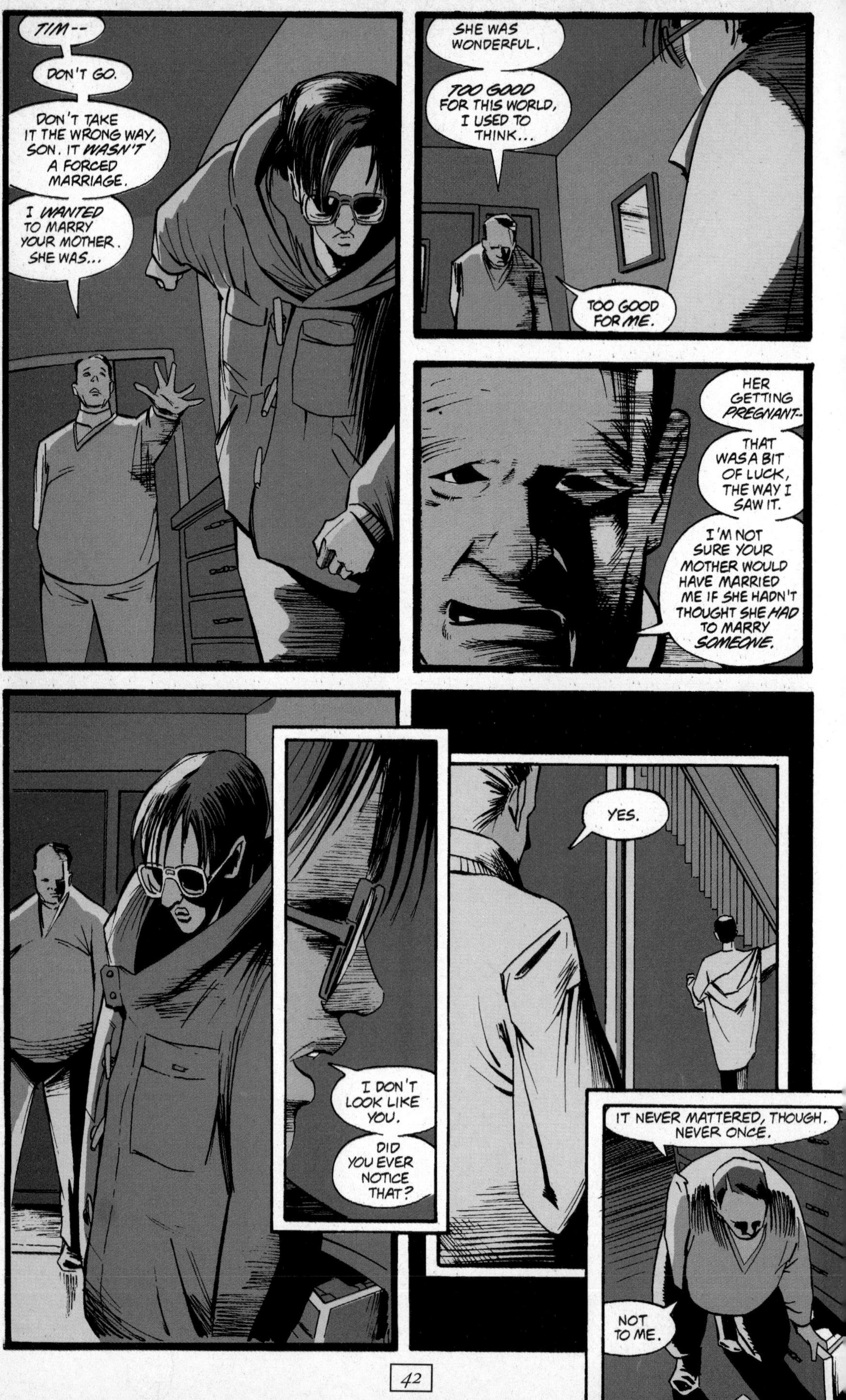
TIM--
DON'T GO.
DON'T TAKE IT THE WRONG WAY, SON. IT WASN'T A FORCED MARRIAGE.
I WANTED TO MARRY YOUR MOTHER. SHE WAS...
SHE WAS WONDERFUL.
TOO GOOD FOR THIS WORLD, I USED TO THINK...
TOO GOOD FOR ME.
HER GETTING PREGNANT--
THAT WAS A BIT OF LUCK, THE WAY I SAW IT.
I'M NOT SURE YOUR MOTHER WOULD HAVE MARRIED ME IF SHE HADN'T THOUGHT SHE HAD TO MARRY SOMEONE.
I DON'T LOOK LIKE YOU.
DID YOU EVER NOTICE THAT?
YES.
IT NEVER MATTERED, THOUGH. NEVER ONCE.
NOT TO ME.

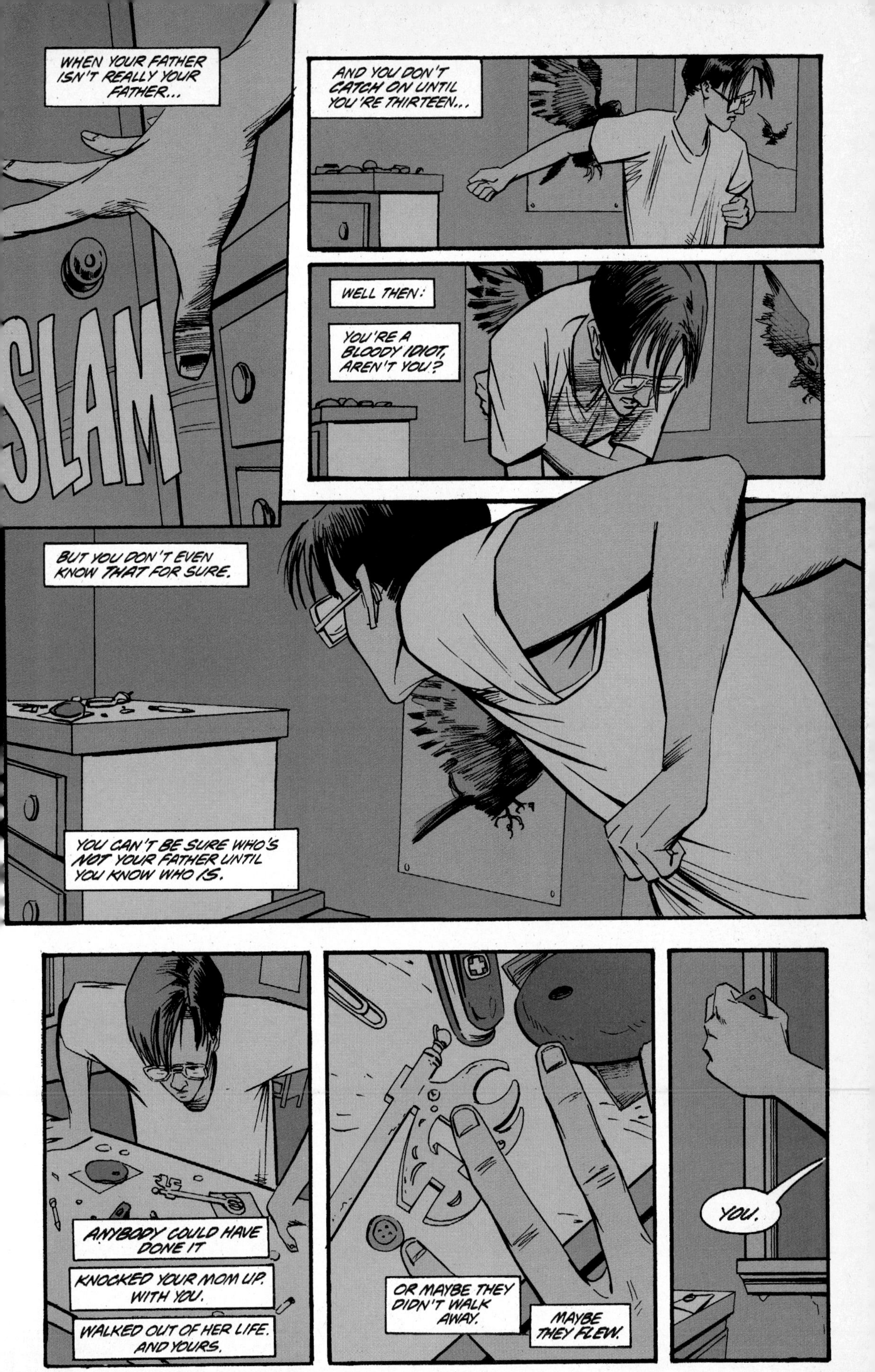
WHEN YOUR FATHER ISN'T REALLY YOUR FATHER...
SLAM
AND YOU DON'T CATCH ON UNTIL YOU'RE THIRTEEN...
WELL THEN:
YOU'RE A BLOODY IDIOT, AREN'T YOU?
BUT YOU DON'T EVEN KNOW THAT FOR SURE.
YOU CAN'T BE SURE WHO'S NOT YOUR FATHER UNTIL YOU KNOW WHO IS.
ANYBODY COULD HAVE DONE IT
KNOCKED YOUR MOM UP. WITH YOU.
WALKED OUT OF HER LIFE. AND YOURS.
OR MAYBE THEY DIDN'T WALK AWAY.
MAYBE THEY FLEW.
YOU.

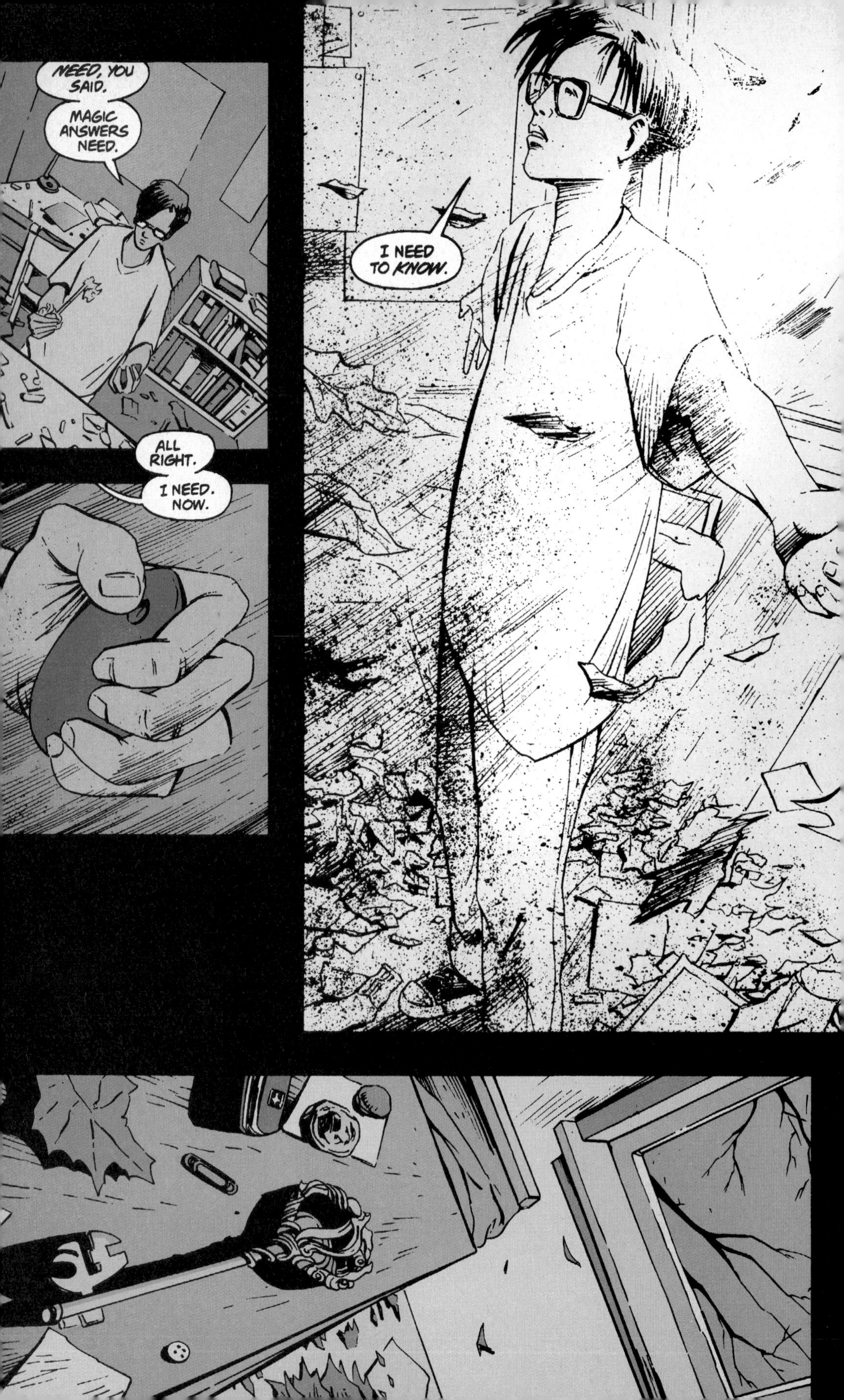
NEED, YOU SAID.
MAGIC ANSWERS NEED.
ALL RIGHT.
I NEED. NOW.
I NEED TO KNOW.

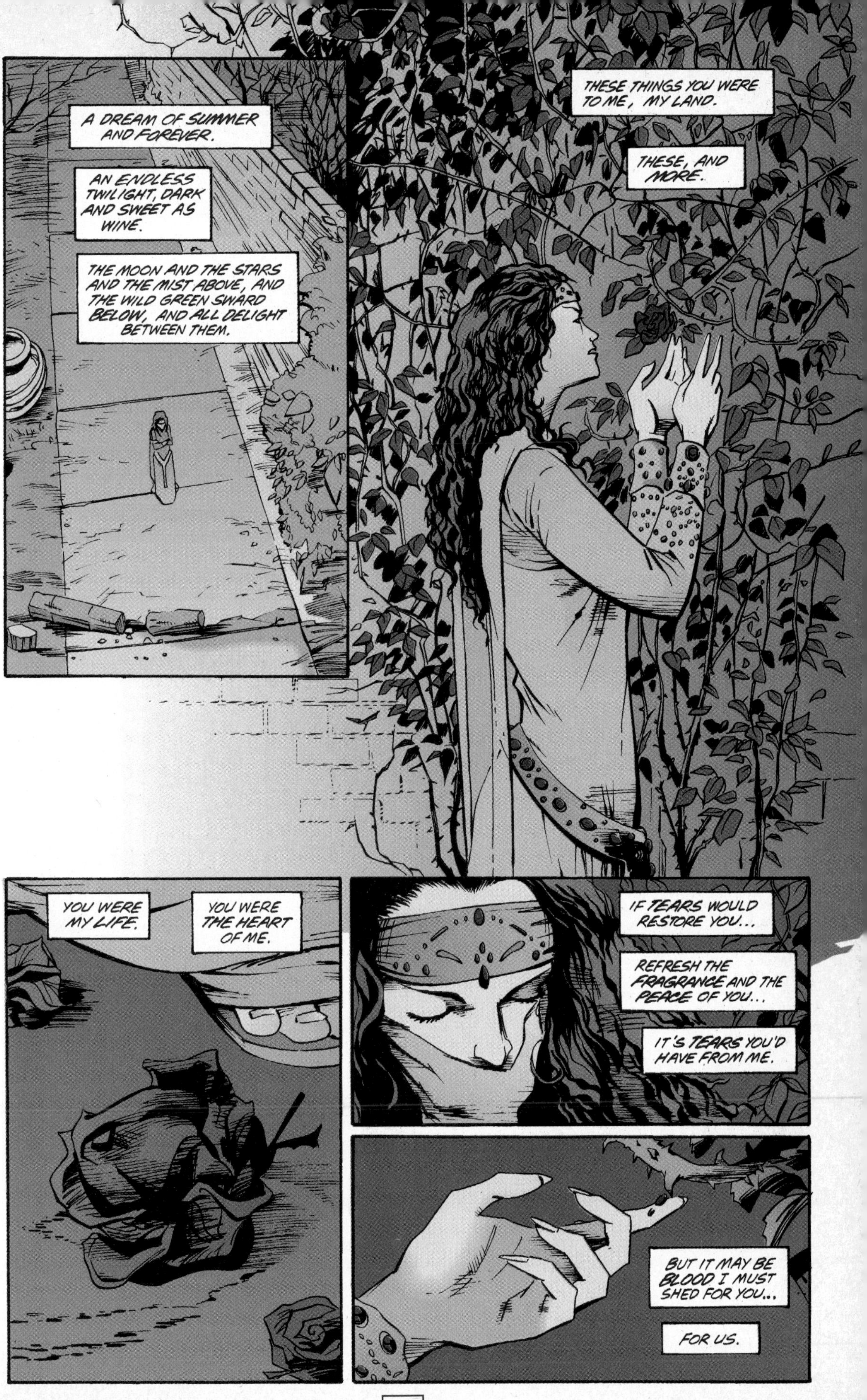
A DREAM OF SUMMER AND FOREVER.
AN ENDLESS TWILIGHT, DARK AND SWEET AS WINE.
THE MOON AND THE STARS AND THE MIST ABOVE, AND THE WILD GREEN SWARD BELOW, AND ALL DELIGHT BETWEEN THEM.
THESE THINGS YOU WERE TO ME, MY LAND.
THESE, AND MORE.
YOU WERE MY LIFE.
YOU WERE THE HEART OF ME.
IF TEARS WOULD RESTORE YOU...
REFRESH THE FRAGRANCE AND THE PEACE OF YOU...
IT'S TEARS YOU'D HAVE FROM ME.
BUT IT MAY BE BLOOD I MUST SHED FOR YOU...
FOR US.

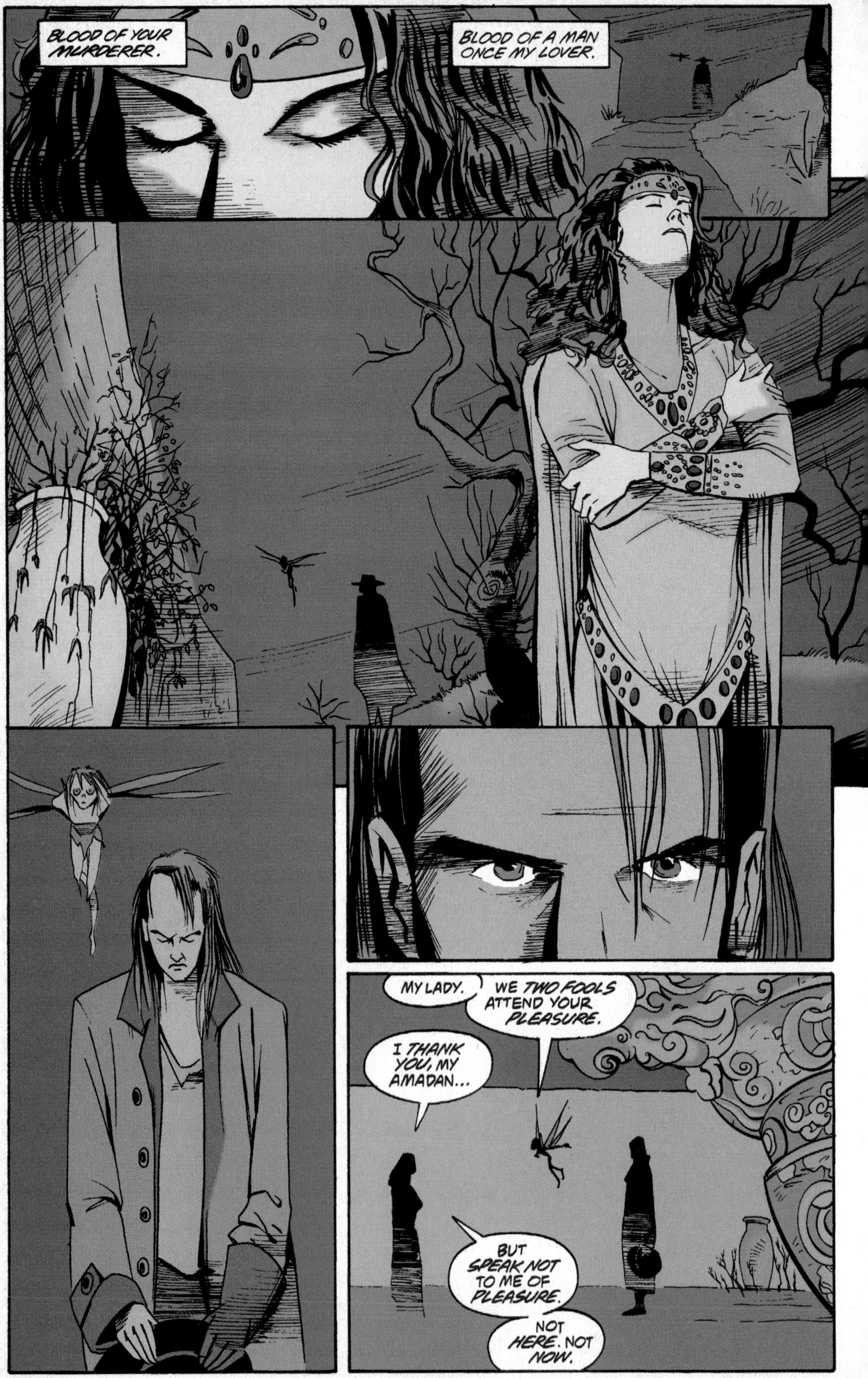
BLOOD OF YOUR MURDERER.
BLOOD OF A MAN ONCE MY LOVER.
MY LADY.
WE TWO FOOLS ATTEND YOUR PLEASURE.
I THANK YOU, MY AMADAN...
BUT SPEAK NOT TO ME OF PLEASURE.
NOT HERE. NOT NOW.

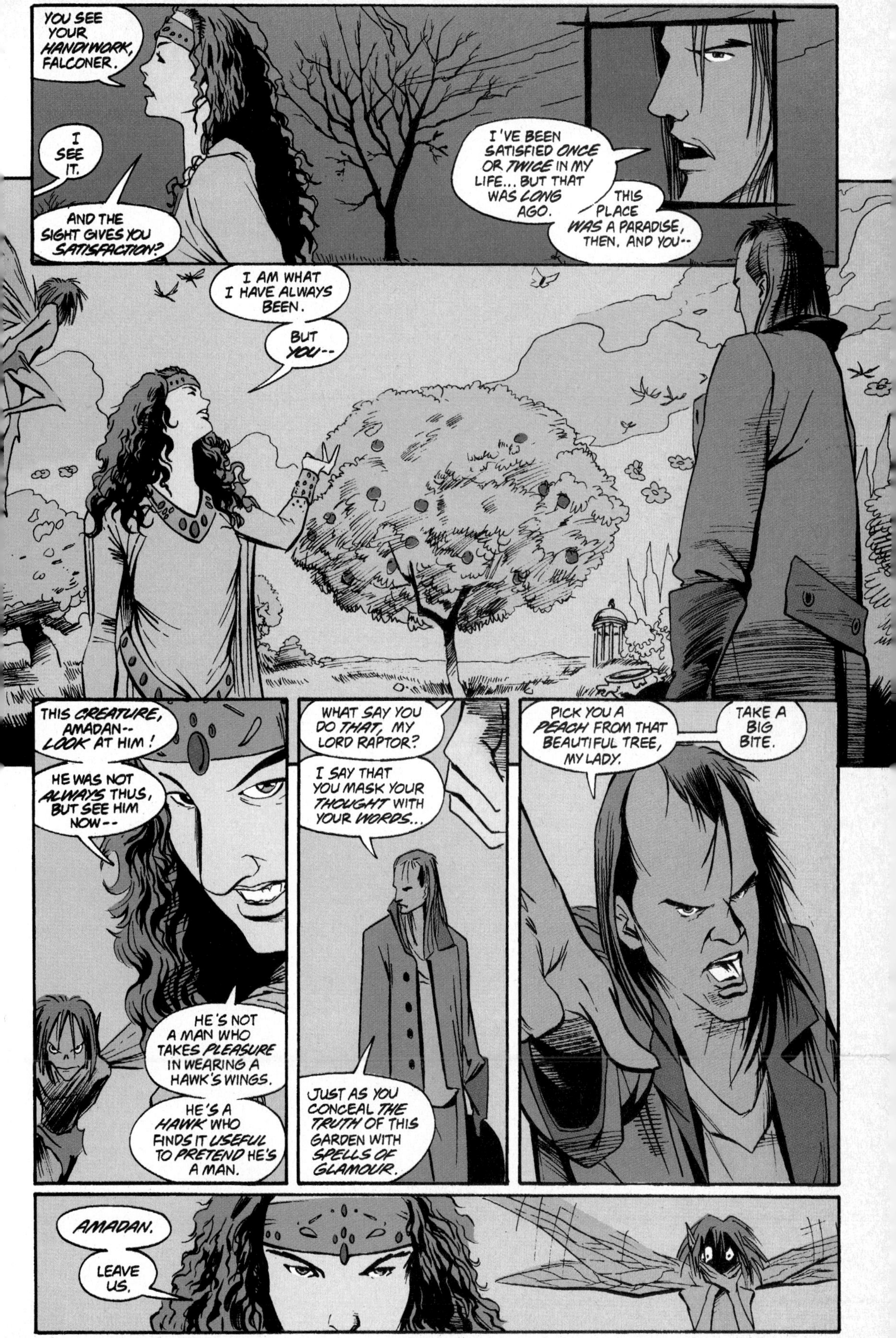
YOU SEE YOUR HANDIWORK, FALCONER.
I SEE IT.
AND THE SIGHT GIVES YOU SATISFACTION?
I'VE BEEN SATISFIED ONCE OR TWICE IN MY LIFE... BUT THAT WAS LONG AGO.
THIS PLACE WAS A PARADISE, THEN. AND YOU--
I AM WHAT I HAVE ALWAYS BEEN.
BUT YOU--
THIS CREATURE, AMADAN-- LOOK AT HIM!
HE WAS NOT ALWAYS THUS, BUT SEE HIM NOW--
HE'S NOT A MAN WHO TAKES PLEASURE IN WEARING A HAWK'S WINGS.
HE'S A HAWK WHO FINDS IT USEFUL TO PRETEND HE'S A MAN.
WHAT SAY YOU DO THAT, MY LORD RAPTOR?
I SAY THAT YOU MASK YOUR THOUGHT WITH YOUR WORDS...
JUST AS YOU CONCEAL THE TRUTH OF THIS GARDEN WITH SPELLS OF GLAMOUR.
PICK YOU A PEACH FROM THAT BEAUTIFUL TREE, MY LADY.
TAKE A BIG BITE.
AMADAN.
LEAVE US.

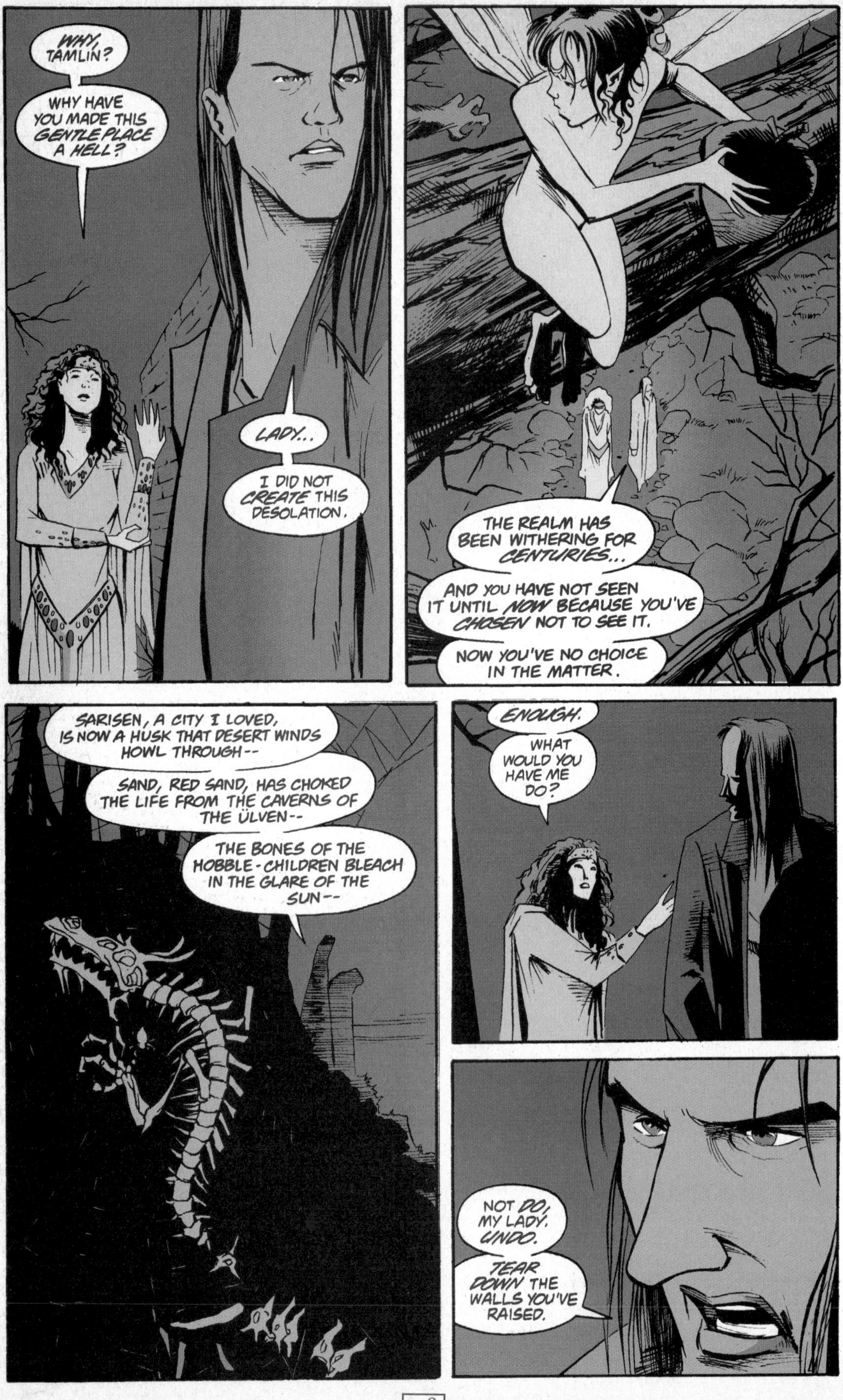
WHY, TAMLIN?
WHY HAVE YOU MADE THIS GENTLE PLACE A HELL?
LADY...
I DID NOT CREATE THIS DESOLATION.
THE REALM HAS BEEN WITHERING FOR CENTURIES...
AND YOU HAVE NOT SEEN IT UNTIL NOW BECAUSE YOU'VE CHOSEN NOT TO SEE IT.
NOW YOU'VE NO CHOICE IN THE MATTER.
SARISEN, A CITY I LOVED, IS NOW A HUSK THAT DESERT WINDS HOWL THROUGH--
SAND, RED SAND, HAS CHOKED THE LIFE FROM THE CAVERNS OF THE ÜLVEN--
THE BONES OF THE HOBBLE-CHILDREN BLEACH IN THE GLARE OF THE SUN--
ENOUGH.
WHAT WOULD YOU HAVE ME DO?
NOT DO, MY LADY. UNDO.
TEAR DOWN THE WALLS YOU'VE RAISED.

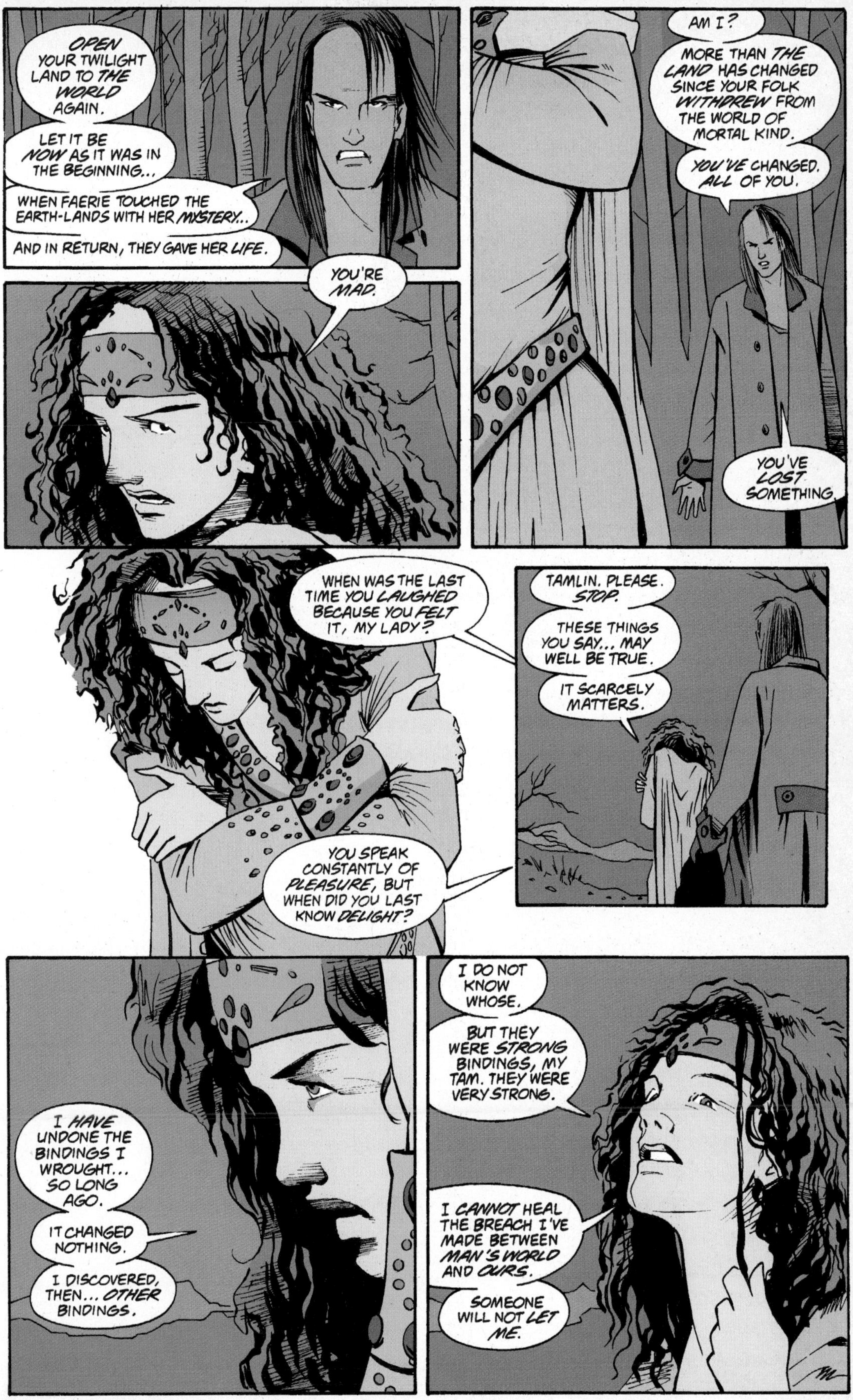
OPEN YOUR TWILIGHT LAND TO THE WORLD AGAIN.
LET IT BE NOW AS IT WAS IN THE BEGINNING...
WHEN FAERIE TOUCHED THE EARTH-LANDS WITH HER MYSTERY...
AND IN RETURN, THEY GAVE HER LIFE.
YOU'RE MAD.
AM I?
MORE THAN THE LAND HAS CHANGED SINCE YOUR FOLK WITHDREW FROM THE WORLD OF MORTAL KIND.
YOU'VE CHANGED. ALL OF YOU.
YOU'VE LOST SOMETHING.
WHEN WAS THE LAST TIME YOU LAUGHED BECAUSE YOU FELT IT, MY LADY?
YOU SPEAK CONSTANTLY OF PLEASURE, BUT WHEN DID YOU LAST KNOW DELIGHT?
TAMLIN. PLEASE. STOP.
THESE THINGS YOU SAY... MAY WELL BE TRUE.
IT SCARCELY MATTERS.
I HAVE UNDONE THE BINDINGS I WROUGHT... SO LONG AGO.
IT CHANGED NOTHING.
I DISCOVERED, THEN... OTHER BINDINGS.
I DO NOT KNOW WHOSE.
BUT THEY WERE STRONG BINDINGS, MY TAM. THEY WERE VERY STRONG.
I CANNOT HEAL THE BREACH I'VE MADE BETWEEN MAN'S WORLD AND OURS.
SOMEONE WILL NOT LET ME.

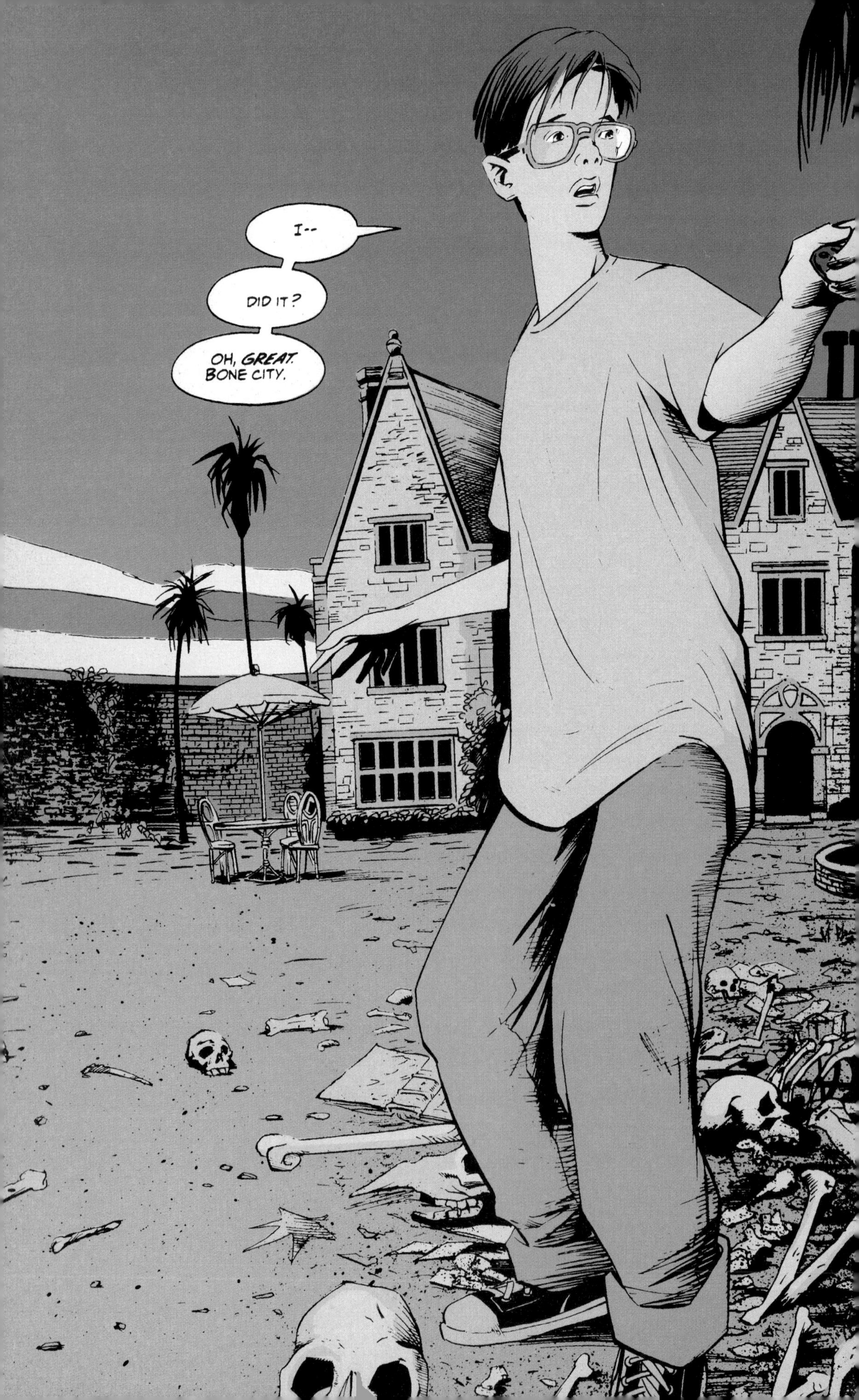
I--
DID IT?
OH, GREAT. BONE CITY.

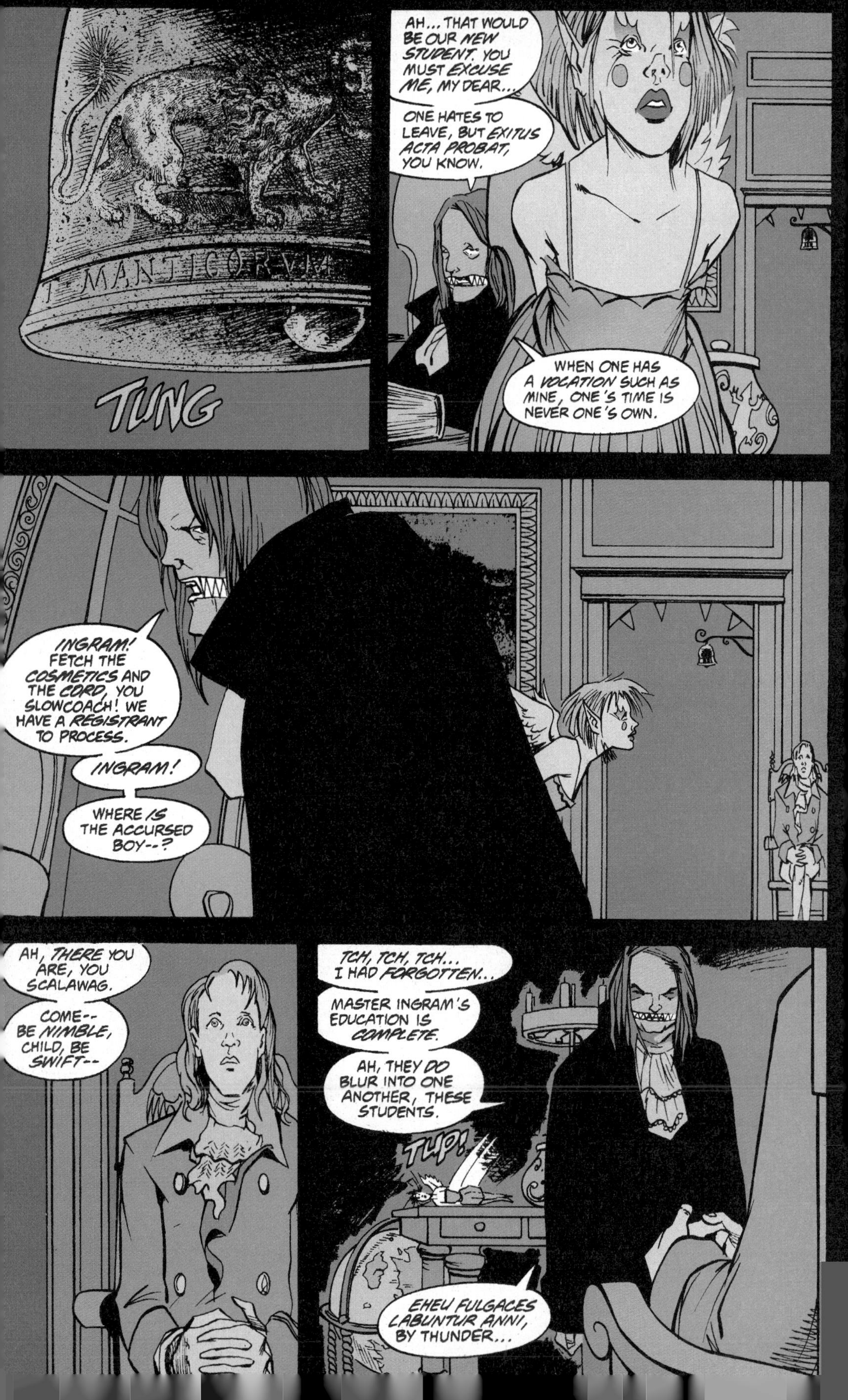
MANTICORVM
TUNG
AH... THAT WOULD BE OUR NEW STUDENT. YOU MUST EXCUSE ME, MY DEAR...
ONE HATES TO LEAVE, BUT EXITUS ACTA PROBAT, YOU KNOW.
WHEN ONE HAS A VOCATION SUCH AS MINE, ONE'S TIME IS NEVER ONE'S OWN.
INGRAM! FETCH THE COSMETICS AND THE CORD, YOU SLOWCOACH! WE HAVE A REGISTRANT TO PROCESS.
INGRAM!
WHERE IS THE ACCURSED BOY--?
AH, THERE YOU ARE, YOU SCALAWAG.
COME-- BE NIMBLE, CHILD, BE SWIFT--
TCH, TCH, TCH... I HAD FORGOTTEN...
MASTER INGRAM'S EDUCATION IS COMPLETE.
AH, THEY DO BLUR INTO ONE ANOTHER, THESE STUDENTS.
TUP!
EHEU FULGACES LABUNTUR ANNI, BY THUNDER...

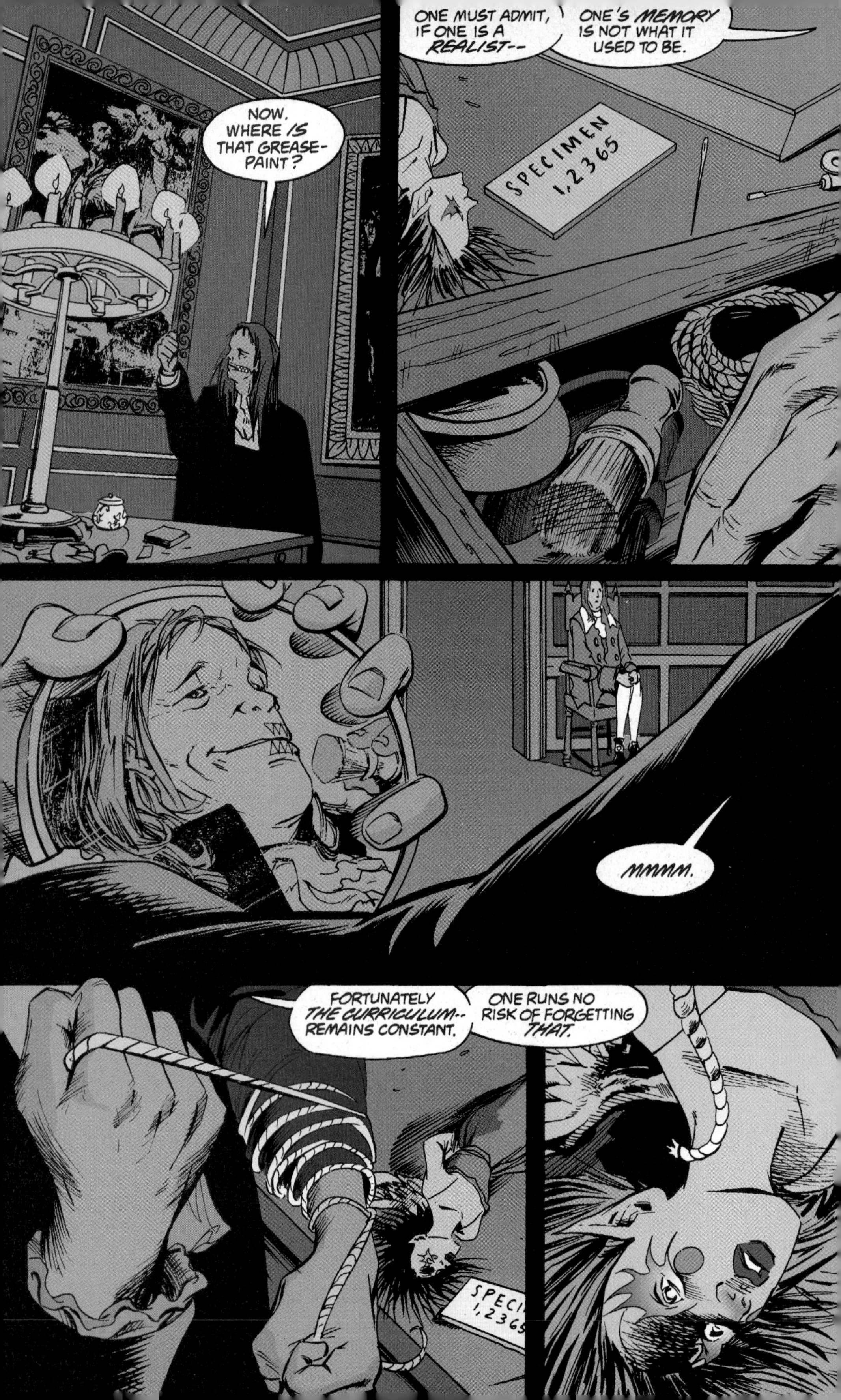
NOW. WHERE IS THAT GREASE-PAINT?
ONE MUST ADMIT, IF ONE IS A REALIST--
ONE'S MEMORY IS NOT WHAT IT USED TO BE.
SPECIMEN 1,2365
MMMM.
FORTUNATELY THE CURRICULUM-- REMAINS CONSTANT.
ONE RUNS NO RISK OF FORGETTING THAT.

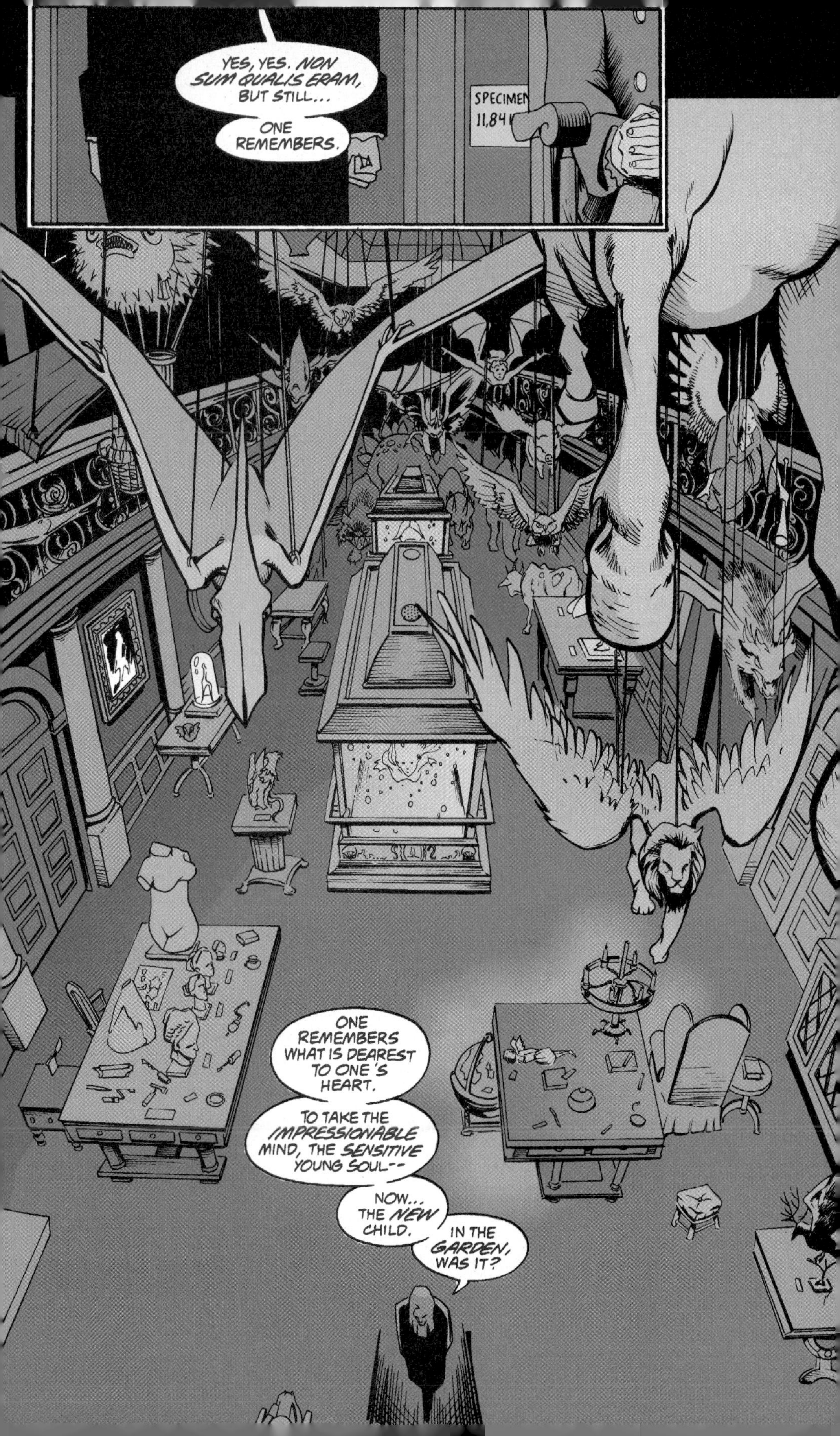
YES, YES. NON SUM QUALIS ERAM, BUT STILL...
ONE REMEMBERS.
SPECIMEN 11,84
ONE REMEMBERS WHAT IS DEAREST TO ONE'S HEART.
TO TAKE THE IMPRESSIONABLE MIND, THE SENSITIVE YOUNG SOUL--
NOW... THE NEW CHILD.
IN THE GARDEN, WAS IT?

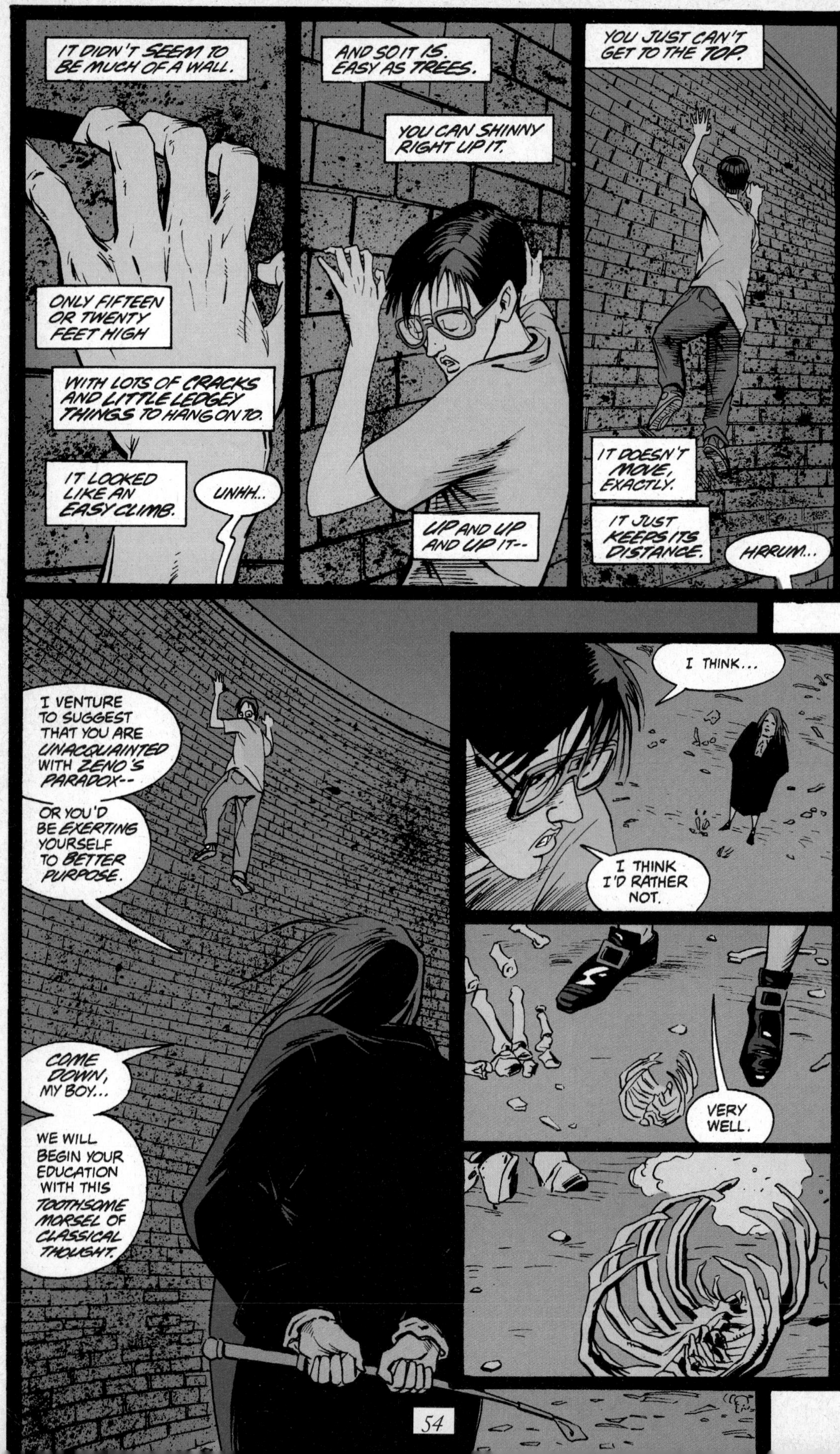
IT DIDN'T SEEM TO BE MUCH OF A WALL.
ONLY FIFTEEN OR TWENTY FEET HIGH
WITH LOTS OF CRACKS AND LITTLE LEDGEY THINGS TO HANG ON TO.
IT LOOKED LIKE AN EASY CLIMB.
UNHH...
AND SO IT IS. EASY AS TREES.
YOU CAN SHINNY RIGHT UP IT.
UP AND UP AND UP IT--
YOU JUST CAN'T GET TO THE TOP.
IT DOESN'T MOVE, EXACTLY.
IT JUST KEEPS ITS DISTANCE.
HRRUM...
I VENTURE TO SUGGEST THAT YOU ARE UNACQUAINTED WITH ZENO'S PARADOX--
OR YOU'D BE EXERTING YOURSELF TO BETTER PURPOSE.
COME DOWN, MY BOY...
WE WILL BEGIN YOUR EDUCATION WITH THIS TOOTHSOME MORSEL OF CLASSICAL THOUGHT.
I THINK...
I THINK I'D RATHER NOT.
VERY WELL.

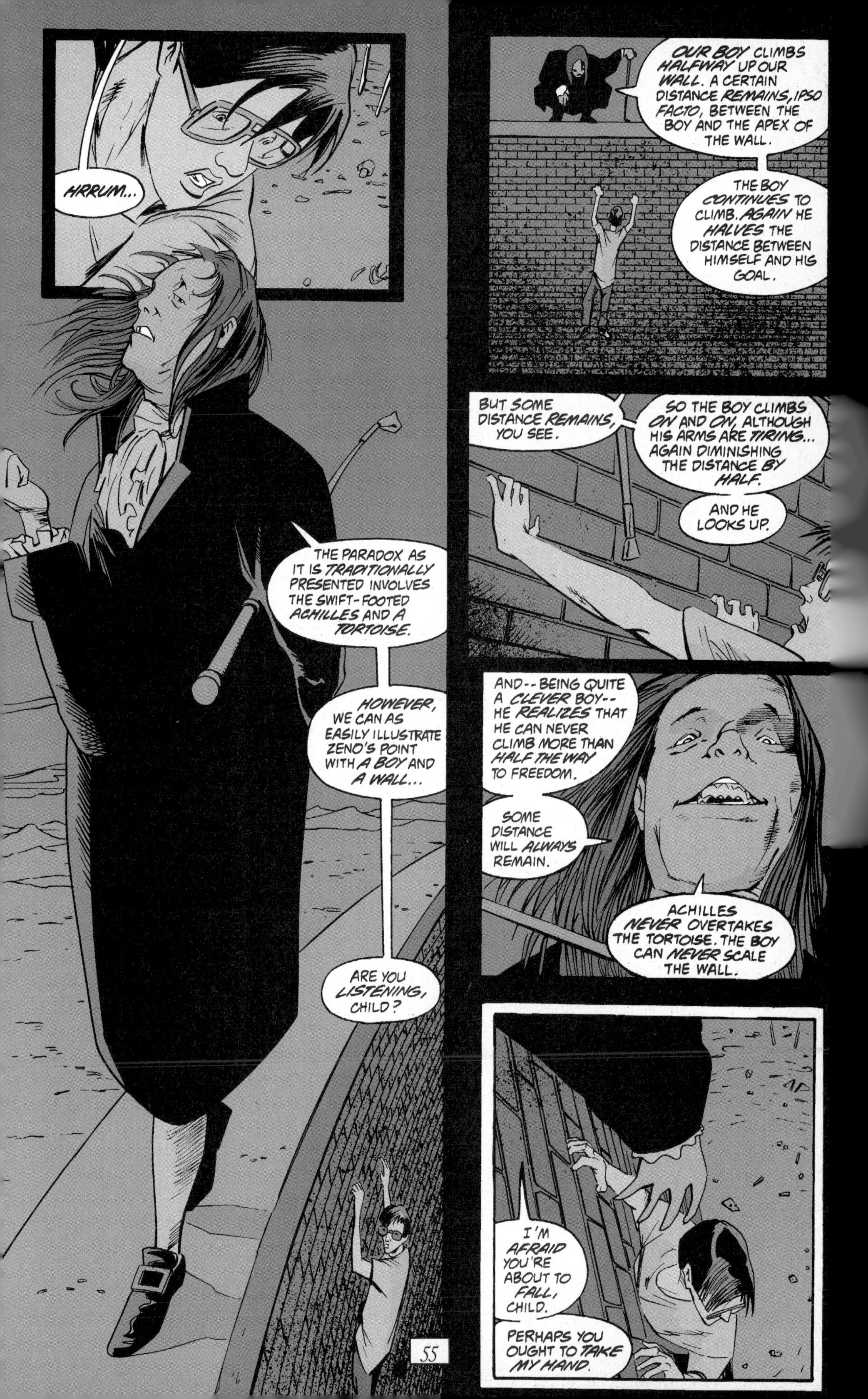
HRRUM...
THE PARADOX AS IT IS TRADITIONALLY PRESENTED INVOLVES THE SWIFT-FOOTED ACHILLES AND A TORTOISE.
HOWEVER, WE CAN AS EASILY ILLUSTRATE ZENO'S POINT WITH A BOY AND A WALL...
ARE YOU LISTENING, CHILD?
OUR BOY CLIMBS HALFWAY UP OUR WALL. A CERTAIN DISTANCE REMAINS, IPSO FACTO, BETWEEN THE BOY AND THE APEX OF THE WALL.
THE BOY CONTINUES TO CLIMB. AGAIN HE HALVES THE DISTANCE BETWEEN HIMSELF AND HIS GOAL.
BUT SOME DISTANCE REMAINS, YOU SEE.
SO THE BOY CLIMBS ON AND ON, ALTHOUGH HIS ARMS ARE TIRING... AGAIN DIMINISHING THE DISTANCE BY HALF.
AND HE LOOKS UP.
AND--BEING QUITE A CLEVER BOY--HE REALIZES THAT HE CAN NEVER CLIMB MORE THAN HALF THE WAY TO FREEDOM.
SOME DISTANCE WILL ALWAYS REMAIN.
ACHILLES NEVER OVERTAKES THE TORTOISE. THE BOY CAN NEVER SCALE THE WALL.
I'M AFRAID YOU'RE ABOUT TO FALL, CHILD.
PERHAPS YOU OUGHT TO TAKE MY HAND.

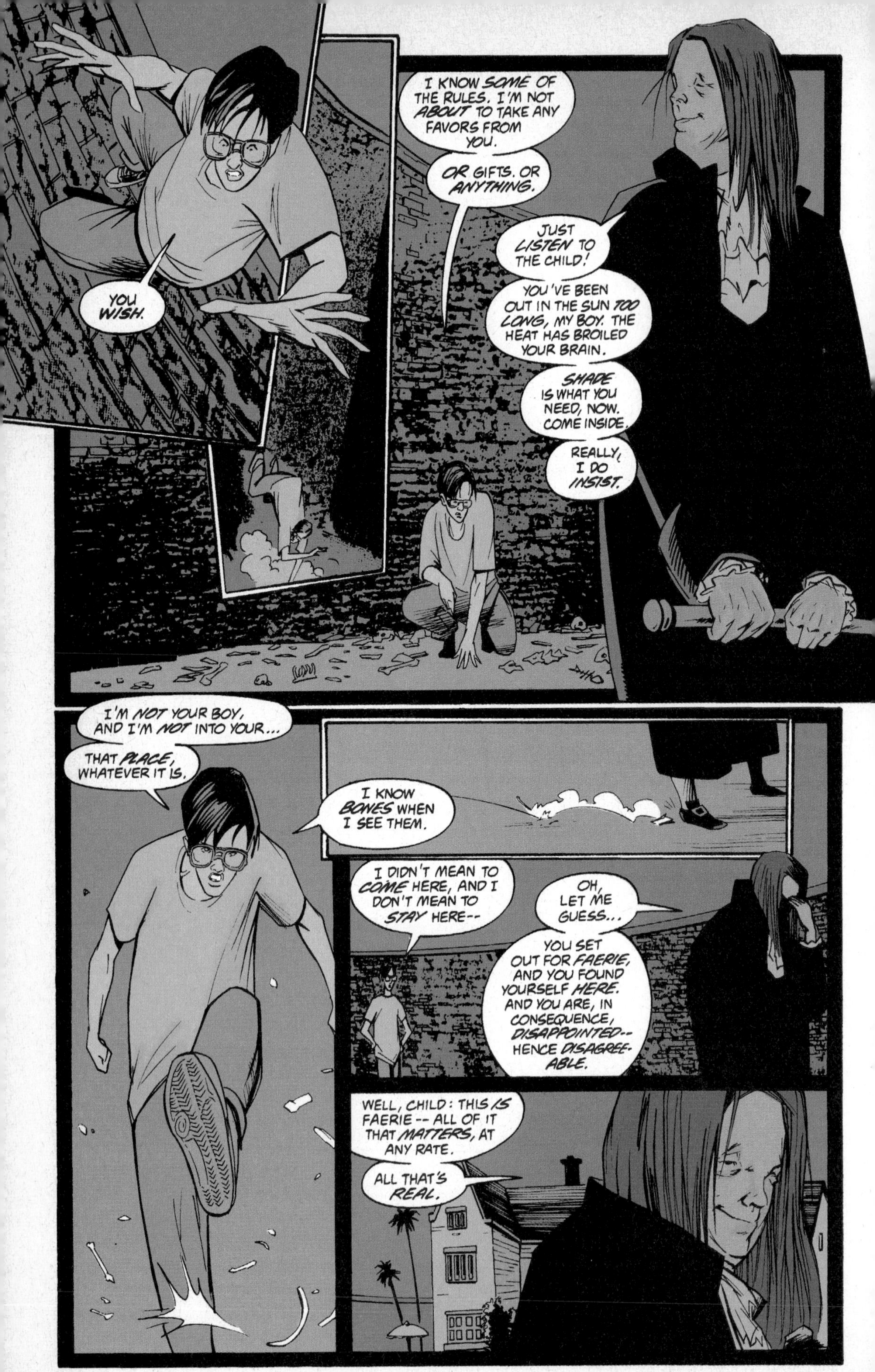
YOU WISH.
I KNOW SOME OF THE RULES. I'M NOT ABOUT TO TAKE ANY FAVORS FROM YOU.
OR GIFTS. OR ANYTHING.
JUST LISTEN TO THE CHILD!
YOU'VE BEEN OUT IN THE SUN TOO LONG, MY BOY. THE HEAT HAS BROILED YOUR BRAIN.
SHADE IS WHAT YOU NEED, NOW. COME INSIDE.
REALLY, I DO INSIST.
I'M NOT YOUR BOY, AND I'M NOT INTO YOUR...
THAT PLACE, WHATEVER IT IS.
I KNOW BONES WHEN I SEE THEM.
I DIDN'T MEAN TO COME HERE, AND I DON'T MEAN TO STAY HERE--
OH, LET ME GUESS...
YOU SET OUT FOR FAERIE, AND YOU FOUND YOURSELF HERE. AND YOU ARE, IN CONSEQUENCE, DISAPPOINTED-- HENCE DISAGREE-ABLE.
WELL, CHILD: THIS IS FAERIE -- ALL OF IT THAT MATTERS, AT ANY RATE.
ALL THAT'S REAL.

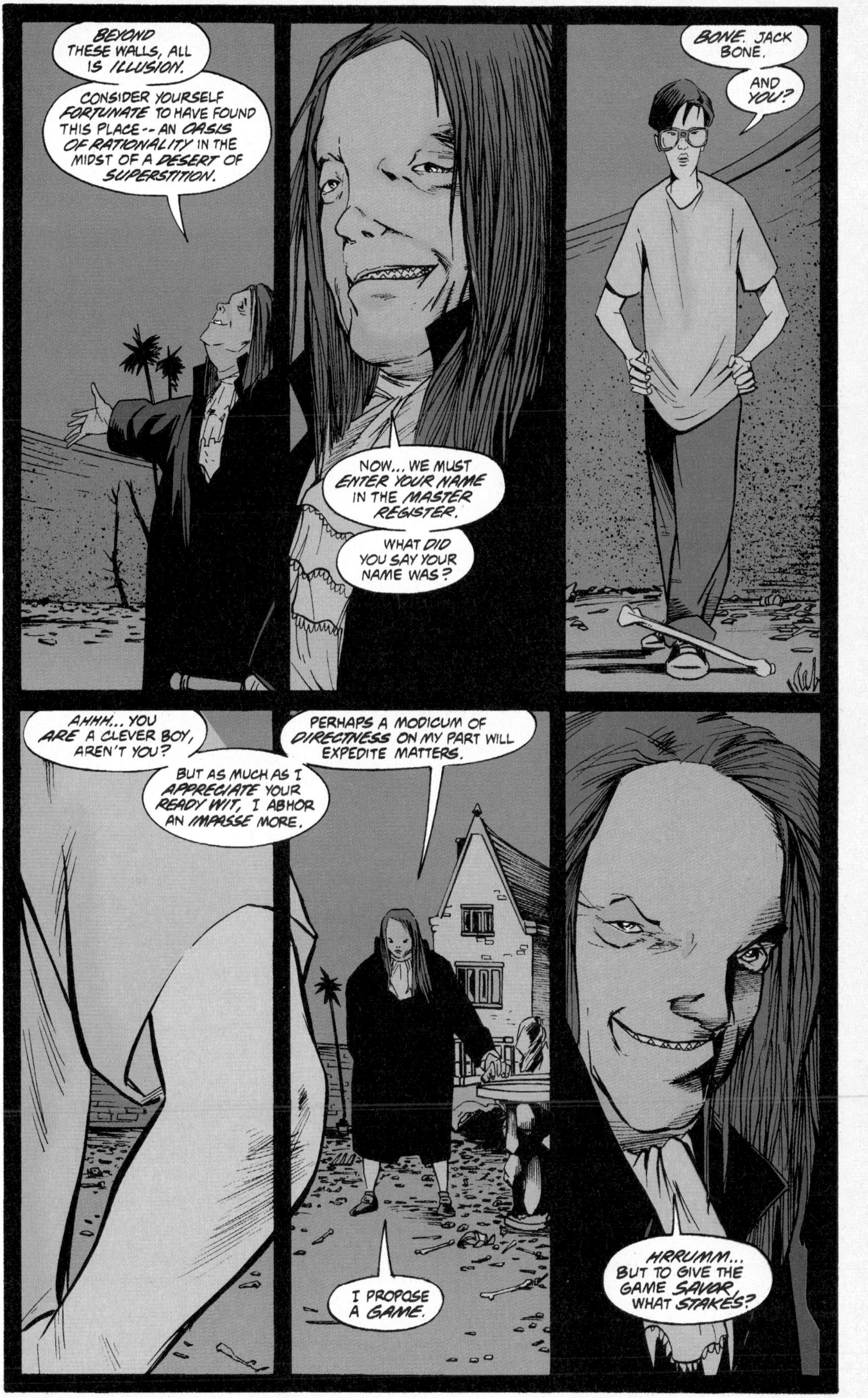
BEYOND THESE WALLS, ALL IS ILLUSION.
CONSIDER YOURSELF FORTUNATE TO HAVE FOUND THIS PLACE-- AN OASIS OF RATIONALITY IN THE MIDST OF A DESERT OF SUPERSTITION.
NOW... WE MUST ENTER YOUR NAME IN THE MASTER REGISTER.
WHAT DID YOU SAY YOUR NAME WAS?
BONE. JACK BONE.
AND YOU?
AHHH... YOU ARE A CLEVER BOY, AREN'T YOU?
BUT AS MUCH AS I APPRECIATE YOUR READY WIT, I ABHOR AN IMPASSE MORE.
PERHAPS A MODICUM OF DIRECTNESS ON MY PART WILL EXPEDITE MATTERS.
I PROPOSE A GAME.
HRRUMM... BUT TO GIVE THE GAME SAVOR, WHAT STAKES?

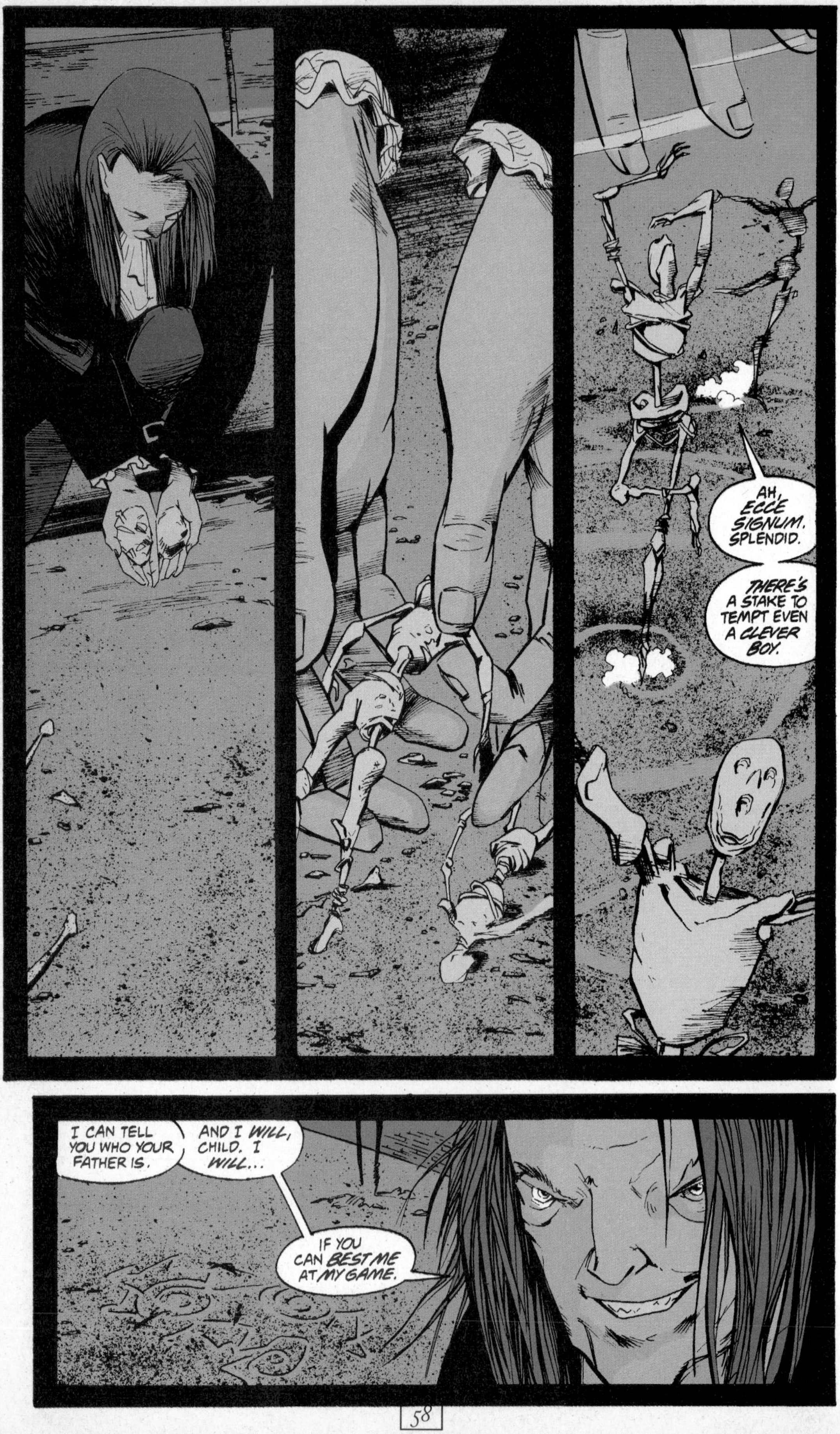
AH, ECCE SIGNUM. SPLENDID.
THERE'S A STAKE TO TEMPT EVEN A CLEVER BOY.
I CAN TELL YOU WHO YOUR FATHER IS.
AND I WILL, CHILD. I WILL...
IF YOU CAN BEST ME AT MY GAME.

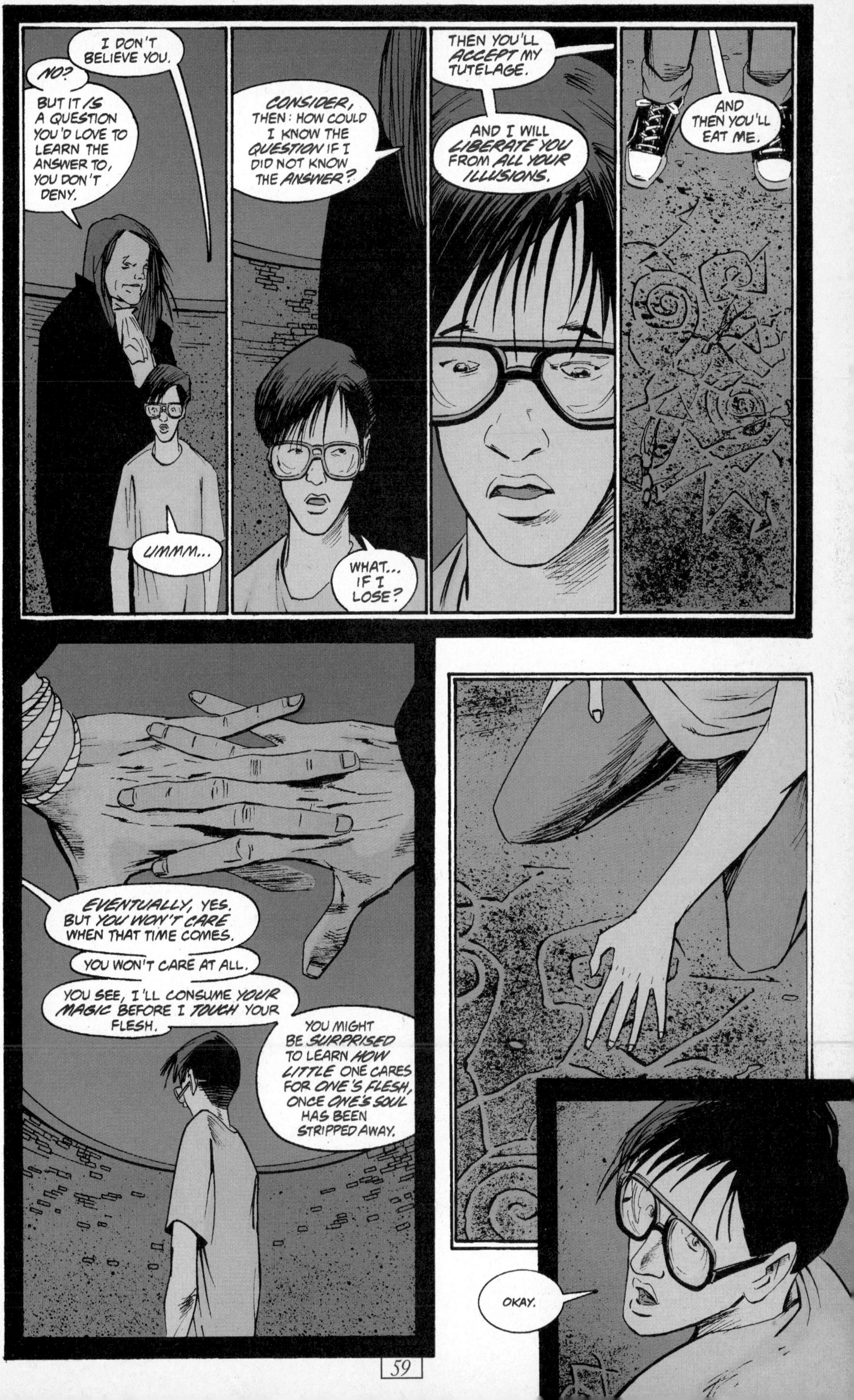
I DON'T BELIEVE YOU.
NO?
BUT IT IS A QUESTION YOU'D LOVE TO LEARN THE ANSWER TO, YOU DON'T DENY.
UMMM...
CONSIDER, THEN: HOW COULD I KNOW THE QUESTION IF I DID NOT KNOW THE ANSWER?
WHAT... IF I LOSE?
THEN YOU'LL ACCEPT MY TUTELAGE.
AND I WILL LIBERATE YOU FROM ALL YOUR ILLUSIONS.
AND THEN YOU'LL EAT ME.
EVENTUALLY, YES. BUT YOU WON'T CARE WHEN THAT TIME COMES.
YOU WON'T CARE AT ALL.
YOU SEE, I'LL CONSUME YOUR MAGIC BEFORE I TOUCH YOUR FLESH.
YOU MIGHT BE SURPRISED TO LEARN HOW LITTLE ONE CARES FOR ONE'S FLESH, ONCE ONE'S SOUL HAS BEEN STRIPPED AWAY.
OKAY.

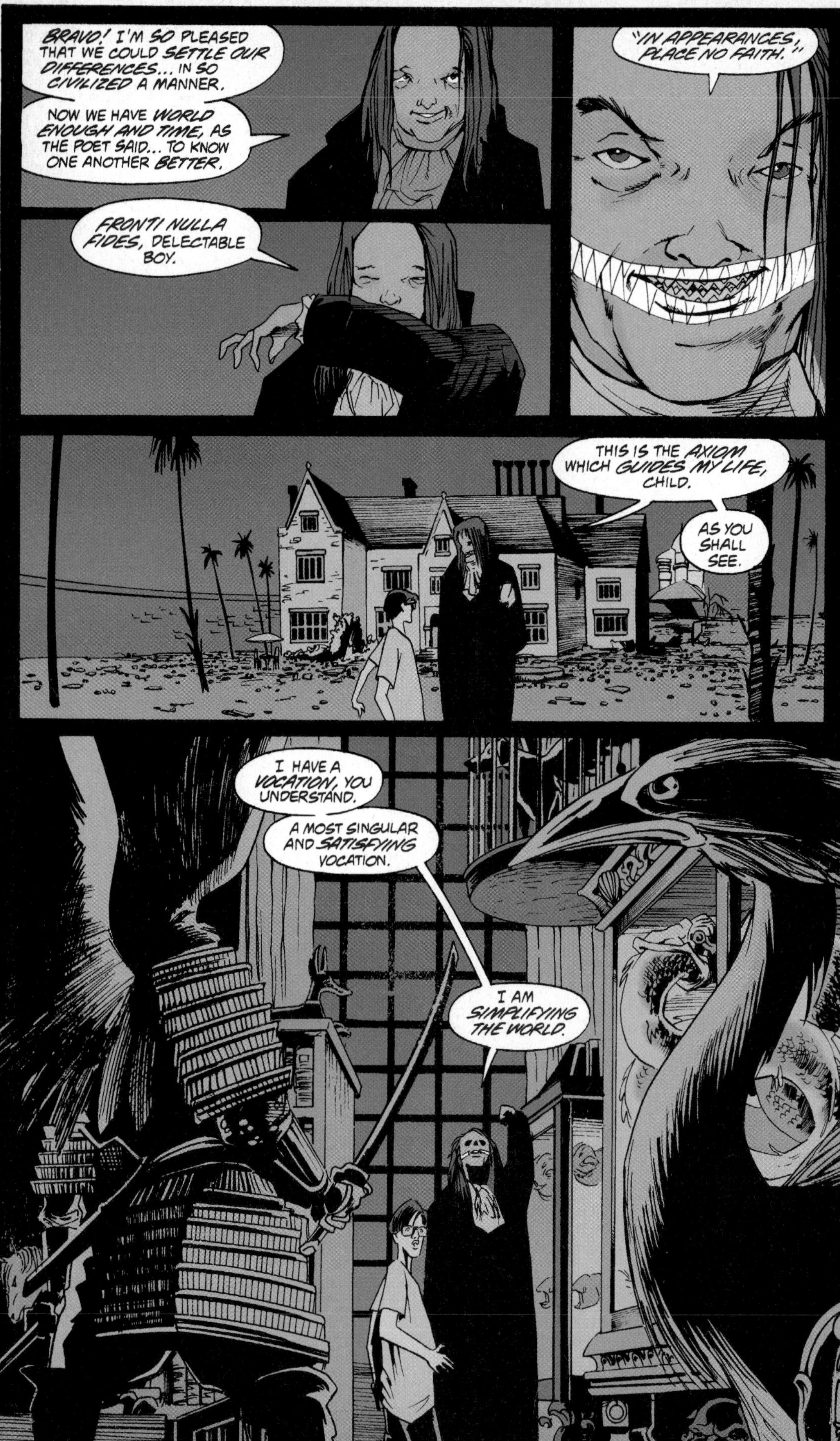
BRAVO! I'M SO PLEASED THAT WE COULD SETTLE OUR DIFFERENCES... IN SO CIVILIZED A MANNER.
NOW WE HAVE WORLD ENOUGH AND TIME, AS THE POET SAID... TO KNOW ONE ANOTHER BETTER.
FRONTI NULLA FIDES, DELECTABLE BOY.
"IN APPEARANCES, PLACE NO FAITH."
THIS IS THE AXIOM WHICH GUIDES MY LIFE, CHILD.
AS YOU SHALL SEE.
I HAVE A VOCATION, YOU UNDERSTAND.
A MOST SINGULAR AND SATISFYING VOCATION.
I AM SIMPLIFYING THE WORLD.

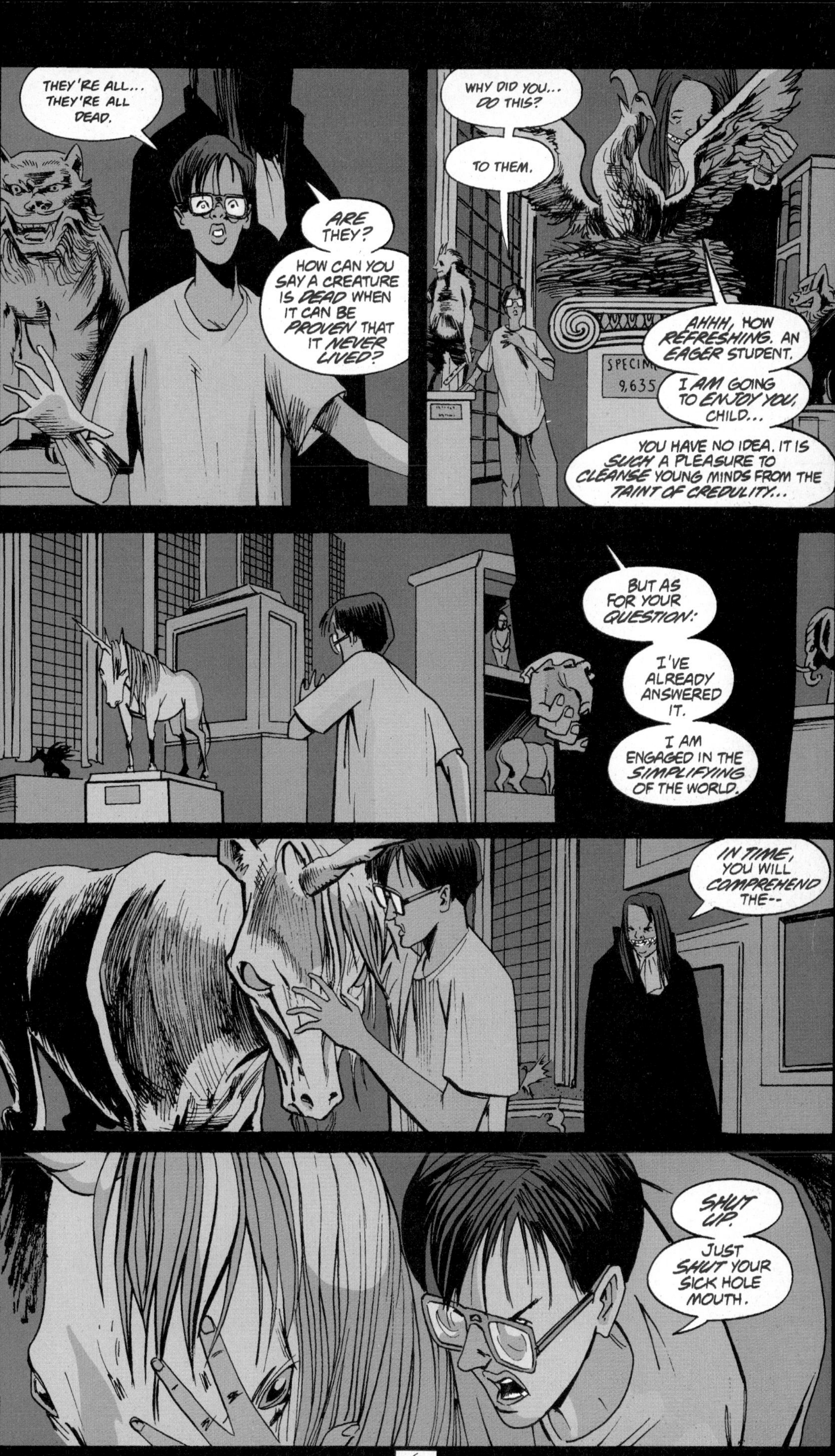

THEY'RE ALL... THEY'RE ALL DEAD.
ARE THEY?
HOW CAN YOU SAY A CREATURE IS DEAD WHEN IT CAN BE PROVEN THAT IT NEVER LIVED?
WHY DID YOU... DO THIS?
TO THEM.
AHHH, HOW REFRESHING. AN EAGER STUDENT.
I AM GOING TO ENJOY YOU, CHILD...
YOU HAVE NO IDEA. IT IS SUCH A PLEASURE TO CLEANSE YOUNG MINDS FROM THE TAINT OF CREDULITY...
BUT AS FOR YOUR QUESTION:
I'VE ALREADY ANSWERED IT.
I AM ENGAGED IN THE SIMPLIFYING OF THE WORLD.
IN TIME, YOU WILL COMPREHEND THE--
SHUT UP.
JUST SHUT YOUR SICK HOLE MOUTH.

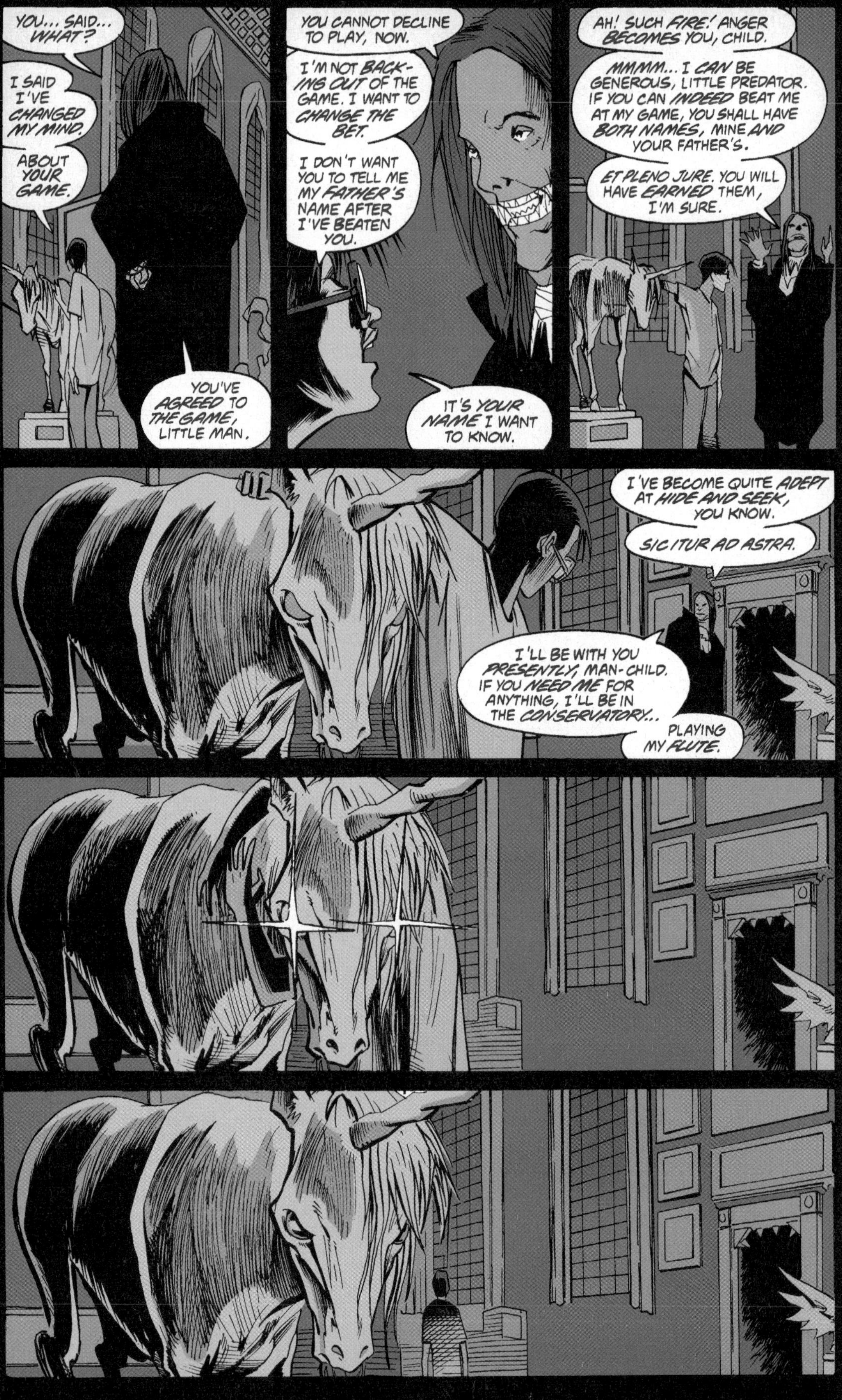

YOU... SAID... WHAT?
I SAID I'VE CHANGED MY MIND.
ABOUT YOUR GAME.
YOU'VE AGREED TO THE GAME, LITTLE MAN.
YOU CANNOT DECLINE TO PLAY, NOW.
I'M NOT BACKING OUT OF THE GAME. I WANT TO CHANGE THE BET.
I DON'T WANT YOU TO TELL ME MY FATHER'S NAME AFTER I'VE BEATEN YOU.
IT'S YOUR NAME I WANT TO KNOW.
AH! SUCH FIRE! ANGER BECOMES YOU, CHILD.
MMMM... I CAN BE GENEROUS, LITTLE PREDATOR. IF YOU CAN INDEED BEAT ME AT MY GAME, YOU SHALL HAVE BOTH NAMES, MINE AND YOUR FATHER'S.
ET PLENO JURE. YOU WILL HAVE EARNED THEM, I'M SURE.
I'VE BECOME QUITE ADEPT AT HIDE AND SEEK, YOU KNOW.
SIC ITUR AD ASTRA.
I'LL BE WITH YOU PRESENTLY, MAN-CHILD. IF YOU NEED ME FOR ANYTHING, I'LL BE IN THE CONSERVATORY...
PLAYING MY FLUTE.

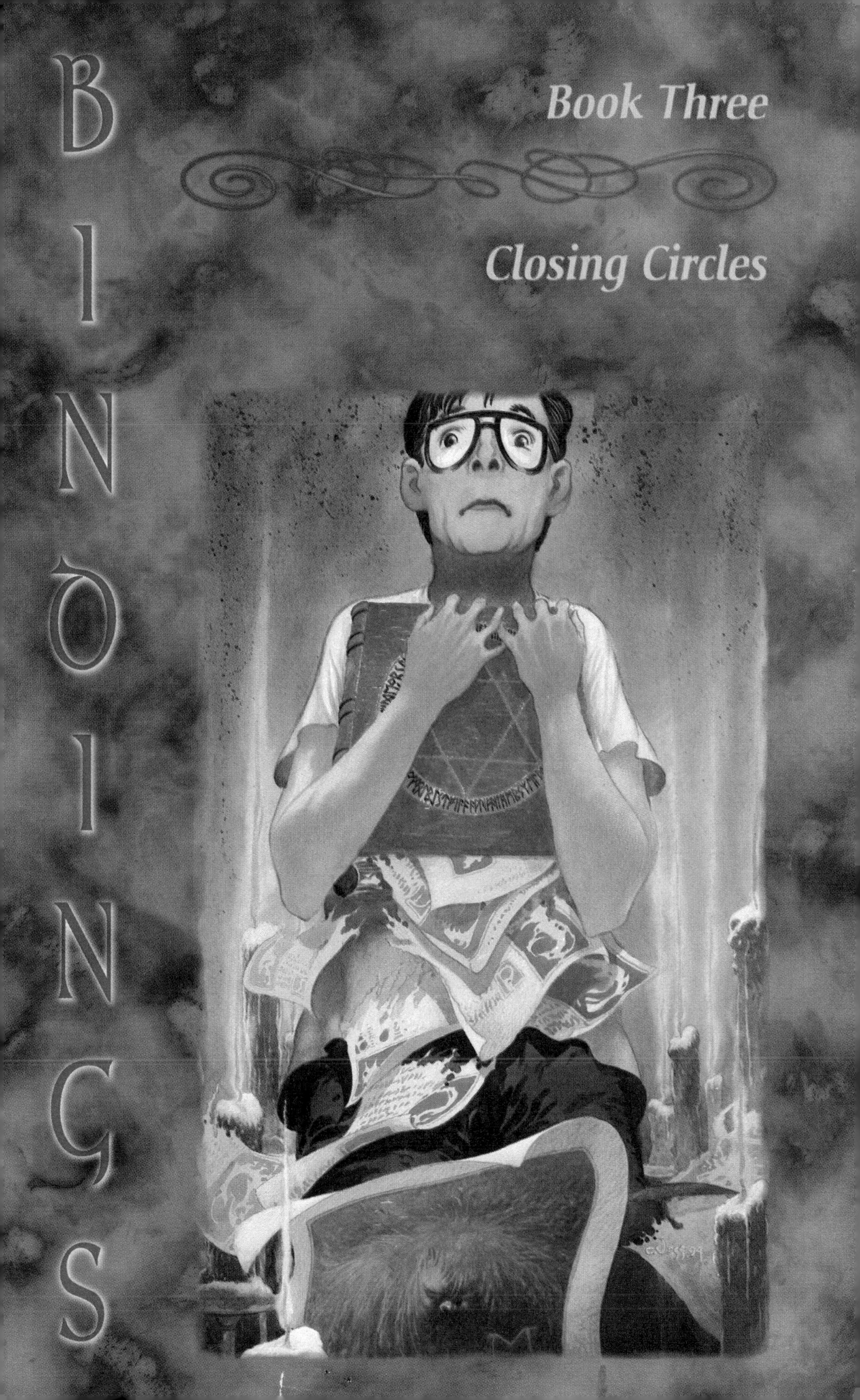
BINDINGS
Book Three
Closing Circles

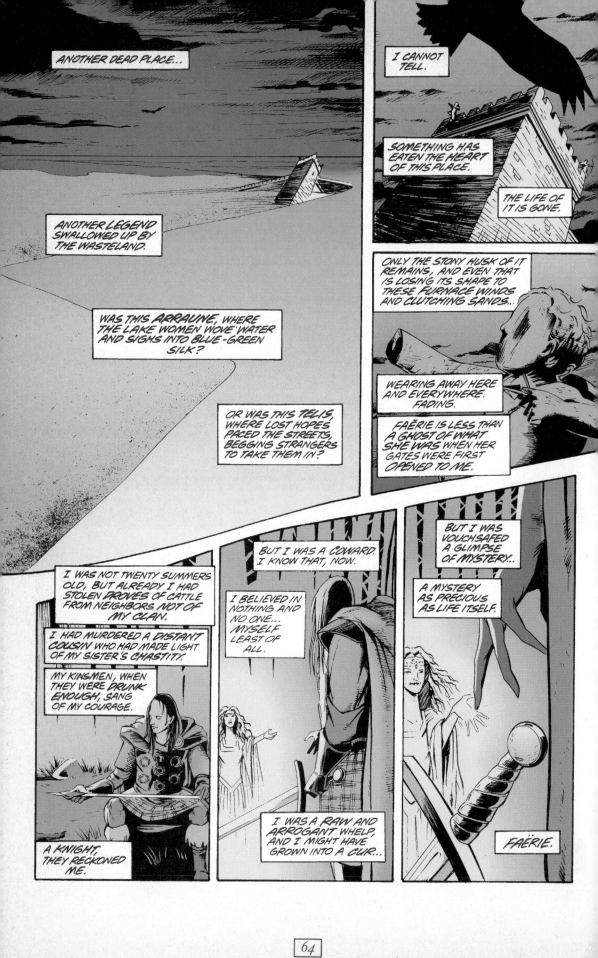

ANOTHER DEAD PLACE...

ANOTHER LEGEND SWALLOWED UP BY THE WASTELAND.

WAS THIS *ARRAUNE*, WHERE THE LAKE WOMEN WOVE WATER AND SIGHS INTO BLUE-GREEN SILK?

OR WAS THIS *TELIS*, WHERE LOST HOPES PACED THE STREETS, BEGGING STRANGERS TO TAKE THEM IN?

I CANNOT TELL.

SOMETHING HAS EATEN THE HEART OF THIS PLACE.

THE LIFE OF IT IS GONE.

ONLY THE STONY HUSK OF IT REMAINS, AND EVEN THAT IS LOSING ITS SHAPE TO THESE *FURNACE WINDS* AND CLUTCHING SANDS...

WEARING AWAY HERE AND EVERYWHERE. FADING.

FAËRIE IS LESS THAN A GHOST OF WHAT SHE WAS WHEN HER GATES WERE FIRST OPENED TO ME.

I WAS NOT TWENTY SUMMERS OLD, BUT ALREADY I HAD STOLEN *DROVES* OF CATTLE FROM NEIGHBORS *NOT OF MY CLAN.*

I HAD MURDERED A DISTANT *COUSIN* WHO HAD MADE LIGHT OF MY SISTER'S *CHASTITY.*

MY KINSMEN, WHEN THEY WERE DRUNK ENOUGH, SANG OF MY COURAGE.

A KNIGHT, THEY RECKONED ME.

BUT I WAS A *COWARD.* I KNOW THAT, NOW.

I BELIEVED IN NOTHING AND NO ONE... MYSELF LEAST OF ALL.

I WAS A RAW AND ARROGANT WHELP, AND I MIGHT HAVE GROWN INTO A *CUR...*

BUT I WAS VOUCHSAFED A GLIMPSE OF *MYSTERY...*

A MYSTERY AS PRECIOUS AS LIFE ITSELF.

FAËRIE.

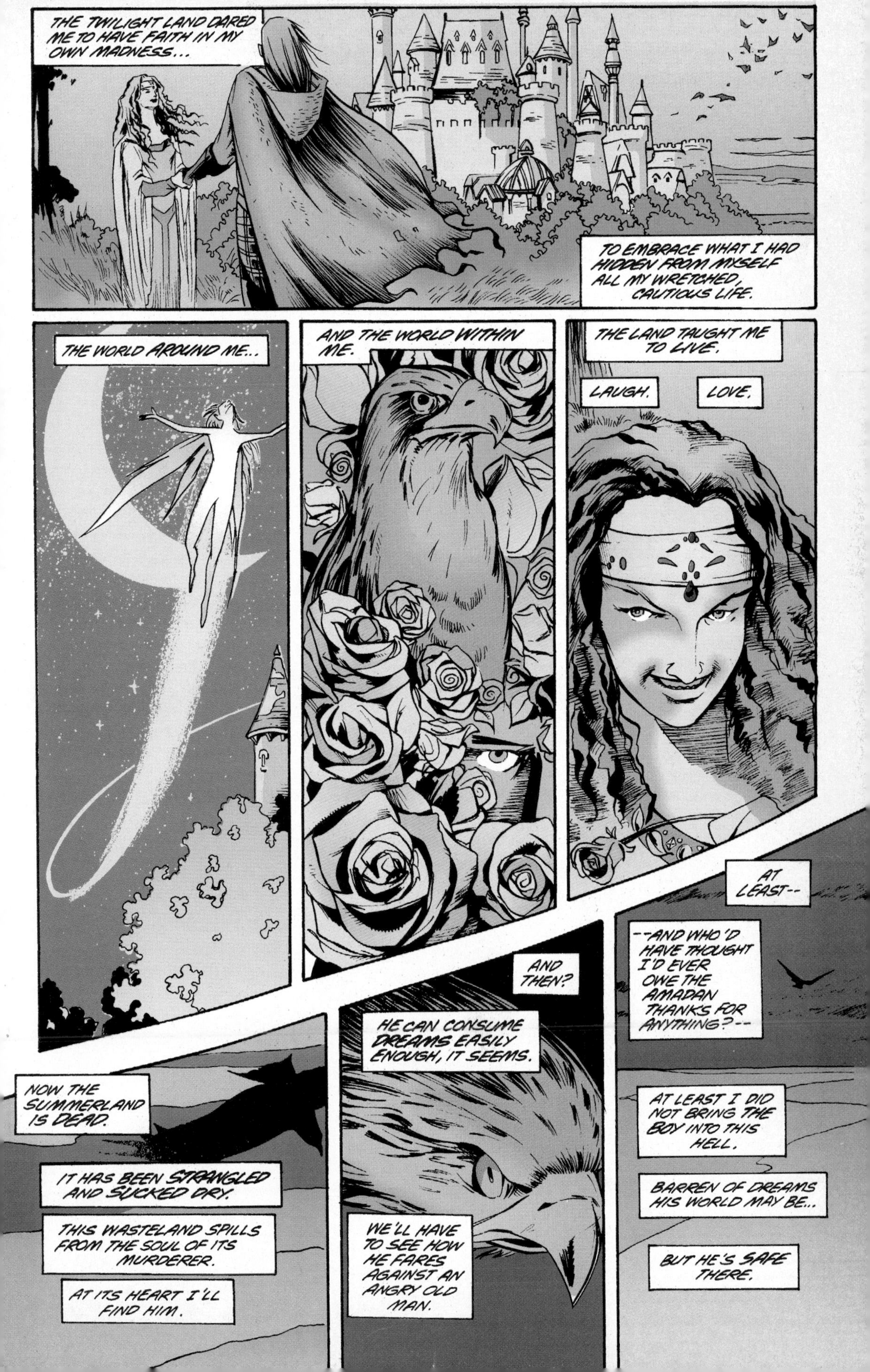
THE TWILIGHT LAND DARED ME TO HAVE FAITH IN MY OWN MADNESS...
TO EMBRACE WHAT I HAD HIDDEN FROM MYSELF ALL MY WRETCHED, CAUTIOUS LIFE.
THE WORLD AROUND ME...
AND THE WORLD WITHIN ME.
THE LAND TAUGHT ME TO LIVE.
LAUGH.
LOVE.
AT LEAST--
--AND WHO'D HAVE THOUGHT I'D EVER OWE THE AMADAN THANKS FOR ANYTHING?--
AND THEN?
HE CAN CONSUME DREAMS EASILY ENOUGH, IT SEEMS.
NOW THE SUMMERLAND IS DEAD.
IT HAS BEEN STRANGLED AND SUCKED DRY.
THIS WASTELAND SPILLS FROM THE SOUL OF ITS MURDERER.
AT ITS HEART I'LL FIND HIM.
WE'LL HAVE TO SEE HOW HE FARES AGAINST AN ANGRY OLD MAN.
AT LEAST I DID NOT BRING THE BOY INTO THIS HELL.
BARREN OF DREAMS HIS WORLD MAY BE...
BUT HE'S SAFE THERE.

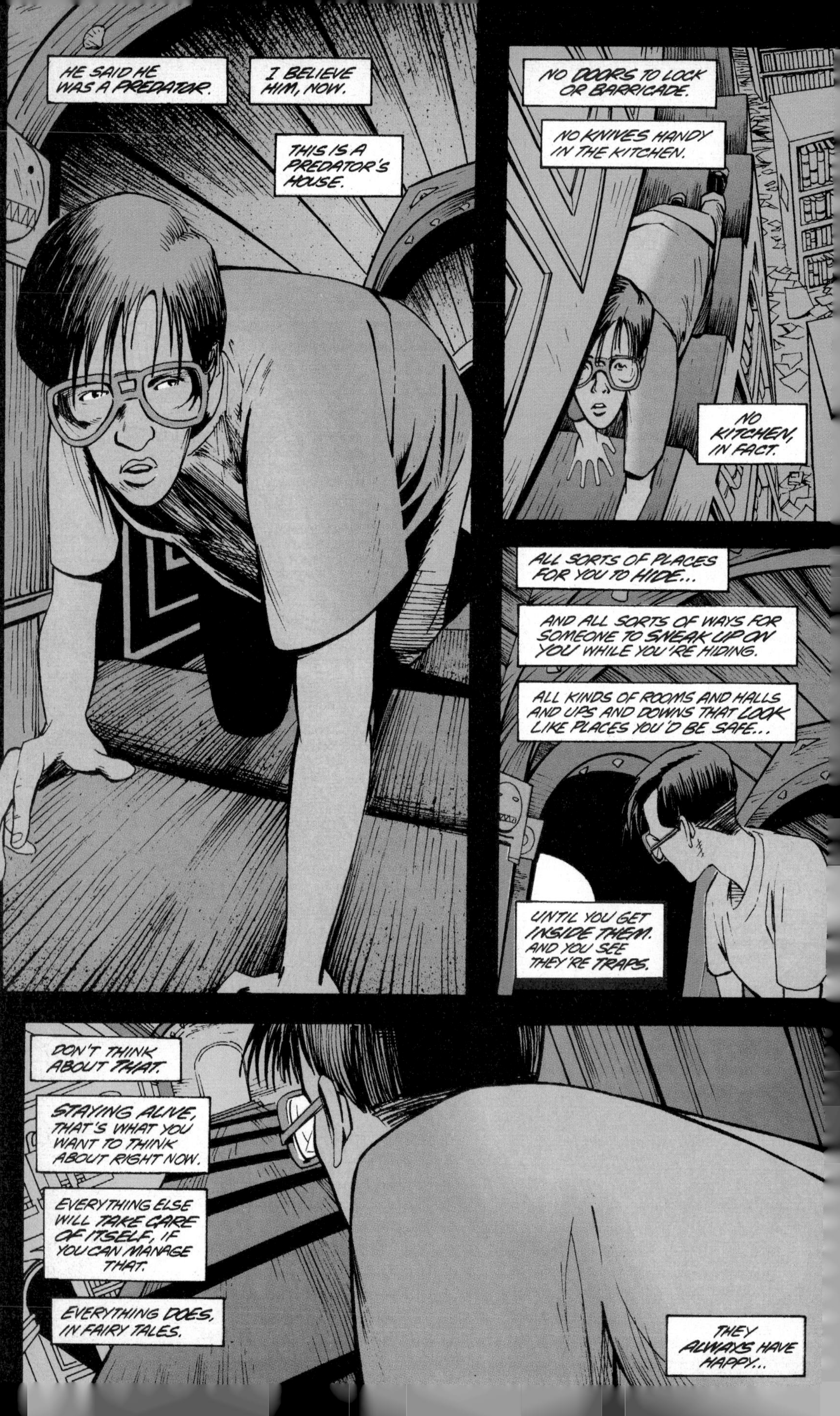
HE SAID HE WAS A PREDATOR.
I BELIEVE HIM, NOW.
THIS IS A PREDATOR'S HOUSE.
NO DOORS TO LOCK OR BARRICADE.
NO KNIVES HANDY IN THE KITCHEN.
NO KITCHEN, IN FACT.
ALL SORTS OF PLACES FOR YOU TO HIDE...
AND ALL SORTS OF WAYS FOR SOMEONE TO SNEAK UP ON YOU WHILE YOU'RE HIDING.
ALL KINDS OF ROOMS AND HALLS AND UPS AND DOWNS THAT LOOK LIKE PLACES YOU'D BE SAFE...
UNTIL YOU GET INSIDE THEM. AND YOU SEE THEY'RE TRAPS.
DON'T THINK ABOUT THAT.
STAYING ALIVE, THAT'S WHAT YOU WANT TO THINK ABOUT RIGHT NOW.
EVERYTHING ELSE WILL TAKE CARE OF ITSELF, IF YOU CAN MANAGE THAT.
EVERYTHING DOES, IN FAIRY TALES.
THEY ALWAYS HAVE HAPPY...

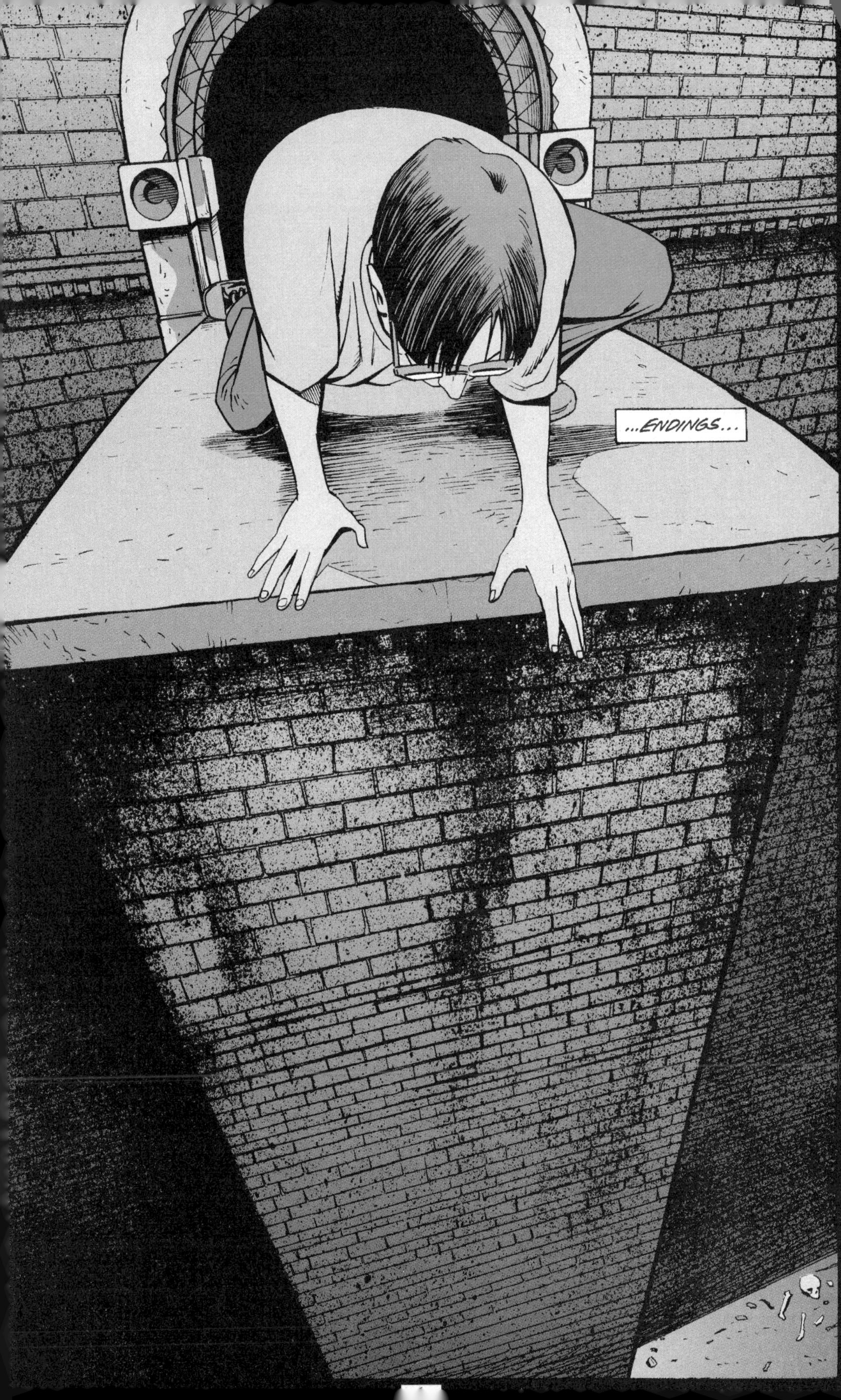
...ENDINGS...

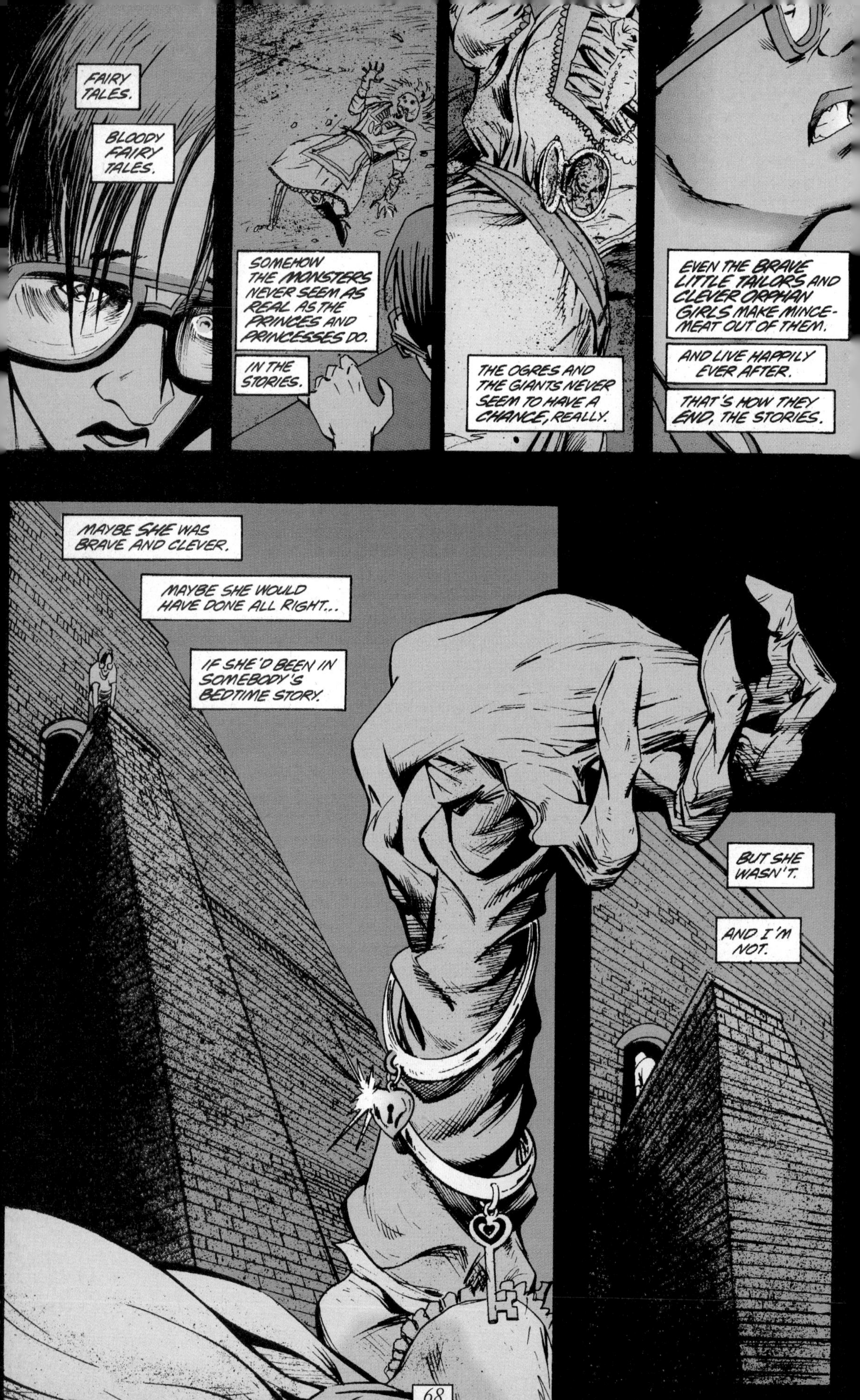
FAIRY TALES.
BLOODY FAIRY TALES.
SOMEHOW THE MONSTERS NEVER SEEM AS REAL AS THE PRINCES AND PRINCESSES DO.
IN THE STORIES.
THE OGRES AND THE GIANTS NEVER SEEM TO HAVE A CHANCE, REALLY.
EVEN THE BRAVE LITTLE TAILORS AND CLEVER ORPHAN GIRLS MAKE MINCE-MEAT OUT OF THEM.
AND LIVE HAPPILY EVER AFTER.
THAT'S HOW THEY END, THE STORIES.
MAYBE SHE WAS BRAVE AND CLEVER.
MAYBE SHE WOULD HAVE DONE ALL RIGHT...
IF SHE'D BEEN IN SOMEBODY'S BEDTIME STORY.
BUT SHE WASN'T.
AND I'M NOT.

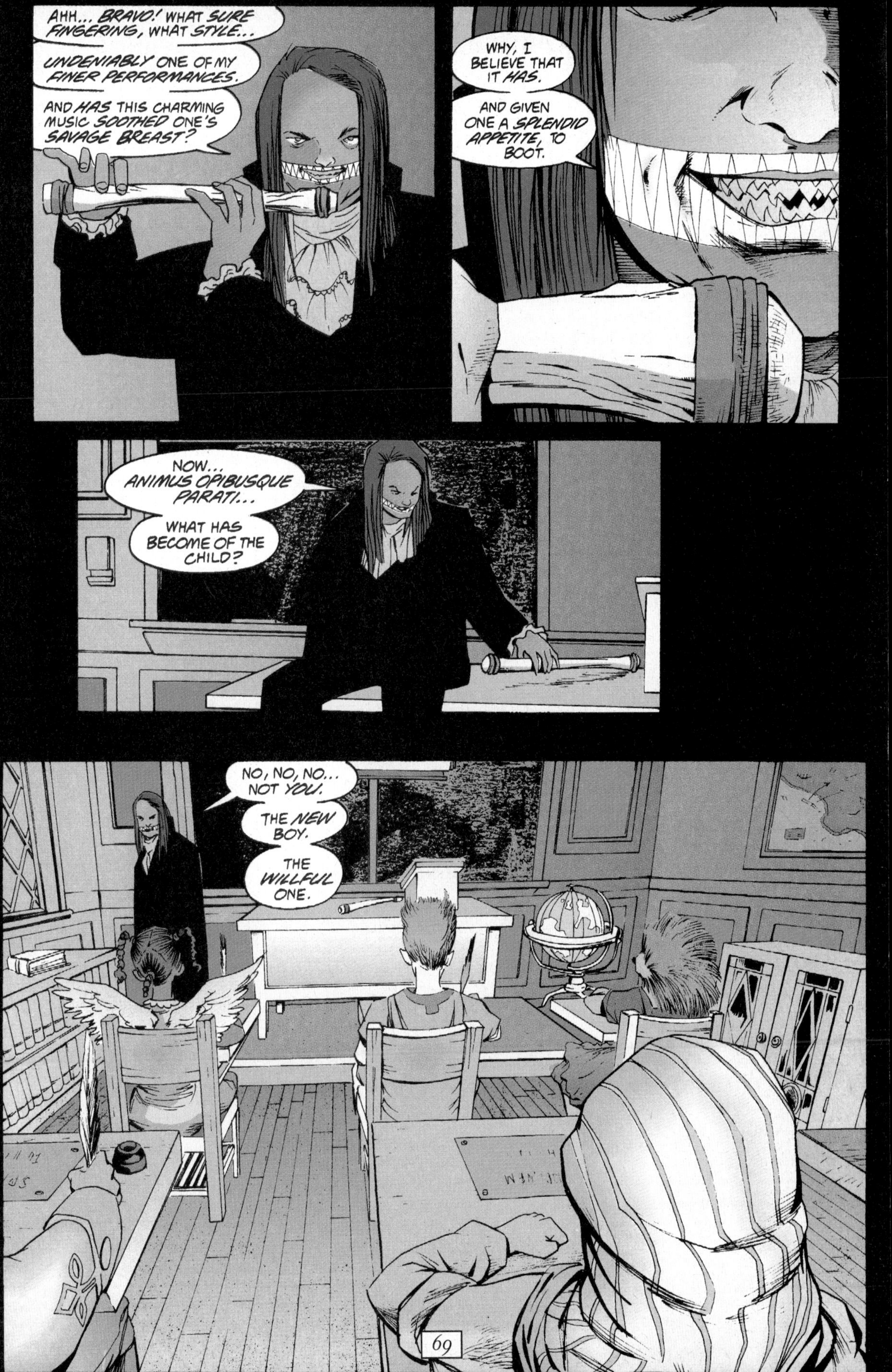
AHH... BRAVO! WHAT SURE FINGERING, WHAT STYLE...
UNDENIABLY ONE OF MY FINER PERFORMANCES.
AND HAS THIS CHARMING MUSIC SOOTHED ONE'S SAVAGE BREAST?
WHY, I BELIEVE THAT IT HAS.
AND GIVEN ONE A SPLENDID APPETITE, TO BOOT.
NOW... ANIMUS OPIBUSQUE PARATI...
WHAT HAS BECOME OF THE CHILD?
NO, NO, NO... NOT YOU.
THE NEW BOY.
THE WILLFUL ONE.

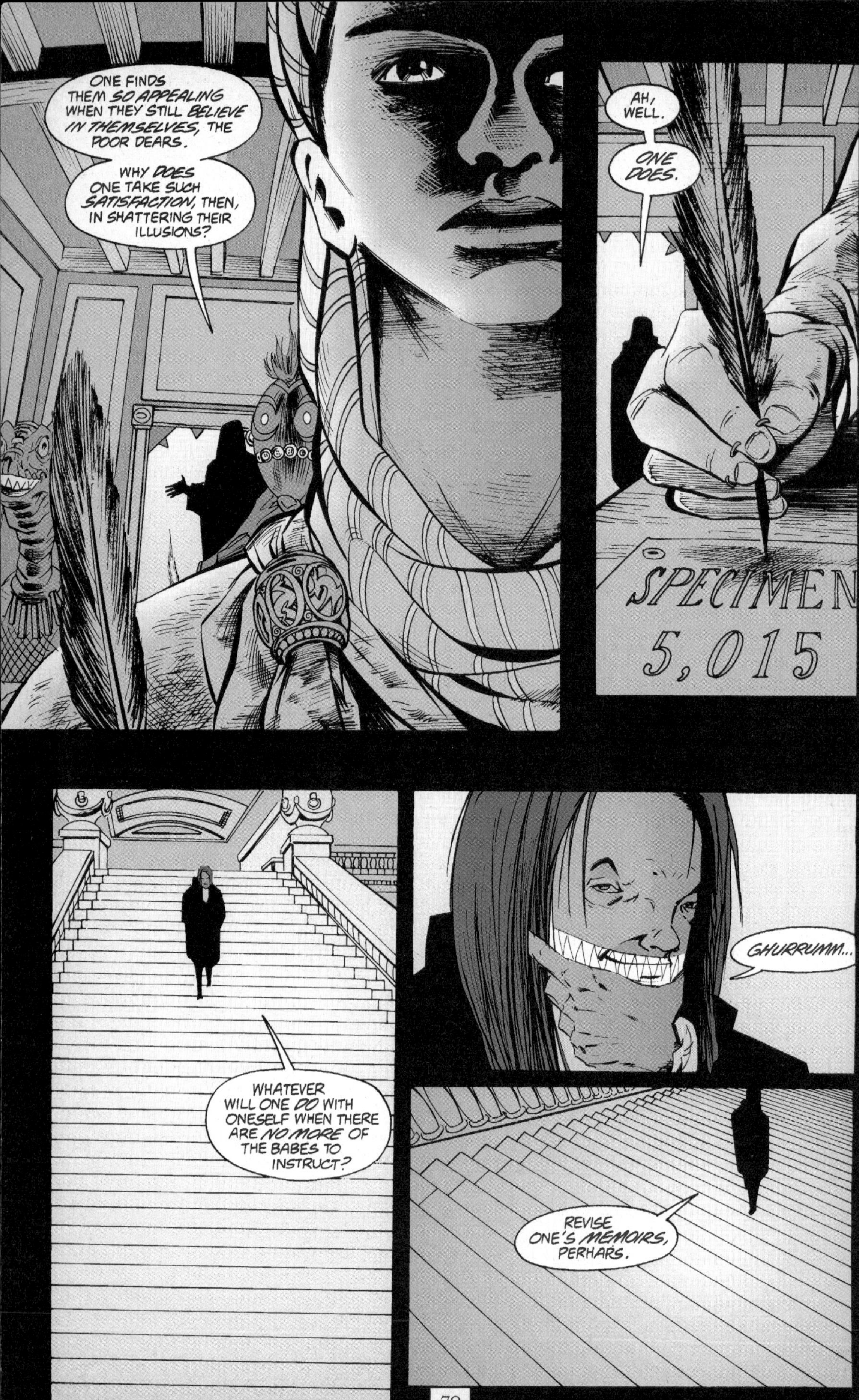
ONE FINDS THEM SO APPEALING WHEN THEY STILL BELIEVE IN THEMSELVES, THE POOR DEARS.
WHY DOES ONE TAKE SUCH SATISFACTION, THEN, IN SHATTERING THEIR ILLUSIONS?
AH, WELL.
ONE DOES.
SPECIMEN
5,015
WHATEVER WILL ONE DO WITH ONESELF WHEN THERE ARE NO MORE OF THE BABES TO INSTRUCT?
GHURRUMM...
REVISE ONE'S MEMOIRS, PERHAPS.

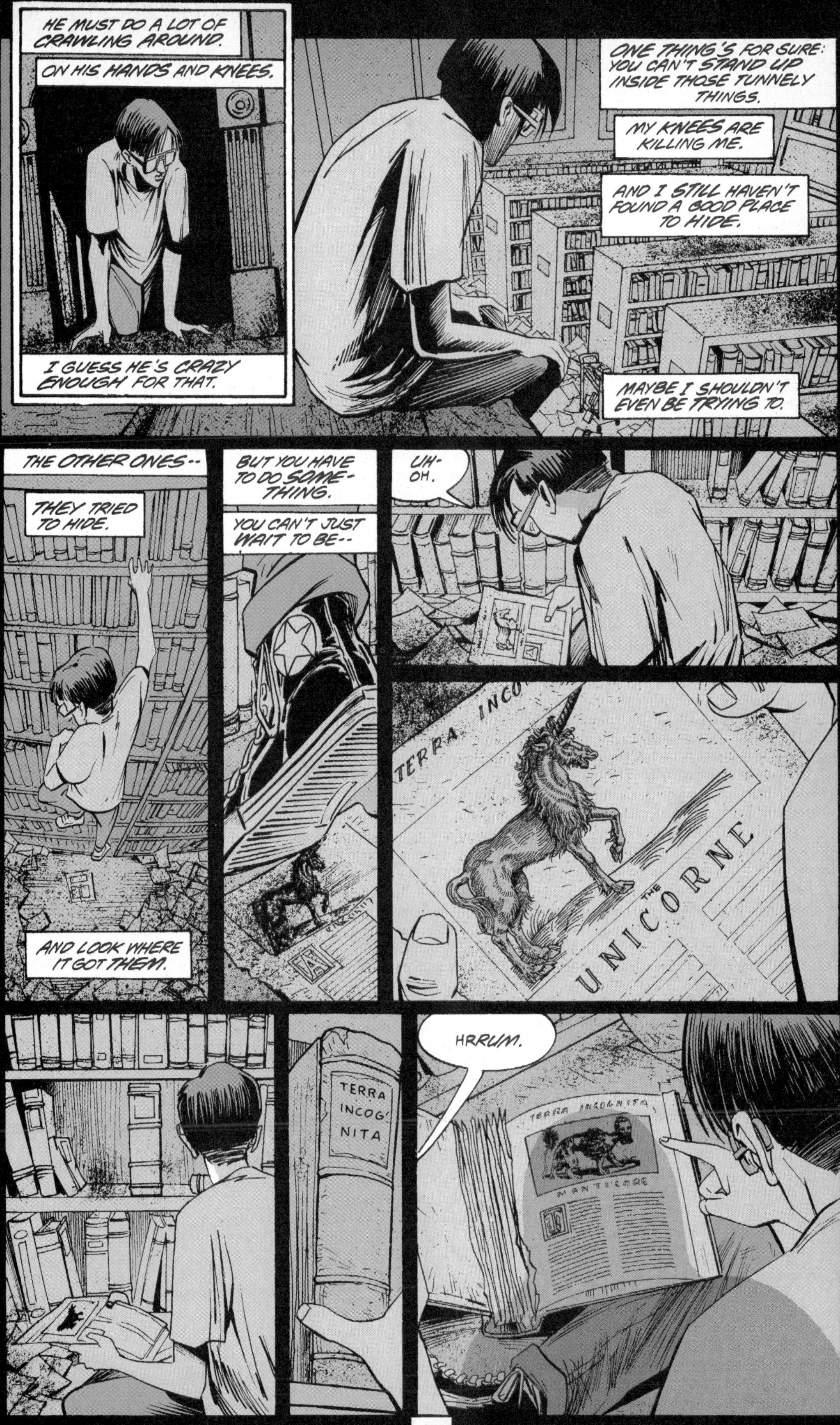

HE MUST DO A LOT OF CRAWLING AROUND.
ON HIS HANDS AND KNEES.
I GUESS HE'S CRAZY ENOUGH FOR THAT.
ONE THING'S FOR SURE: YOU CAN'T STAND UP INSIDE THOSE TUNNELY THINGS.
MY KNEES ARE KILLING ME.
AND I STILL HAVEN'T FOUND A GOOD PLACE TO HIDE.
MAYBE I SHOULDN'T EVEN BE TRYING TO.
THE OTHER ONES--
THEY TRIED TO HIDE.
AND LOOK WHERE IT GOT THEM.
BUT YOU HAVE TO DO SOME-THING.
YOU CAN'T JUST WAIT TO BE--
UH-OH.
TERRA INCO
THE UNICORNE
TERRA INCOG NITA
HRRUM.
TERRA INCOGNITA
MANTICORE

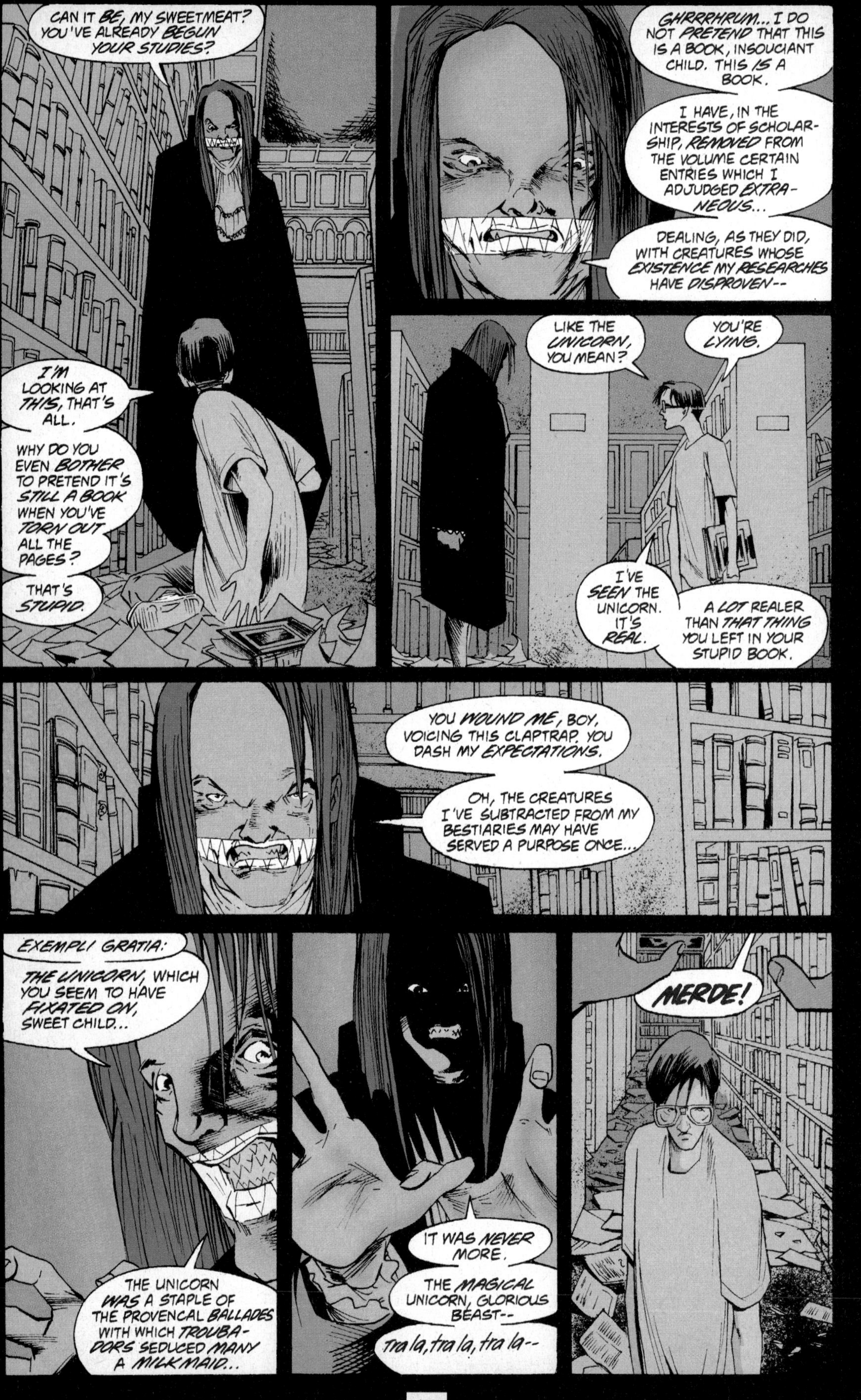
CAN IT BE, MY SWEETMEAT? YOU'VE ALREADY BEGUN YOUR STUDIES?
I'M LOOKING AT THIS, THAT'S ALL.
WHY DO YOU EVEN BOTHER TO PRETEND IT'S STILL A BOOK WHEN YOU'VE TORN OUT ALL THE PAGES?
THAT'S STUPID.
GHRRRHRUM... I DO NOT PRETEND THAT THIS IS A BOOK, INSOUCIANT CHILD. THIS IS A BOOK.
I HAVE, IN THE INTERESTS OF SCHOLARSHIP, REMOVED FROM THE VOLUME CERTAIN ENTRIES WHICH I ADJUDGED EXTRANEOUS...
DEALING, AS THEY DID, WITH CREATURES WHOSE EXISTENCE MY RESEARCHES HAVE DISPROVEN--
LIKE THE UNICORN, YOU MEAN?
YOU'RE LYING.
I'VE SEEN THE UNICORN. IT'S REAL.
A LOT REALER THAN THAT THING YOU LEFT IN YOUR STUPID BOOK.
YOU WOUND ME, BOY, VOICING THIS CLAPTRAP. YOU DASH MY EXPECTATIONS.
OH, THE CREATURES I'VE SUBTRACTED FROM MY BESTIARIES MAY HAVE SERVED A PURPOSE ONCE...
EXEMPLI GRATIA:
THE UNICORN, WHICH YOU SEEM TO HAVE FIXATED ON, SWEET CHILD...
THE UNICORN WAS A STAPLE OF THE PROVENCAL BALLADES WITH WHICH TROUBADORS SEDUCED MANY A MILKMAID...
IT WAS NEVER MORE.
THE MAGICAL UNICORN, GLORIOUS BEAST--
tra la, tra la, tra la--
MERDE!

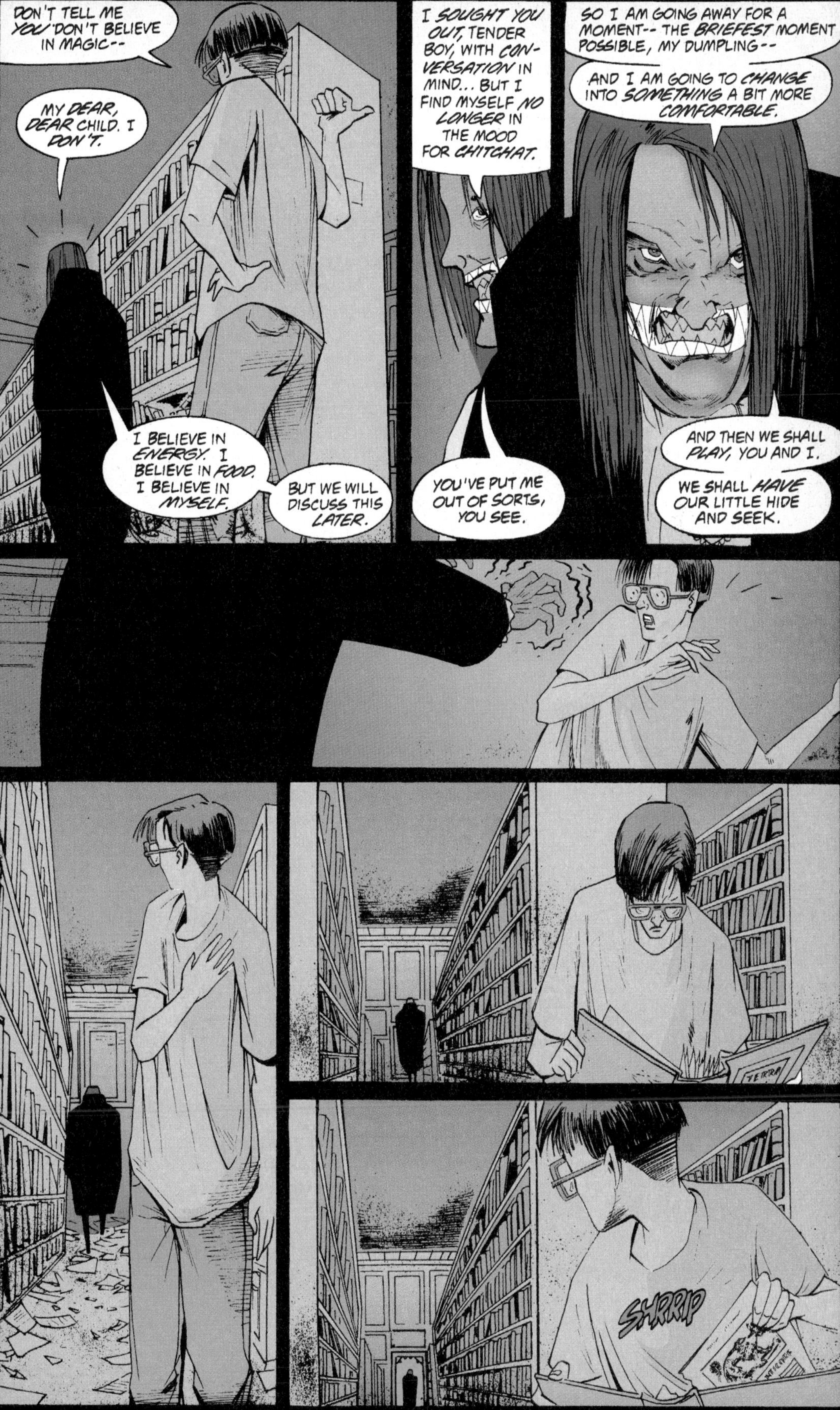

DON'T TELL ME YOU DON'T BELIEVE IN MAGIC--
MY DEAR, DEAR CHILD. I DON'T.
I BELIEVE IN ENERGY. I BELIEVE IN FOOD. I BELIEVE IN MYSELF.
BUT WE WILL DISCUSS THIS LATER.
I SOUGHT YOU OUT, TENDER BOY, WITH CONVERSATION IN MIND... BUT I FIND MYSELF NO LONGER IN THE MOOD FOR CHITCHAT.
YOU'VE PUT ME OUT OF SORTS, YOU SEE.
SO I AM GOING AWAY FOR A MOMENT-- THE BRIEFEST MOMENT POSSIBLE, MY DUMPLING--
AND I AM GOING TO CHANGE INTO SOMETHING A BIT MORE COMFORTABLE.
AND THEN WE SHALL PLAY, YOU AND I.
WE SHALL HAVE OUR LITTLE HIDE AND SEEK.
TERRA
SHRRIP

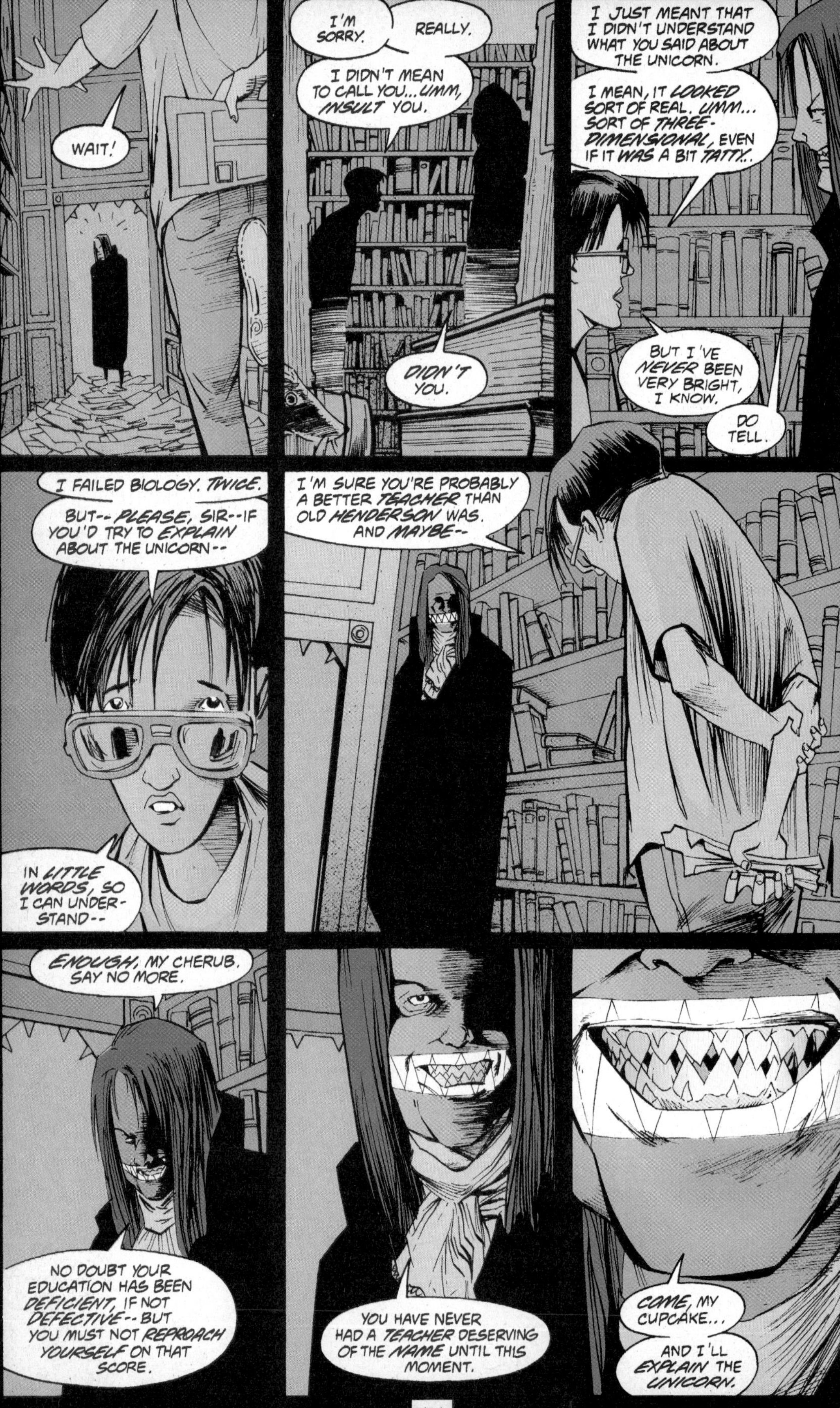
WAIT!
I'M SORRY.
REALLY.
I DIDN'T MEAN TO CALL YOU... UMM, INSULT YOU.
DIDN'T YOU.
I JUST MEANT THAT I DIDN'T UNDERSTAND WHAT YOU SAID ABOUT THE UNICORN.
I MEAN, IT LOOKED SORT OF REAL. UMM... SORT OF THREE-DIMENSIONAL, EVEN IF IT WAS A BIT TATTY...
BUT I'VE NEVER BEEN VERY BRIGHT, I KNOW.
DO TELL.
I FAILED BIOLOGY. TWICE.
BUT-- PLEASE, SIR-- IF YOU'D TRY TO EXPLAIN ABOUT THE UNICORN--
IN LITTLE WORDS, SO I CAN UNDER-STAND--
I'M SURE YOU'RE PROBABLY A BETTER TEACHER THAN OLD HENDERSON WAS. AND MAYBE--
ENOUGH, MY CHERUB. SAY NO MORE.
NO DOUBT YOUR EDUCATION HAS BEEN DEFICIENT, IF NOT DEFECTIVE-- BUT YOU MUST NOT REPROACH YOURSELF ON THAT SCORE.
YOU HAVE NEVER HAD A TEACHER DESERVING OF THE NAME UNTIL THIS MOMENT.
COME, MY CUPCAKE...
AND I'LL EXPLAIN THE UNICORN.

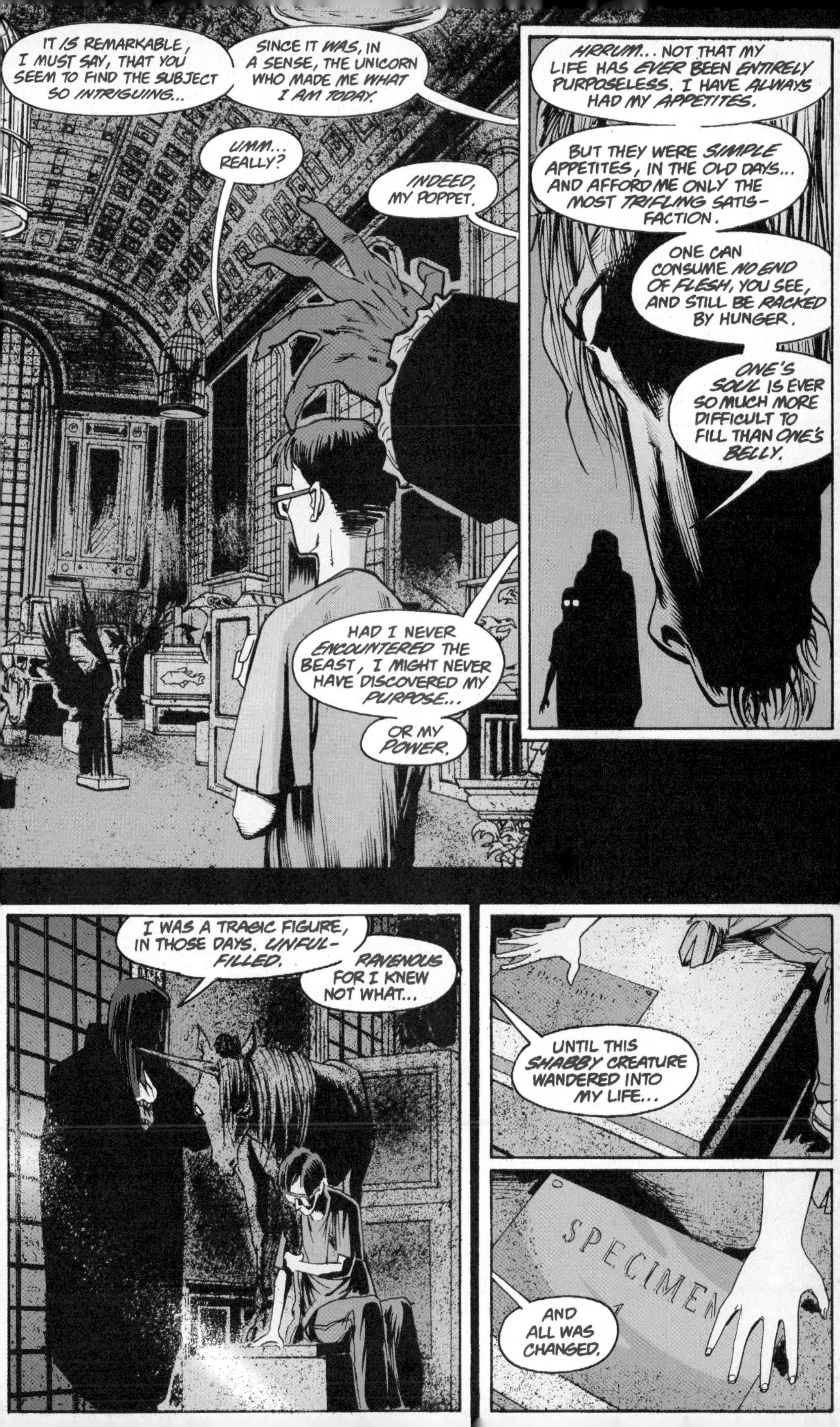
IT IS REMARKABLE, I MUST SAY, THAT YOU SEEM TO FIND THE SUBJECT SO INTRIGUING...
SINCE IT WAS, IN A SENSE, THE UNICORN WHO MADE ME WHAT I AM TODAY.
UMM... REALLY?
INDEED, MY POPPET.
HAD I NEVER ENCOUNTERED THE BEAST, I MIGHT NEVER HAVE DISCOVERED MY PURPOSE...
OR MY POWER.
HRRUM... NOT THAT MY LIFE HAS EVER BEEN ENTIRELY PURPOSELESS. I HAVE ALWAYS HAD MY APPETITES.
BUT THEY WERE SIMPLE APPETITES, IN THE OLD DAYS... AND AFFORD ME ONLY THE MOST TRIFLING SATIS-FACTION.
ONE CAN CONSUME NO END OF FLESH, YOU SEE, AND STILL BE RACKED BY HUNGER.
ONE'S SOUL IS EVER SO MUCH MORE DIFFICULT TO FILL THAN ONE'S BELLY.
I WAS A TRAGIC FIGURE, IN THOSE DAYS. UNFUL-FILLED.
RAVENOUS FOR I KNEW NOT WHAT...
UNTIL THIS SHABBY CREATURE WANDERED INTO MY LIFE...
SPECIMEN
AND ALL WAS CHANGED.

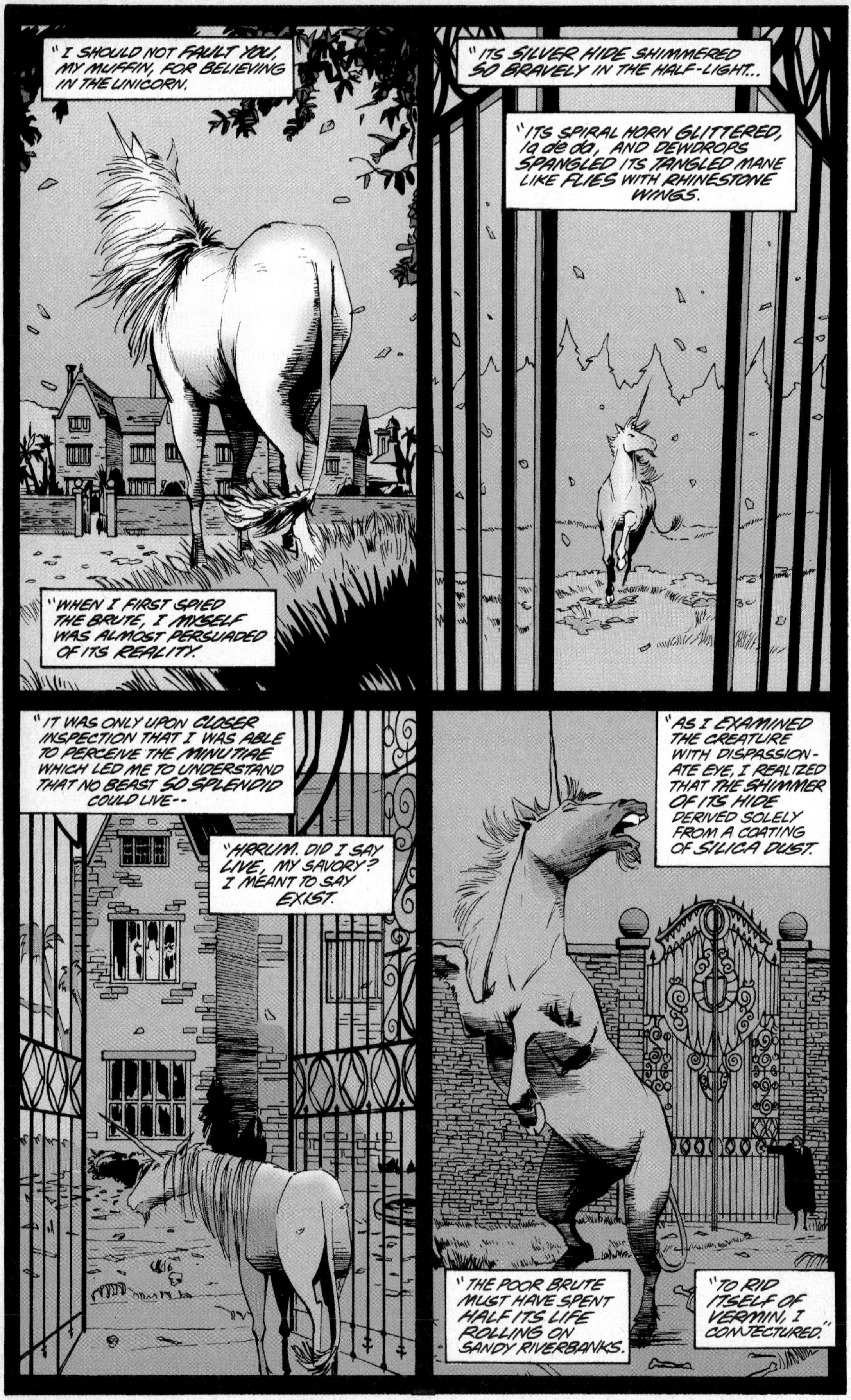
"I SHOULD NOT FAULT YOU, MY MUFFIN, FOR BELIEVING IN THE UNICORN.
"WHEN I FIRST SPIED THE BRUTE, I MYSELF WAS ALMOST PERSUADED OF ITS REALITY.
"ITS SILVER HIDE SHIMMERED SO BRAVELY IN THE HALF-LIGHT...
"ITS SPIRAL HORN GLITTERED, la de da, AND DEWDROPS SPANGLED ITS TANGLED MANE LIKE FLIES WITH RHINESTONE WINGS.
"IT WAS ONLY UPON CLOSER INSPECTION THAT I WAS ABLE TO PERCEIVE THE MINUTIAE WHICH LED ME TO UNDERSTAND THAT NO BEAST SO SPLENDID COULD LIVE--
"HRRUM. DID I SAY LIVE, MY SAVORY? I MEANT TO SAY EXIST.
"AS I EXAMINED THE CREATURE WITH DISPASSION-ATE EYE, I REALIZED THAT THE SHIMMER OF ITS HIDE DERIVED SOLELY FROM A COATING OF SILICA DUST.
"THE POOR BRUTE MUST HAVE SPENT HALF ITS LIFE ROLLING ON SANDY RIVERBANKS.
"TO RID ITSELF OF VERMIN, I CONJECTURED."

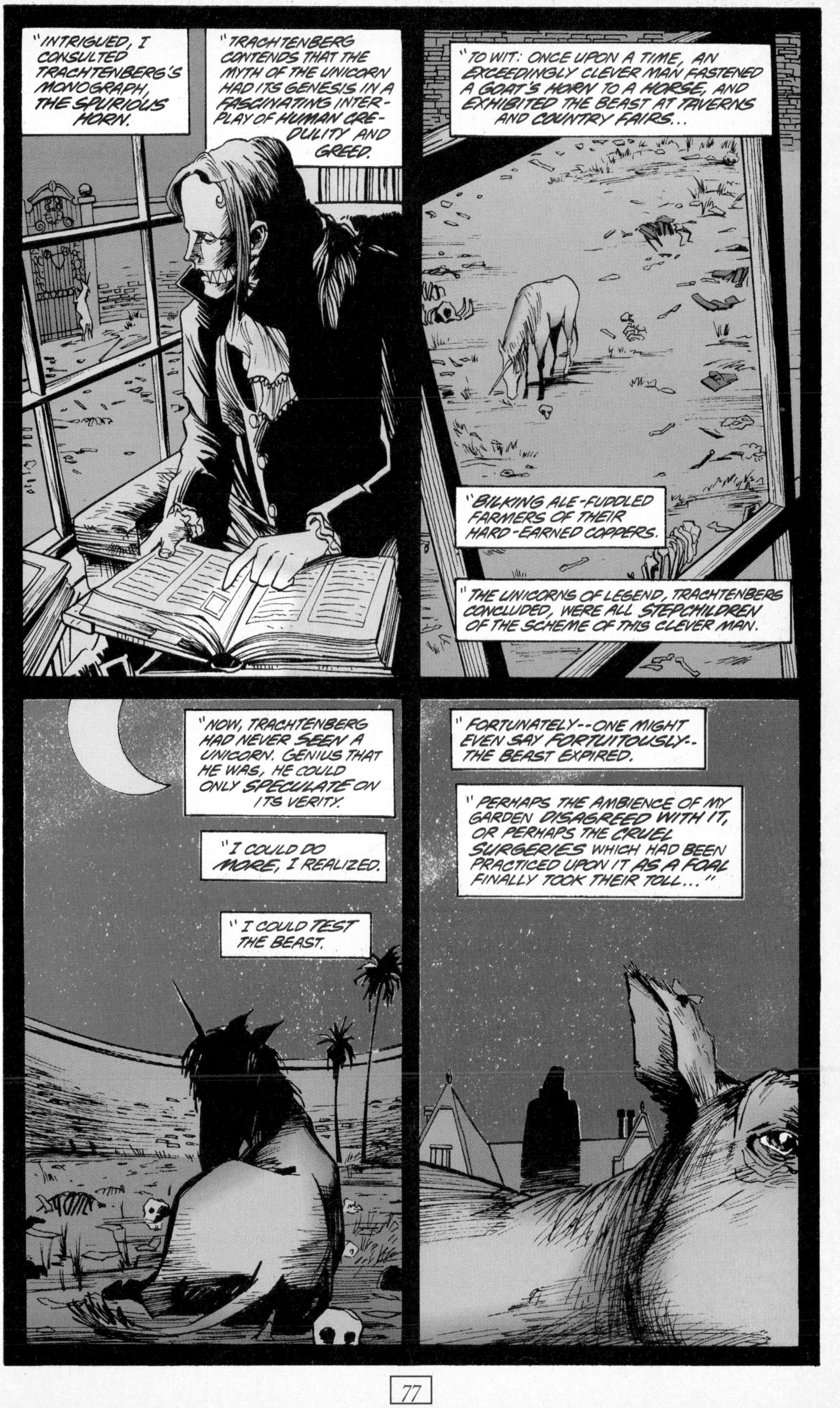
"INTRIGUED, I CONSULTED TRACHTENBERG'S MONOGRAPH, THE SPURIOUS HORN.
"TRACHTENBERG CONTENDS THAT THE MYTH OF THE UNICORN HAD ITS GENESIS IN A FASCINATING INTERPLAY OF HUMAN CREDULITY AND GREED.
"TO WIT: ONCE UPON A TIME, AN EXCEEDINGLY CLEVER MAN FASTENED A GOAT'S HORN TO A HORSE, AND EXHIBITED THE BEAST AT TAVERNS AND COUNTRY FAIRS...
"BILKING ALE-FUDDLED FARMERS OF THEIR HARD-EARNED COPPERS.
"THE UNICORNS OF LEGEND, TRACHTENBERG CONCLUDED, WERE ALL STEPCHILDREN OF THE SCHEME OF THIS CLEVER MAN.
"NOW, TRACHTENBERG HAD NEVER SEEN A UNICORN. GENIUS THAT HE WAS, HE COULD ONLY SPECULATE ON ITS VERITY.
"I COULD DO MORE, I REALIZED.
"I COULD TEST THE BEAST.
"FORTUNATELY--ONE MIGHT EVEN SAY FORTUITOUSLY--THE BEAST EXPIRED.
"PERHAPS THE AMBIENCE OF MY GARDEN DISAGREED WITH IT, OR PERHAPS THE CRUEL SURGERIES WHICH HAD BEEN PRACTICED UPON IT AS A FOAL FINALLY TOOK THEIR TOLL..."

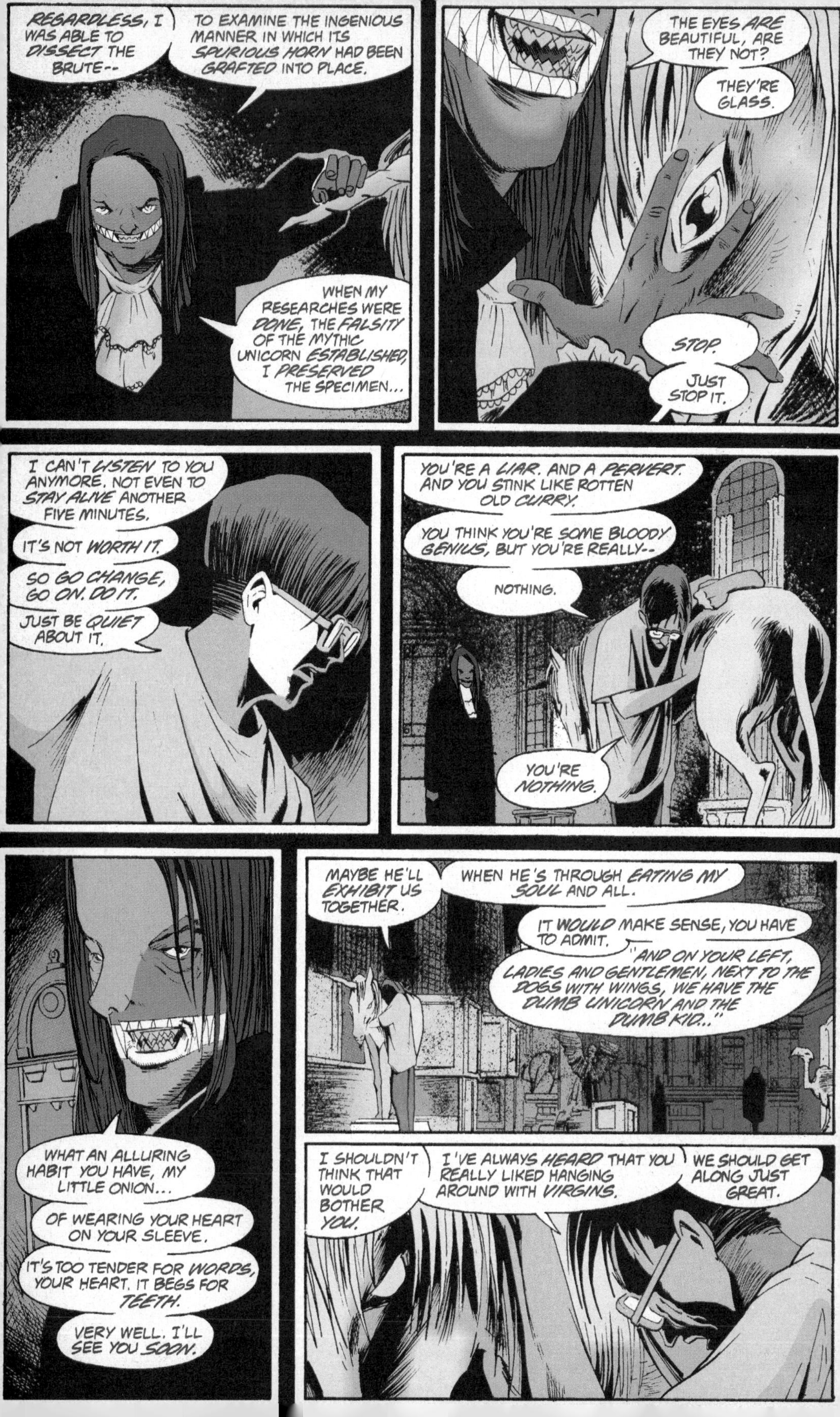
REGARDLESS, I WAS ABLE TO DISSECT THE BRUTE--
TO EXAMINE THE INGENIOUS MANNER IN WHICH ITS SPURIOUS HORN HAD BEEN GRAFTED INTO PLACE.
WHEN MY RESEARCHES WERE DONE, THE FALSITY OF THE MYTHIC UNICORN ESTABLISHED, I PRESERVED THE SPECIMEN...
THE EYES ARE BEAUTIFUL, ARE THEY NOT?
THEY'RE GLASS.
STOP.
JUST STOP IT.
I CAN'T LISTEN TO YOU ANYMORE. NOT EVEN TO STAY ALIVE ANOTHER FIVE MINUTES.
IT'S NOT WORTH IT.
SO GO CHANGE, GO ON. DO IT.
JUST BE QUIET ABOUT IT.
YOU'RE A LIAR. AND A PERVERT. AND YOU STINK LIKE ROTTEN OLD CURRY.
YOU THINK YOU'RE SOME BLOODY GENIUS, BUT YOU'RE REALLY--
NOTHING.
YOU'RE NOTHING.
WHAT AN ALLURING HABIT YOU HAVE, MY LITTLE ONION...
OF WEARING YOUR HEART ON YOUR SLEEVE.
IT'S TOO TENDER FOR WORDS, YOUR HEART. IT BEGS FOR TEETH.
VERY WELL. I'LL SEE YOU SOON.
MAYBE HE'LL EXHIBIT US TOGETHER.
WHEN HE'S THROUGH EATING MY SOUL AND ALL.
IT WOULD MAKE SENSE, YOU HAVE TO ADMIT.
"AND ON YOUR LEFT, LADIES AND GENTLEMEN, NEXT TO THE DOGS WITH WINGS, WE HAVE THE DUMB UNICORN AND THE DUMB KID..."
I SHOULDN'T THINK THAT WOULD BOTHER YOU.
I'VE ALWAYS HEARD THAT YOU REALLY LIKED HANGING AROUND WITH VIRGINS.
WE SHOULD GET ALONG JUST GREAT.

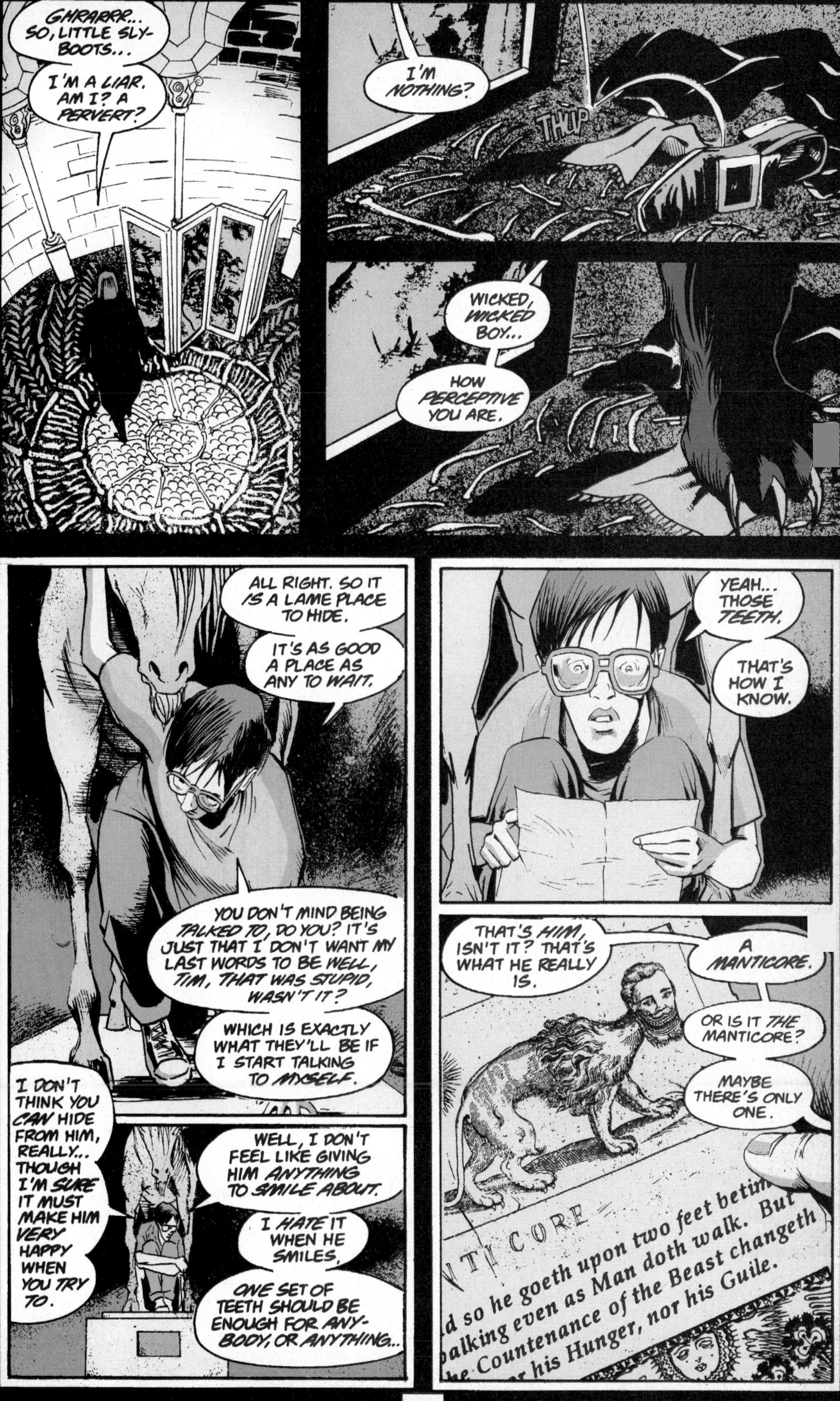
GHRARRR... SO, LITTLE SLY-BOOTS...
I'M A LIAR. AM I? A PERVERT?
I'M NOTHING?
THUP
WICKED, WICKED BOY...
HOW PERCEPTIVE YOU ARE.
ALL RIGHT. SO IT IS A LAME PLACE TO HIDE.
IT'S AS GOOD A PLACE AS ANY TO WAIT.
YOU DON'T MIND BEING TALKED TO, DO YOU? IT'S JUST THAT I DON'T WANT MY LAST WORDS TO BE WELL, TIM, THAT WAS STUPID, WASN'T IT?
WHICH IS EXACTLY WHAT THEY'LL BE IF I START TALKING TO MYSELF.
YEAH... THOSE TEETH.
THAT'S HOW I KNOW.
I DON'T THINK YOU CAN HIDE FROM HIM, REALLY... THOUGH I'M SURE IT MUST MAKE HIM VERY HAPPY WHEN YOU TRY TO.
WELL, I DON'T FEEL LIKE GIVING HIM ANYTHING TO SMILE ABOUT.
I HATE IT WHEN HE SMILES.
ONE SET OF TEETH SHOULD BE ENOUGH FOR ANY-BODY, OR ANYTHING...
THAT'S HIM, ISN'T IT? THAT'S WHAT HE REALLY IS.
A MANTICORE.
OR IS IT THE MANTICORE?
MAYBE THERE'S ONLY ONE.
NTICORE
d so he goeth upon two feet betim
walking even as Man doth walk. But
he Countenance of the Beast changeth
nor his Hunger, nor his Guile.

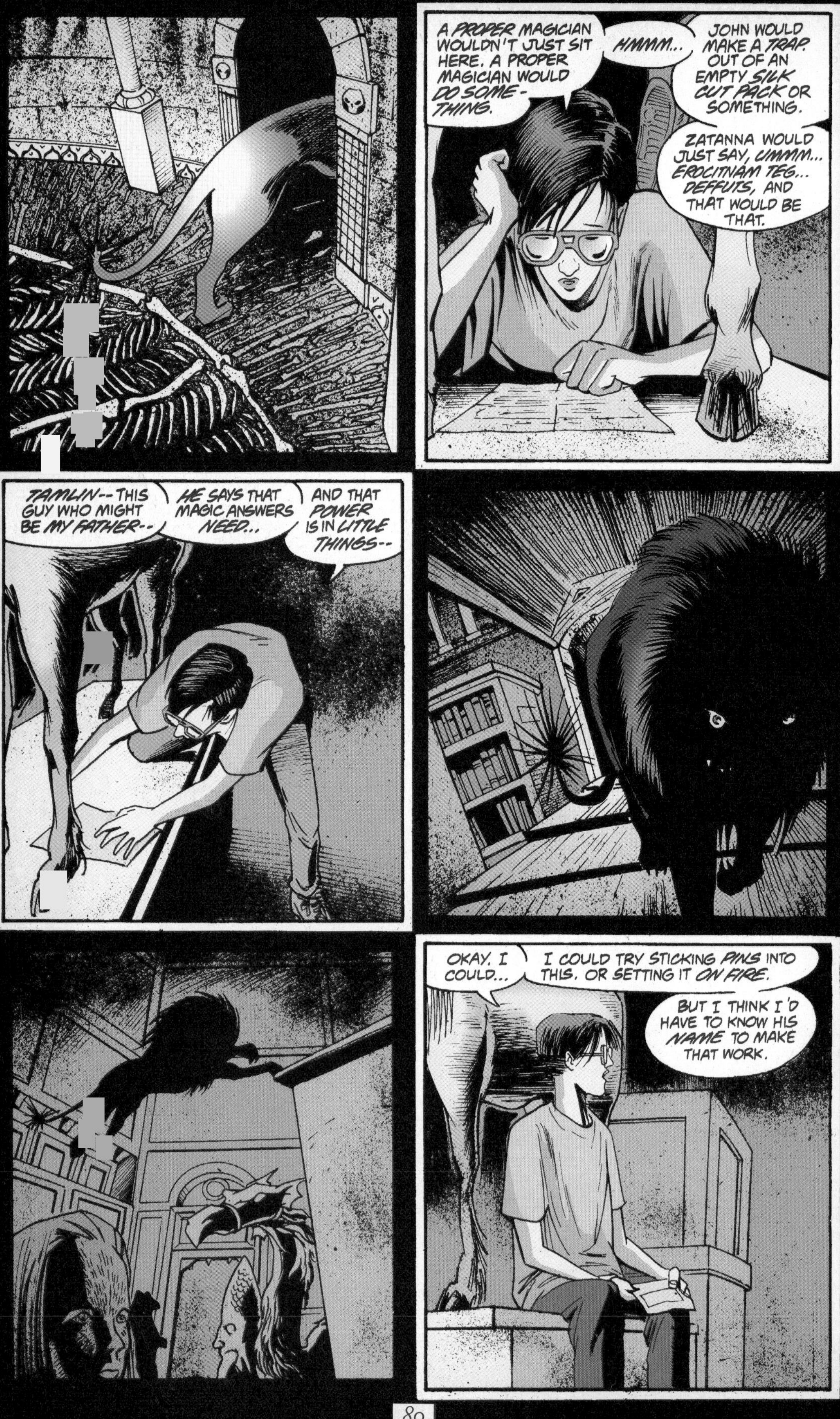
A PROPER MAGICIAN WOULDN'T JUST SIT HERE. A PROPER MAGICIAN WOULD DO SOME-THING.
HMMM...
JOHN WOULD MAKE A TRAP OUT OF AN EMPTY SILK CUT PACK OR SOMETHING.
ZATANNA WOULD JUST SAY, UMMM... EROCITNAM TEG... DEFFUTS, AND THAT WOULD BE THAT.
TAMLIN--THIS GUY WHO MIGHT BE MY FATHER--
HE SAYS THAT MAGIC ANSWERS NEED...
AND THAT POWER IS IN LITTLE THINGS--
OKAY. I COULD...
I COULD TRY STICKING PINS INTO THIS. OR SETTING IT ON FIRE.
BUT I THINK I'D HAVE TO KNOW HIS NAME TO MAKE THAT WORK.

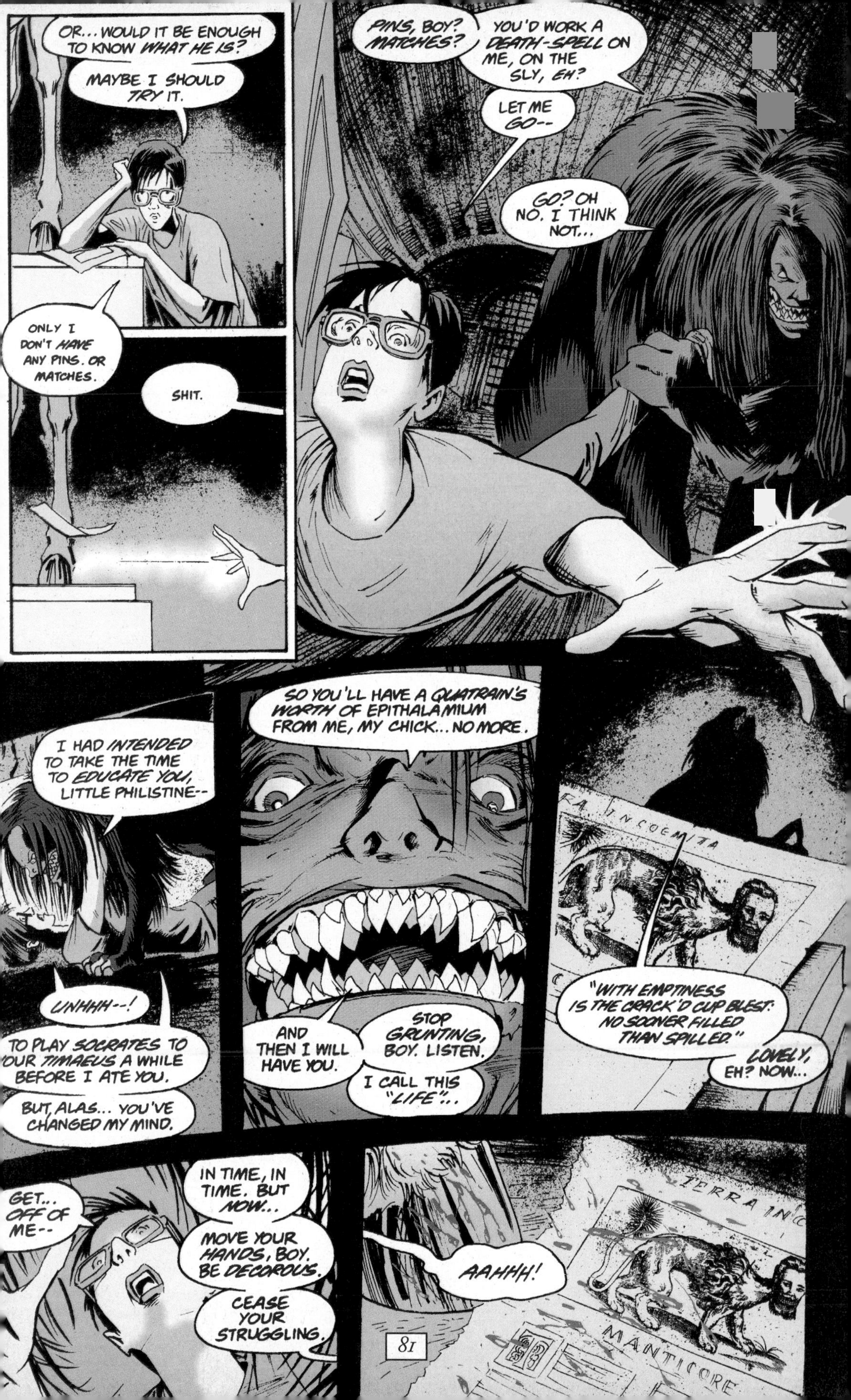

OR... WOULD IT BE ENOUGH TO KNOW WHAT HE IS?
MAYBE I SHOULD TRY IT.
ONLY I DON'T HAVE ANY PINS. OR MATCHES.
SHIT.
PINS, BOY? MATCHES?
YOU'D WORK A DEATH-SPELL ON ME, ON THE SLY, EH?
LET ME GO--
GO? OH NO. I THINK NOT...
I HAD INTENDED TO TAKE THE TIME TO EDUCATE YOU, LITTLE PHILISTINE--
UNHHH--!
TO PLAY SOCRATES TO YOUR TIMAEUS A WHILE BEFORE I ATE YOU.
BUT, ALAS... YOU'VE CHANGED MY MIND.
SO YOU'LL HAVE A QUATRAIN'S WORTH OF EPITHALAMIUM FROM ME, MY CHICK... NO MORE.
AND THEN I WILL HAVE YOU.
STOP GRUNTING, BOY. LISTEN.
I CALL THIS "LIFE"...
"WITH EMPTINESS IS THE CRACK'D CUP BLEST: NO SOONER FILLED THAN SPILLED."
LOVELY, EH? NOW...
GET... OFF OF ME--
IN TIME, IN TIME. BUT NOW...
MOVE YOUR HANDS, BOY. BE DECOROUS.
CEASE YOUR STRUGGLING.
AAHHH!
TERRA IN
MANTICORE

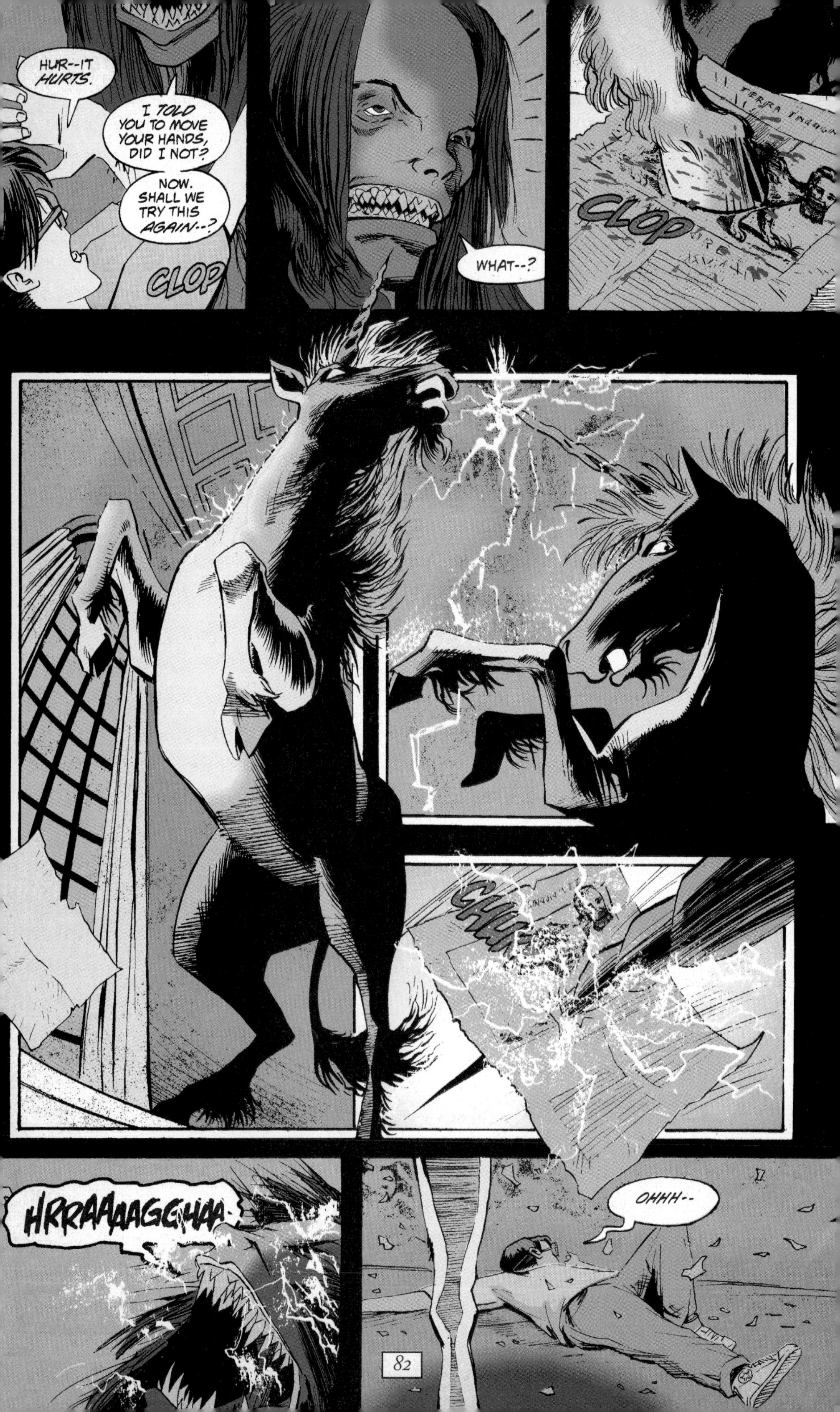
HUR--IT HURTS.
I TOLD YOU TO MOVE YOUR HANDS, DID I NOT?
NOW. SHALL WE TRY THIS AGAIN--?
CLOP
WHAT--?
CLOP
CHUK
HRRAAAAGGHAA
OHHH--

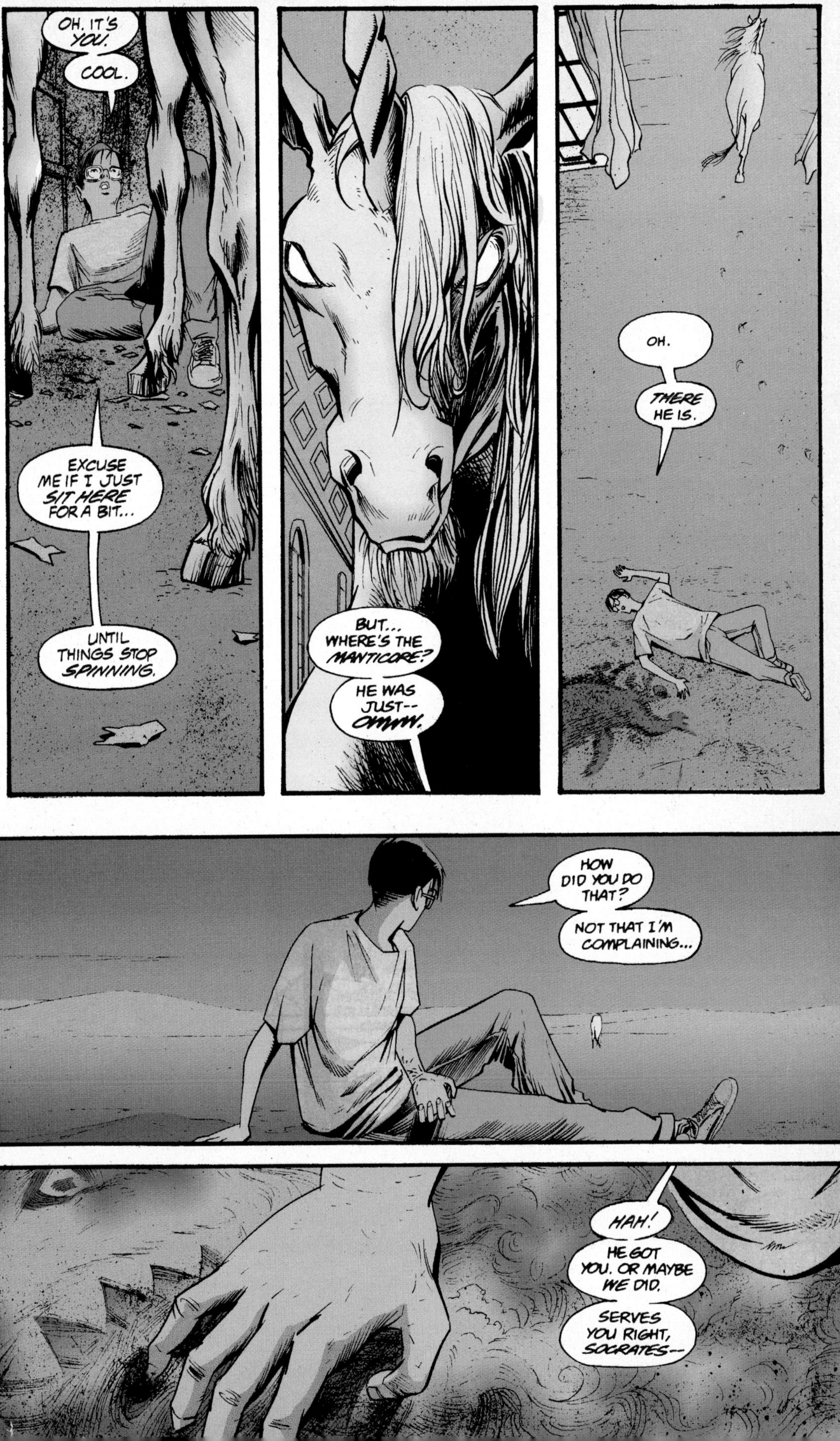
OH. IT'S YOU.
COOL.
EXCUSE ME IF I JUST SIT HERE FOR A BIT...
UNTIL THINGS STOP SPINNING.
BUT... WHERE'S THE MANTICORE?
HE WAS JUST-- OWWW.
OH.
THERE HE IS.
HOW DID YOU DO THAT?
NOT THAT I'M COMPLAINING...
HAH!
HE GOT YOU. OR MAYBE WE DID.
SERVES YOU RIGHT, SOCRATES--

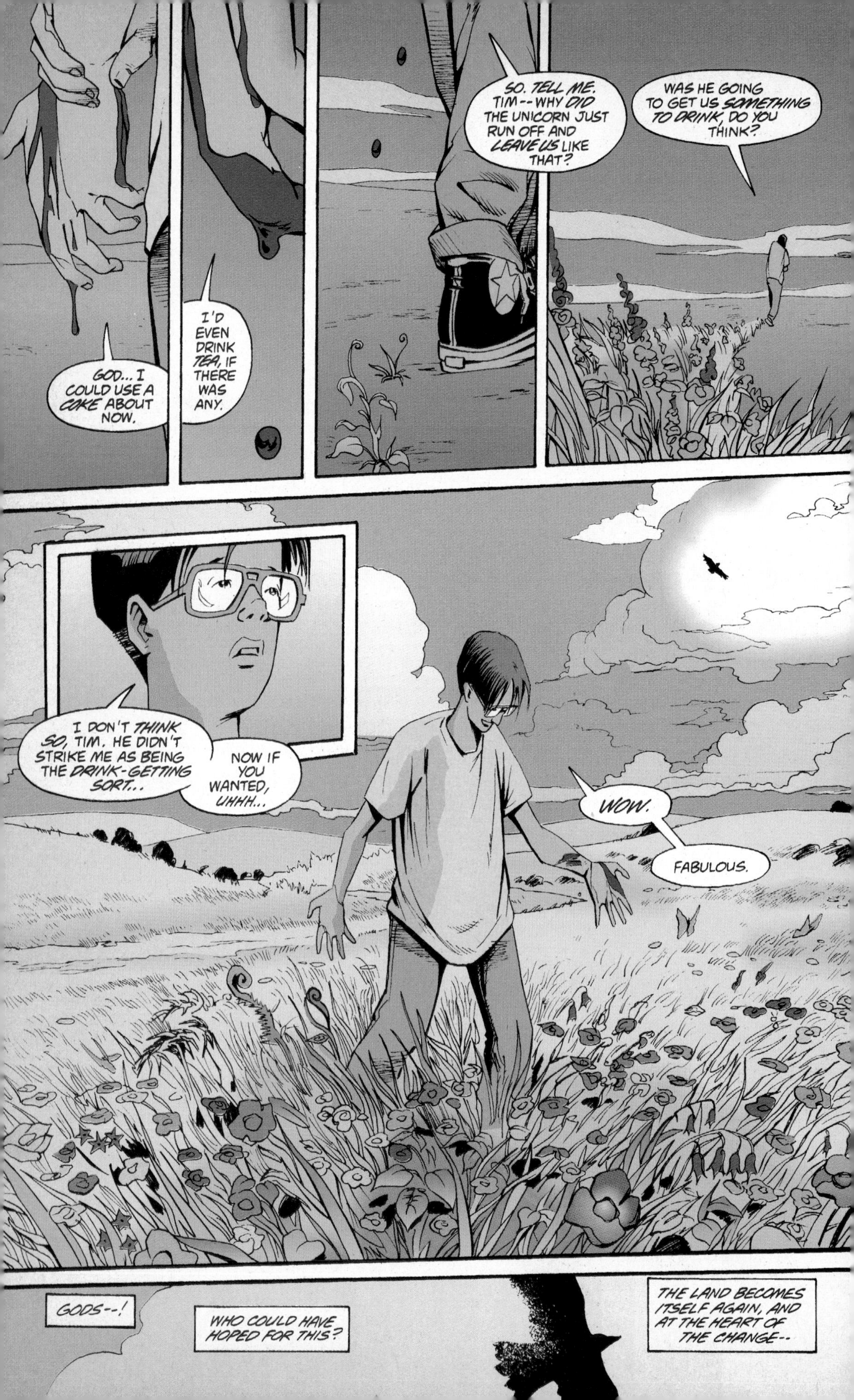
GOD... I COULD USE A COKE ABOUT NOW.
I'D EVEN DRINK TEA, IF THERE WAS ANY.
SO. TELL ME. TIM--WHY DID THE UNICORN JUST RUN OFF AND LEAVE US LIKE THAT?
WAS HE GOING TO GET US SOMETHING TO DRINK, DO YOU THINK?
I DON'T THINK SO, TIM. HE DIDN'T STRIKE ME AS BEING THE DRINK-GETTING SORT...
NOW IF YOU WANTED, UHHH...
WOW.
FABULOUS.
GODS--!
WHO COULD HAVE HOPED FOR THIS?
THE LAND BECOMES ITSELF AGAIN, AND AT THE HEART OF THE CHANGE--

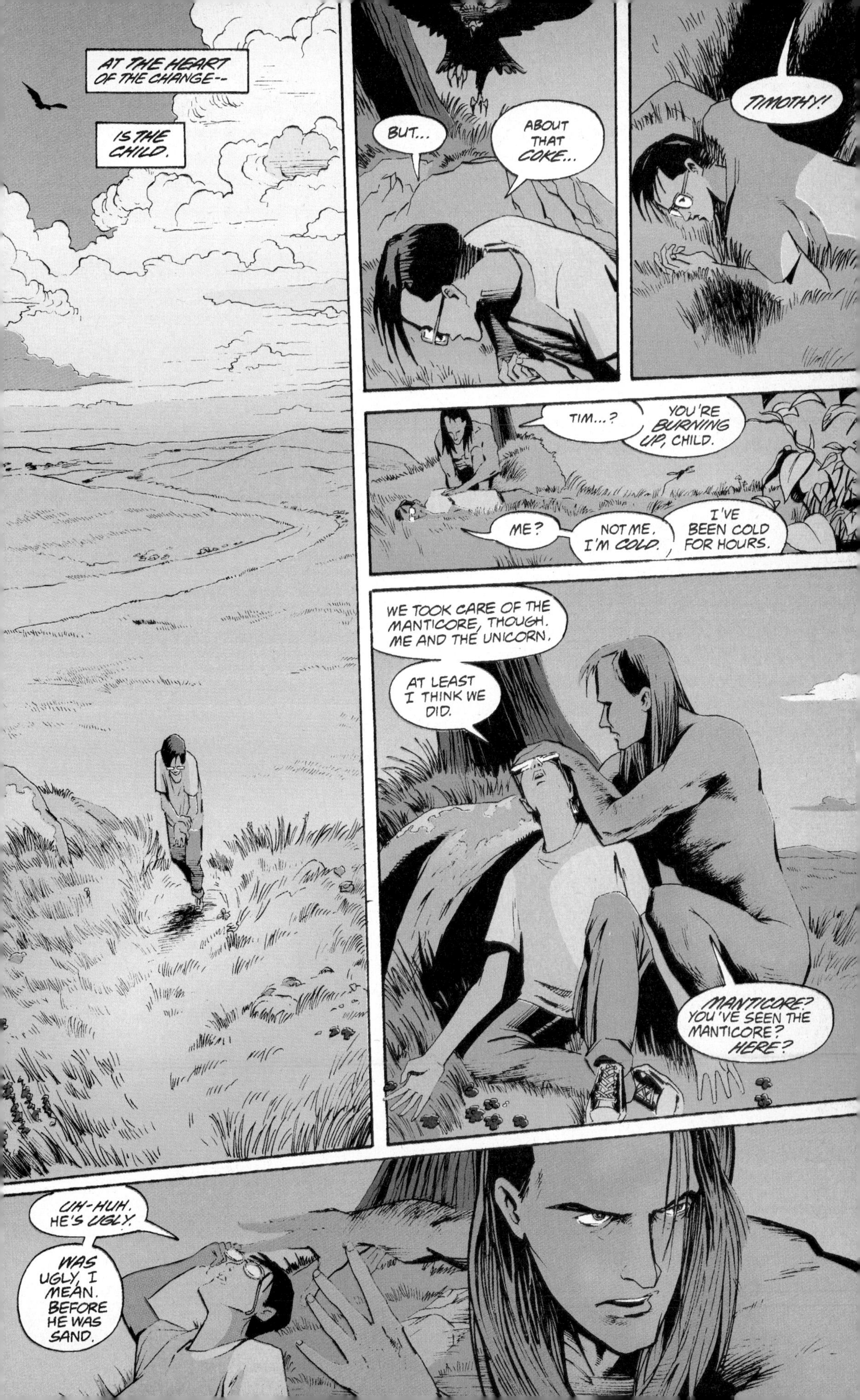
AT THE HEART OF THE CHANGE--
IS THE CHILD.
BUT...
ABOUT THAT COKE...
TIMOTHY!
TIM...?
YOU'RE BURNING UP, CHILD.
ME?
NOT ME. I'M COLD.
I'VE BEEN COLD FOR HOURS.
WE TOOK CARE OF THE MANTICORE, THOUGH. ME AND THE UNICORN.
AT LEAST I THINK WE DID.
MANTICORE? YOU'VE SEEN THE MANTICORE? HERE?
UH-HUH. HE'S UGLY.
WAS UGLY, I MEAN. BEFORE HE WAS SAND.

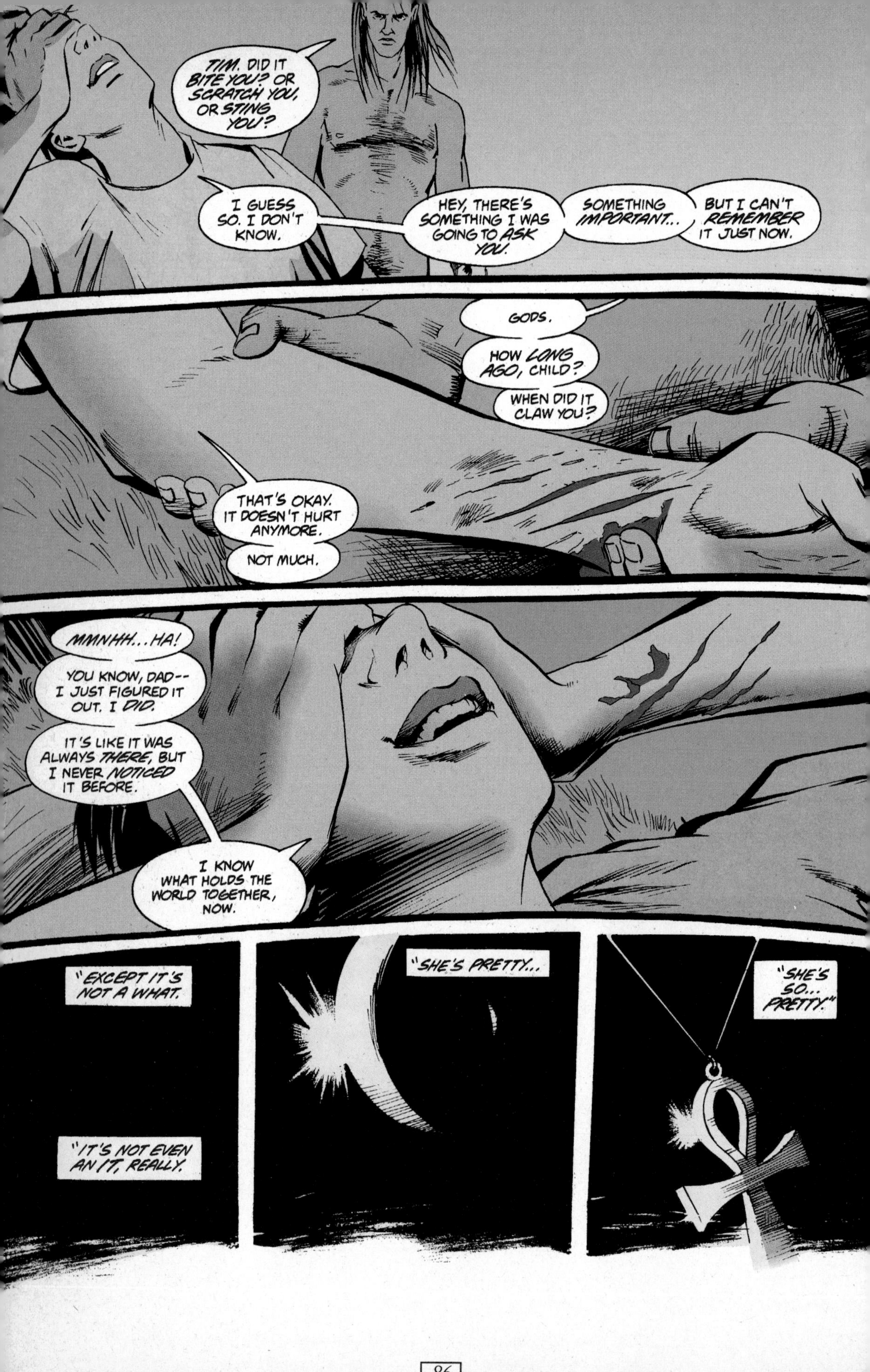
TIM. DID IT BITE YOU? OR SCRATCH YOU, OR STING YOU?
I GUESS SO. I DON'T KNOW.
HEY, THERE'S SOMETHING I WAS GOING TO ASK YOU.
SOMETHING IMPORTANT...
BUT I CAN'T REMEMBER IT JUST NOW.
GODS.
HOW LONG AGO, CHILD?
WHEN DID IT CLAW YOU?
THAT'S OKAY. IT DOESN'T HURT ANYMORE.
NOT MUCH.
MMNHH...HA!
YOU KNOW, DAD-- I JUST FIGURED IT OUT. I DID.
IT'S LIKE IT WAS ALWAYS THERE, BUT I NEVER NOTICED IT BEFORE.
I KNOW WHAT HOLDS THE WORLD TOGETHER, NOW.
"EXCEPT IT'S NOT A WHAT.
"IT'S NOT EVEN AN IT, REALLY.
"SHE'S PRETTY...
"SHE'S SO... PRETTY."

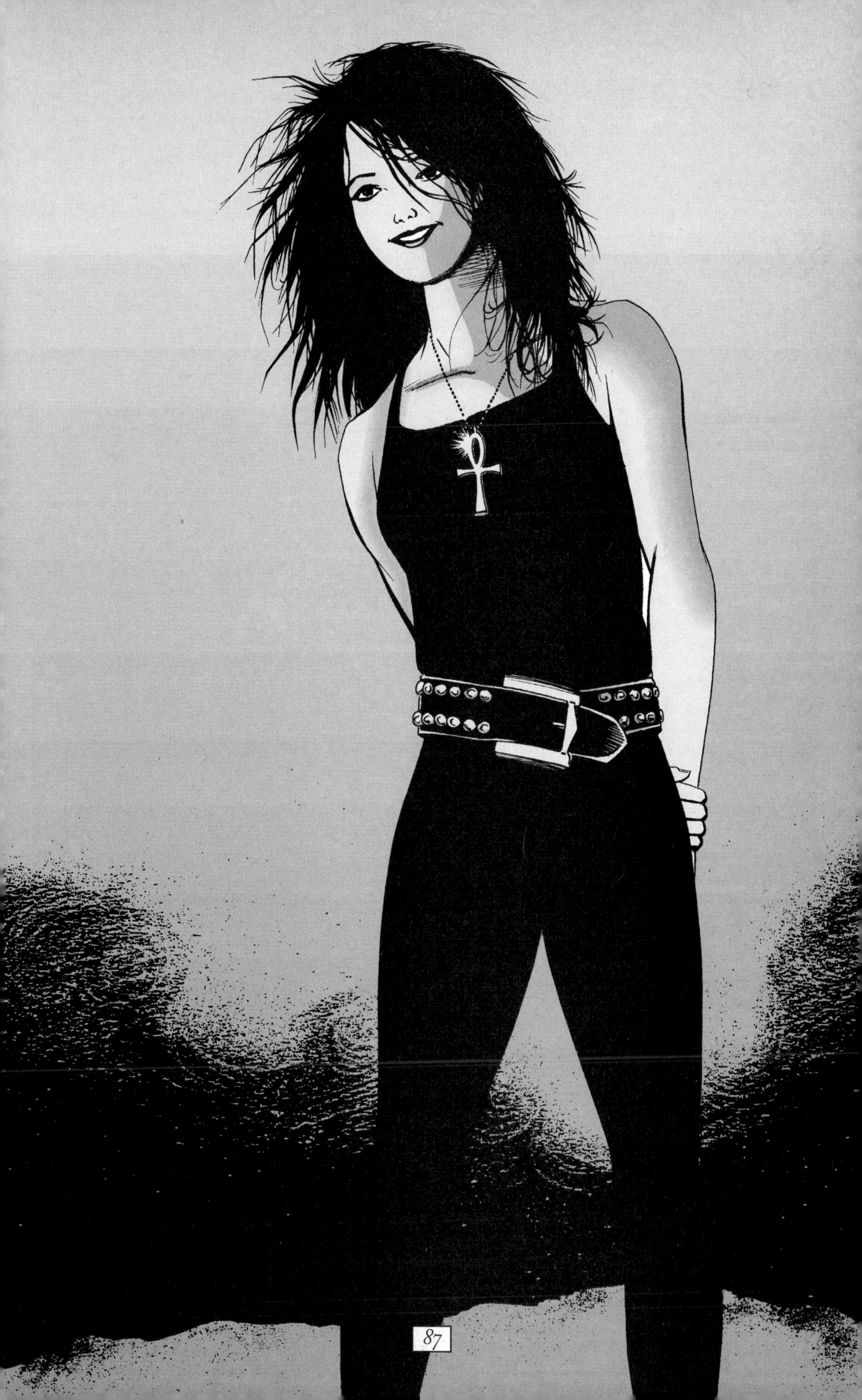

BINDINGS

Epilogue

Lost Causes

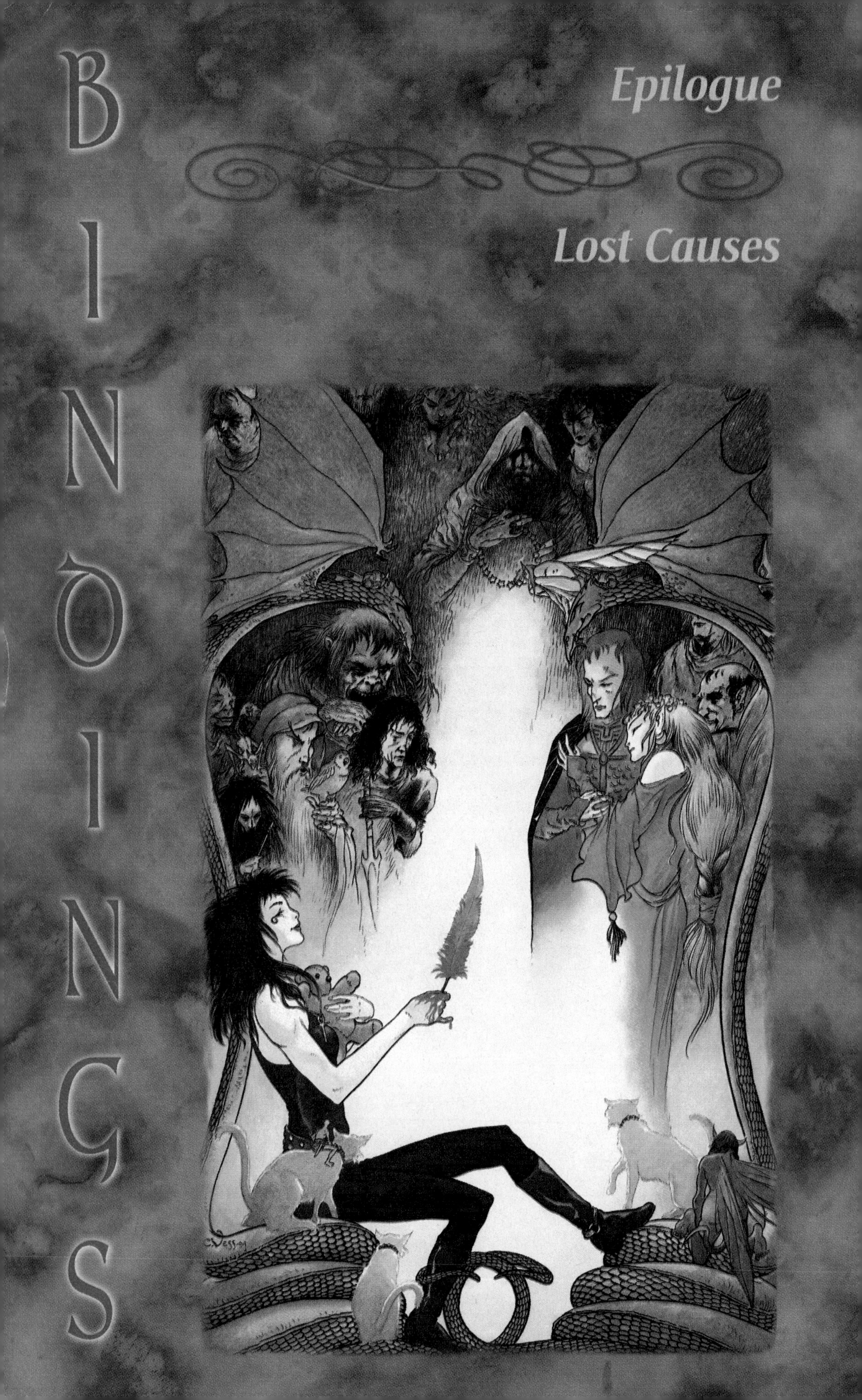

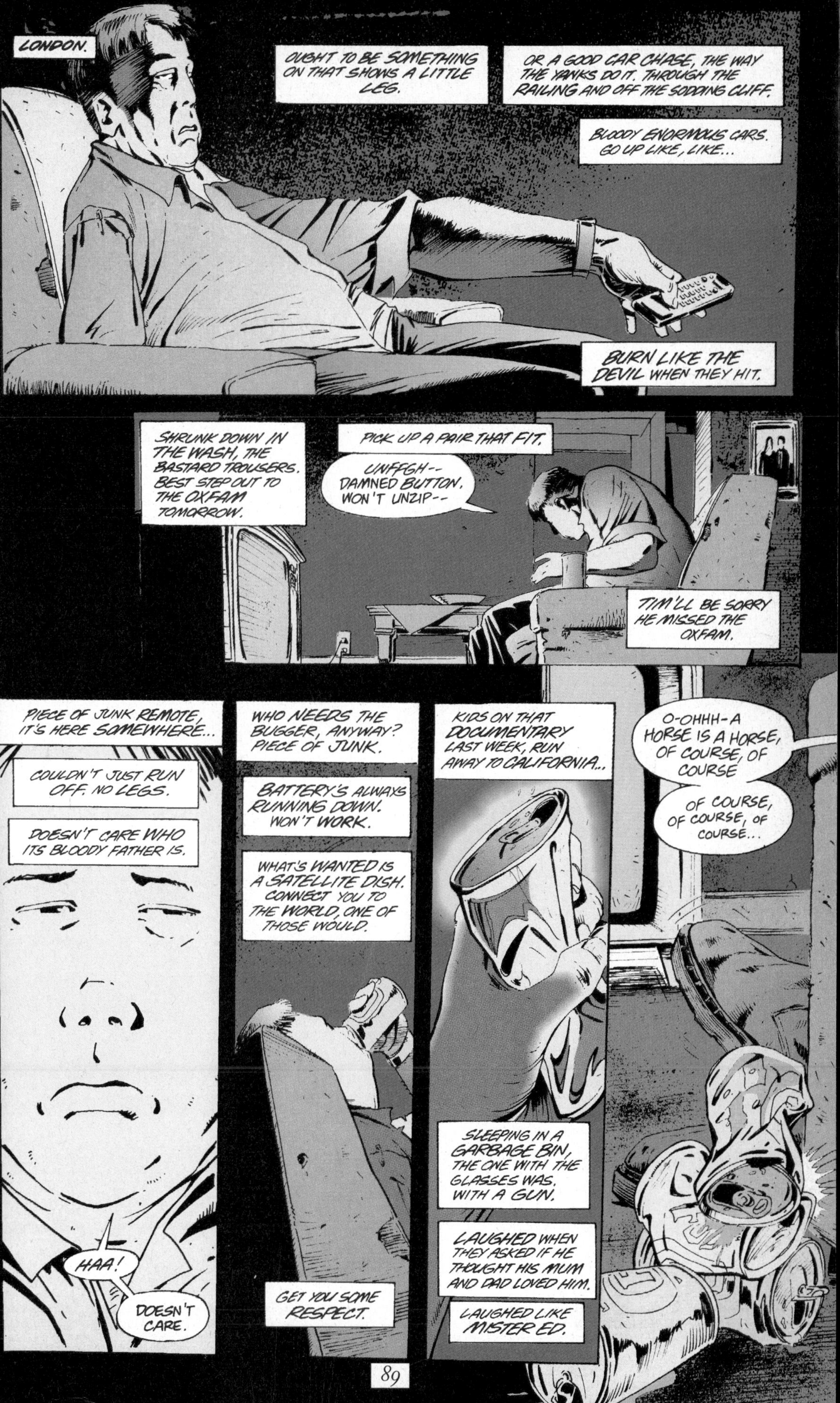
LONDON.
OUGHT TO BE SOMETHING ON THAT SHOWS A LITTLE LEG.
OR A GOOD CAR CHASE, THE WAY THE YANKS DO IT. THROUGH THE RAILING AND OFF THE SODDING CLIFF.
BLOODY ENORMOUS CARS. GO UP LIKE, LIKE...
BURN LIKE THE DEVIL WHEN THEY HIT.
SHRUNK DOWN IN THE WASH, THE BASTARD TROUSERS. BEST STEP OUT TO THE OXFAM TOMORROW.
PICK UP A PAIR THAT FIT.
UNFFGH-- DAMNED BUTTON. WON'T UNZIP--
TIM'LL BE SORRY HE MISSED THE OXFAM.
PIECE OF JUNK REMOTE, IT'S HERE SOMEWHERE...
COULDN'T JUST RUN OFF. NO LEGS.
DOESN'T CARE WHO ITS BLOODY FATHER IS.
HAA!
DOESN'T CARE.
WHO NEEDS THE BUGGER, ANYWAY? PIECE OF JUNK.
BATTERY'S ALWAYS RUNNING DOWN. WON'T WORK.
WHAT'S WANTED IS A SATELLITE DISH. CONNECT YOU TO THE WORLD, ONE OF THOSE WOULD.
GET YOU SOME RESPECT.
KIDS ON THAT DOCUMENTARY LAST WEEK, RUN AWAY TO CALIFORNIA...
SLEEPING IN A GARBAGE BIN, THE ONE WITH THE GLASSES WAS. WITH A GUN.
LAUGHED WHEN THEY ASKED IF HE THOUGHT HIS MUM AND DAD LOVED HIM.
LAUGHED LIKE MISTER ED.
O-OHHH--A HORSE IS A HORSE, OF COURSE, OF COURSE
OF COURSE, OF COURSE, OF COURSE...

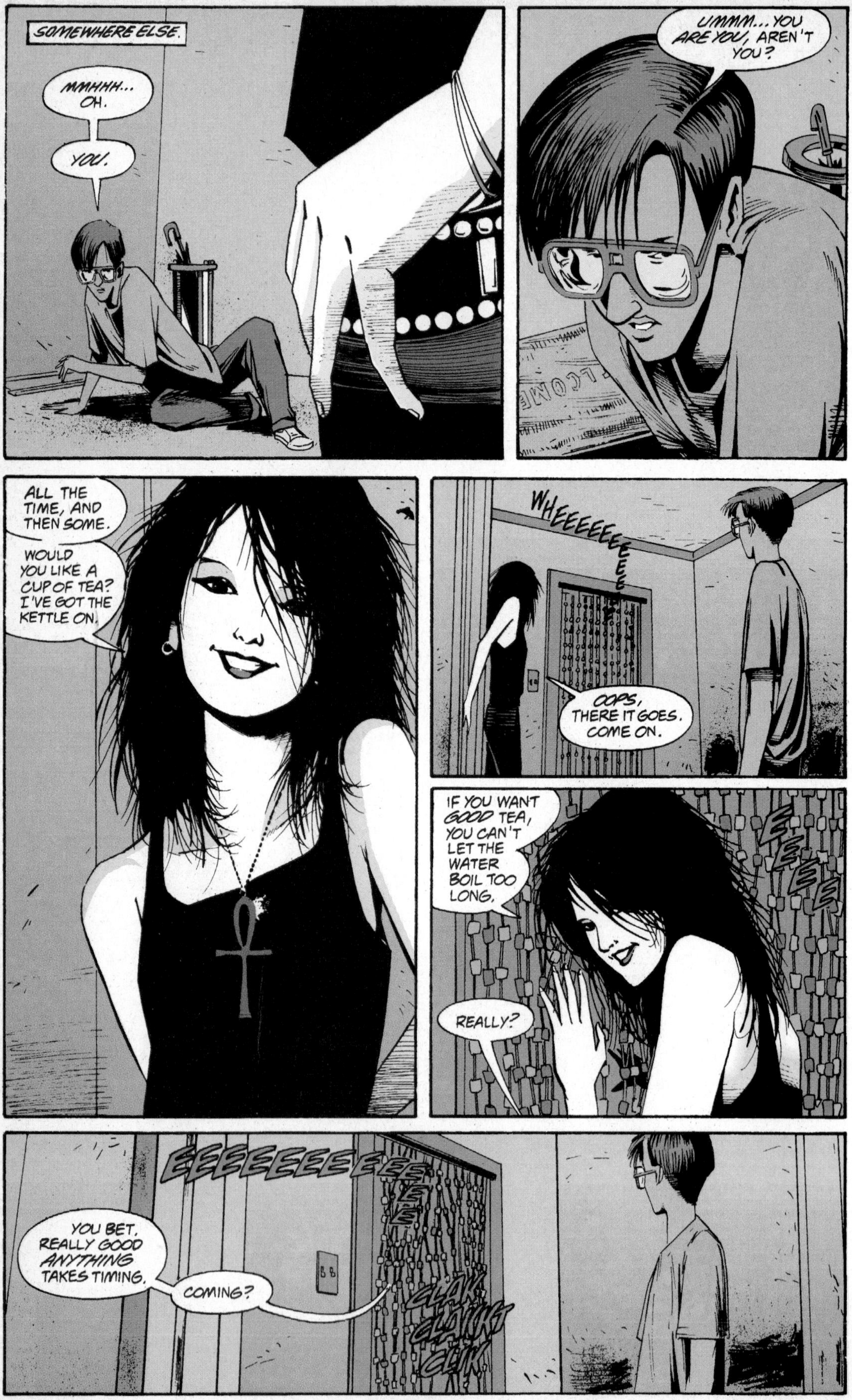
SOMEWHERE ELSE.
MMHHH... OH.
YOU.
UMMM... YOU ARE YOU, AREN'T YOU?
ALL THE TIME, AND THEN SOME.
WOULD YOU LIKE A CUP OF TEA? I'VE GOT THE KETTLE ON.
WHEEEEEEEEEE
OOPS, THERE IT GOES. COME ON.
IF YOU WANT GOOD TEA, YOU CAN'T LET THE WATER BOIL TOO LONG.
REALLY?
EEEEEEEEEEEEEEE
YOU BET. REALLY GOOD ANYTHING TAKES TIMING.
COMING?
CLAK CLAKK CLIK

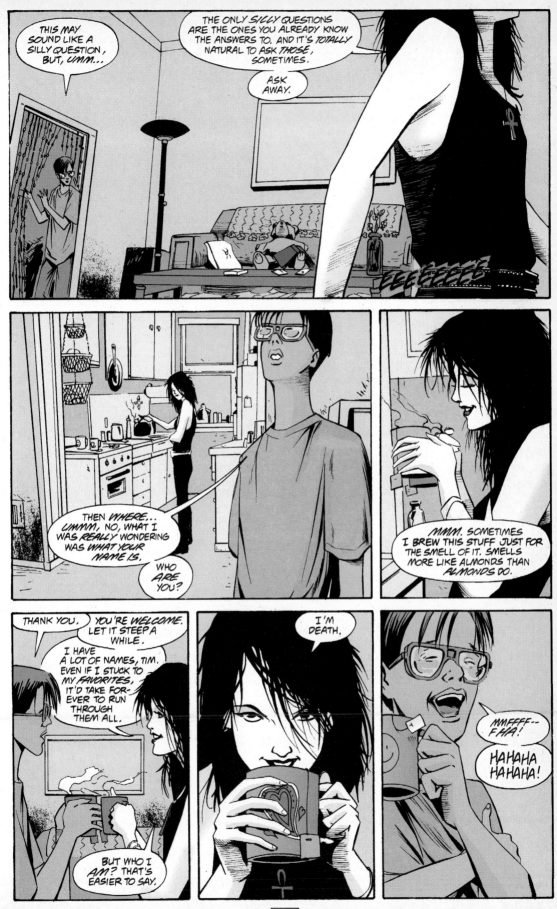

THIS MAY SOUND LIKE A SILLY QUESTION, BUT, UMM...

THE ONLY *SILLY* QUESTIONS ARE THE ONES YOU ALREADY KNOW THE ANSWERS TO, AND IT'S *TOTALLY* NATURAL TO ASK *THOSE*, SOMETIMES.

ASK AWAY.

THEN *WHERE*... UMM, NO, WHAT I WAS *REALLY* WONDERING WAS *WHAT YOUR NAME IS.*

WHO ARE YOU?

MMM. SOMETIMES I BREW THIS STUFF JUST FOR THE SMELL OF IT. SMELLS MORE LIKE ALMONDS THAN *ALMONDS* DO.

THANK YOU.

YOU'RE *WELCOME.* LET IT STEEP A WHILE.

I HAVE A LOT OF NAMES, TIM. EVEN IF I STUCK TO MY *FAVORITES*, IT'D TAKE FOR- EVER TO RUN THROUGH THEM ALL.

BUT WHO I *AM?* THAT'S EASIER TO SAY.

I'M DEATH.

MMFFFF-- F.HA!

HAHAHA HAHAHA!

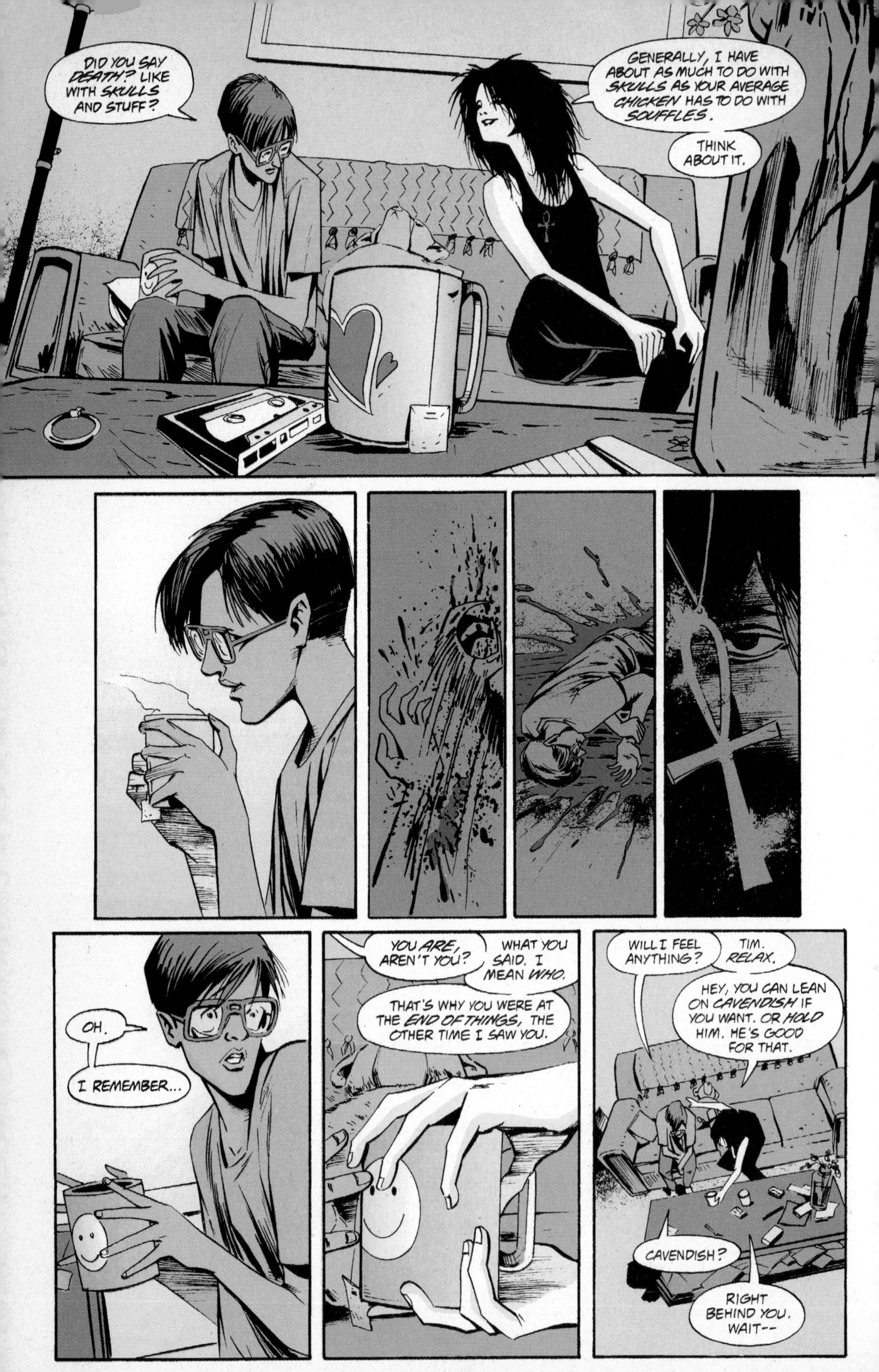

DID YOU SAY DEATH? LIKE WITH SKULLS AND STUFF?
GENERALLY, I HAVE ABOUT AS MUCH TO DO WITH SKULLS AS YOUR AVERAGE CHICKEN HAS TO DO WITH SOUFFLES.
THINK ABOUT IT.
OH.
I REMEMBER...
YOU ARE, AREN'T YOU?
WHAT YOU SAID. I MEAN WHO.
THAT'S WHY YOU WERE AT THE END OF THINGS, THE OTHER TIME I SAW YOU.
WILL I FEEL ANYTHING?
TIM. RELAX.
HEY, YOU CAN LEAN ON CAVENDISH IF YOU WANT. OR HOLD HIM. HE'S GOOD FOR THAT.
CAVENDISH?
RIGHT BEHIND YOU. WAIT--

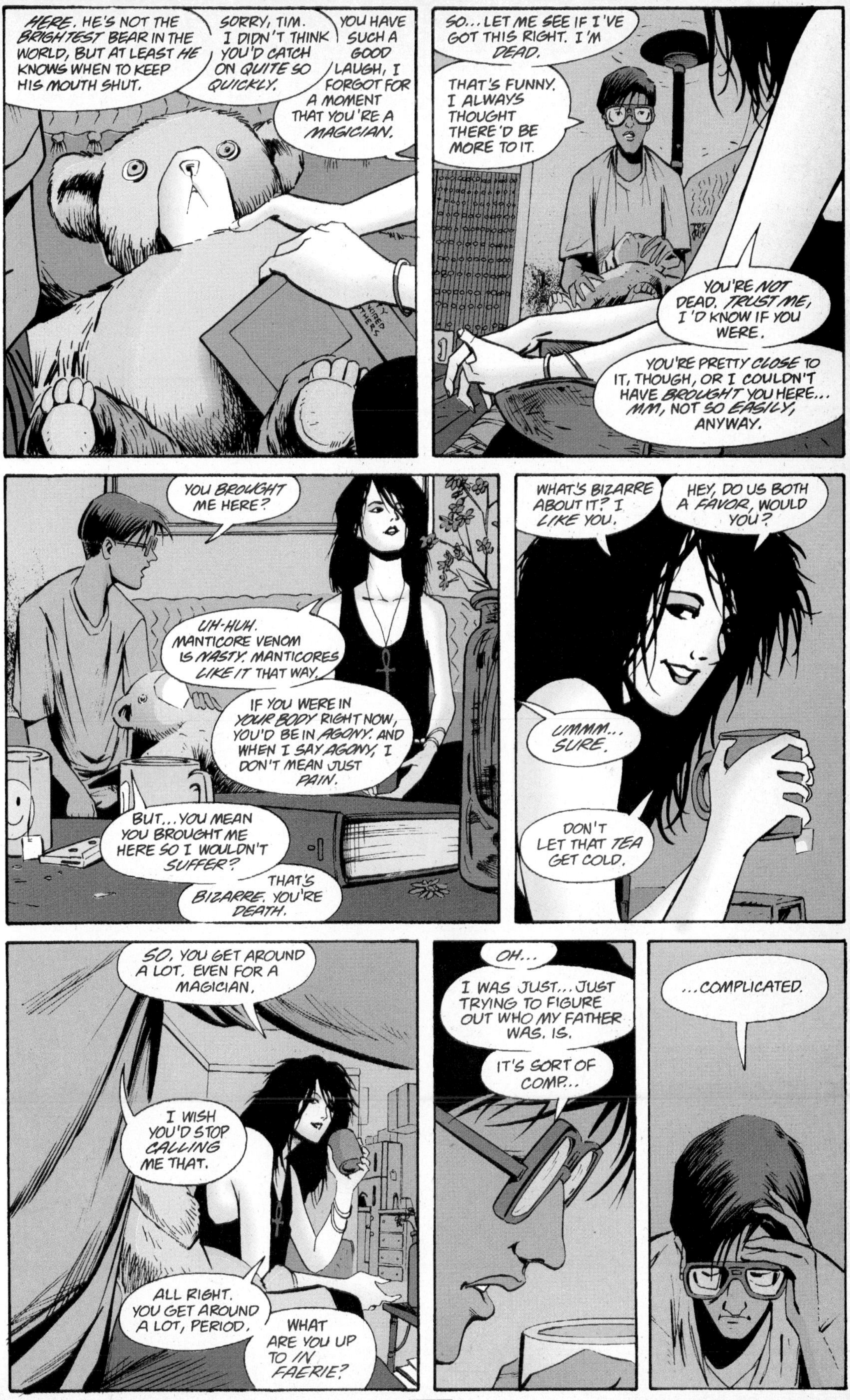
HERE. HE'S NOT THE BRIGHTEST BEAR IN THE WORLD, BUT AT LEAST HE KNOWS WHEN TO KEEP HIS MOUTH SHUT.
SORRY, TIM. I DIDN'T THINK YOU'D CATCH ON QUITE SO QUICKLY.
YOU HAVE SUCH A GOOD LAUGH, I FORGOT FOR A MOMENT THAT YOU'RE A MAGICIAN.
SO... LET ME SEE IF I'VE GOT THIS RIGHT. I'M DEAD.
THAT'S FUNNY. I ALWAYS THOUGHT THERE'D BE MORE TO IT.
YOU'RE NOT DEAD. TRUST ME, I'D KNOW IF YOU WERE.
YOU'RE PRETTY CLOSE TO IT, THOUGH, OR I COULDN'T HAVE BROUGHT YOU HERE... MM, NOT SO EASILY, ANYWAY.
YOU BROUGHT ME HERE?
UH-HUH. MANTICORE VENOM IS NASTY. MANTICORES LIKE IT THAT WAY.
IF YOU WERE IN YOUR BODY RIGHT NOW, YOU'D BE IN AGONY. AND WHEN I SAY AGONY, I DON'T MEAN JUST PAIN.
BUT... YOU MEAN YOU BROUGHT ME HERE SO I WOULDN'T SUFFER?
THAT'S BIZARRE. YOU'RE DEATH.
WHAT'S BIZARRE ABOUT IT? I LIKE YOU.
HEY, DO US BOTH A FAVOR, WOULD YOU?
UMMM... SURE.
DON'T LET THAT TEA GET COLD.
SO, YOU GET AROUND A LOT. EVEN FOR A MAGICIAN.
I WISH YOU'D STOP CALLING ME THAT.
ALL RIGHT. YOU GET AROUND A LOT, PERIOD.
WHAT ARE YOU UP TO IN FAERIE?
OH...
I WAS JUST... JUST TRYING TO FIGURE OUT WHO MY FATHER WAS. IS.
IT'S SORT OF COMP...
...COMPLICATED.

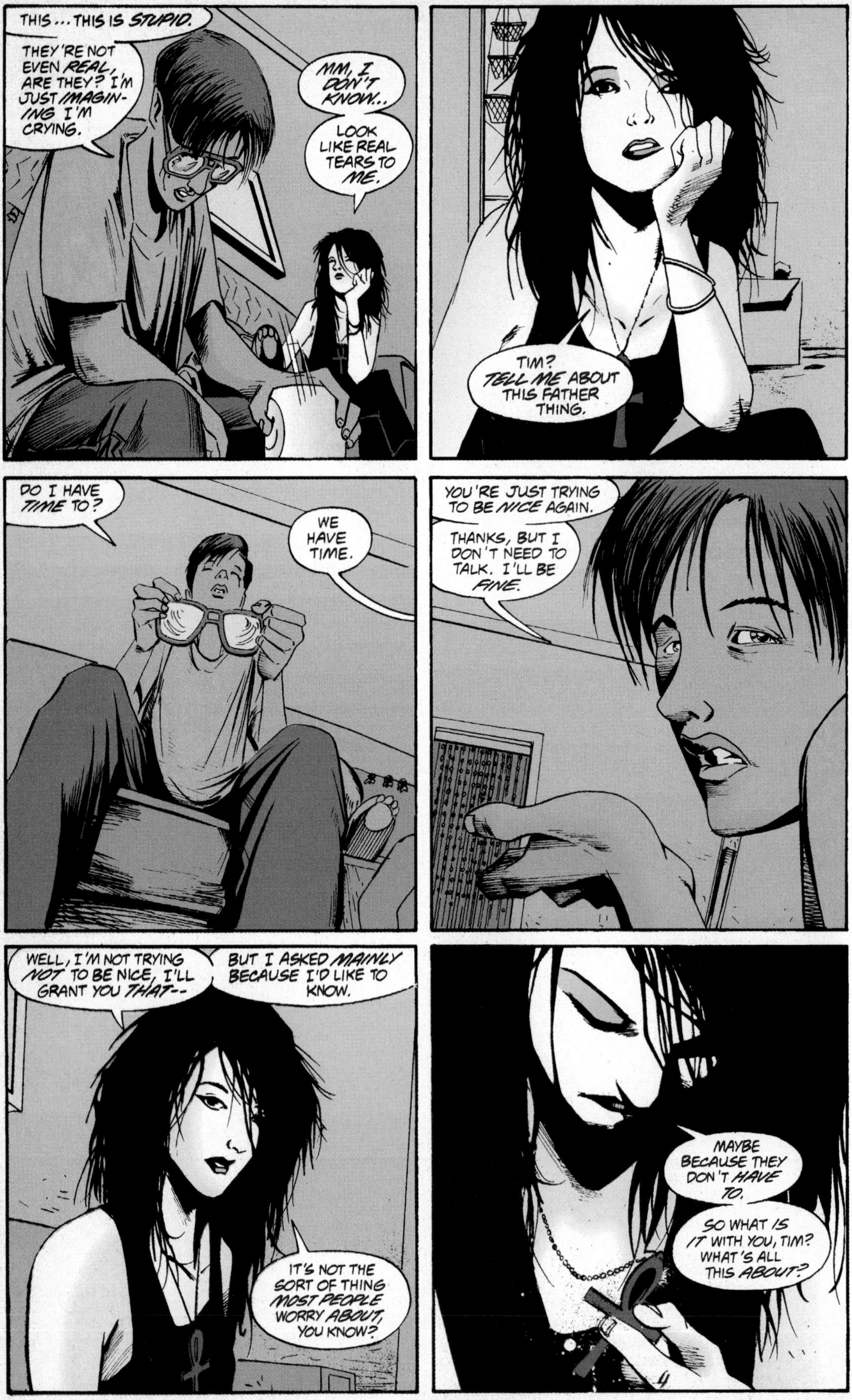

THIS ... THIS IS STUPID.
THEY'RE NOT EVEN REAL, ARE THEY? I'M JUST IMAGINING I'M CRYING.
MM, I DON'T KNOW..
LOOK LIKE REAL TEARS TO ME.
TIM? TELL ME ABOUT THIS FATHER THING.
DO I HAVE TIME TO?
WE HAVE TIME.
YOU'RE JUST TRYING TO BE NICE AGAIN.
THANKS, BUT I DON'T NEED TO TALK. I'LL BE FINE.
WELL, I'M NOT TRYING NOT TO BE NICE, I'LL GRANT YOU THAT--
BUT I ASKED MAINLY BECAUSE I'D LIKE TO KNOW.
IT'S NOT THE SORT OF THING MOST PEOPLE WORRY ABOUT, YOU KNOW?
MAYBE BECAUSE THEY DON'T HAVE TO.
SO WHAT IS IT WITH YOU, TIM? WHAT'S ALL THIS ABOUT?

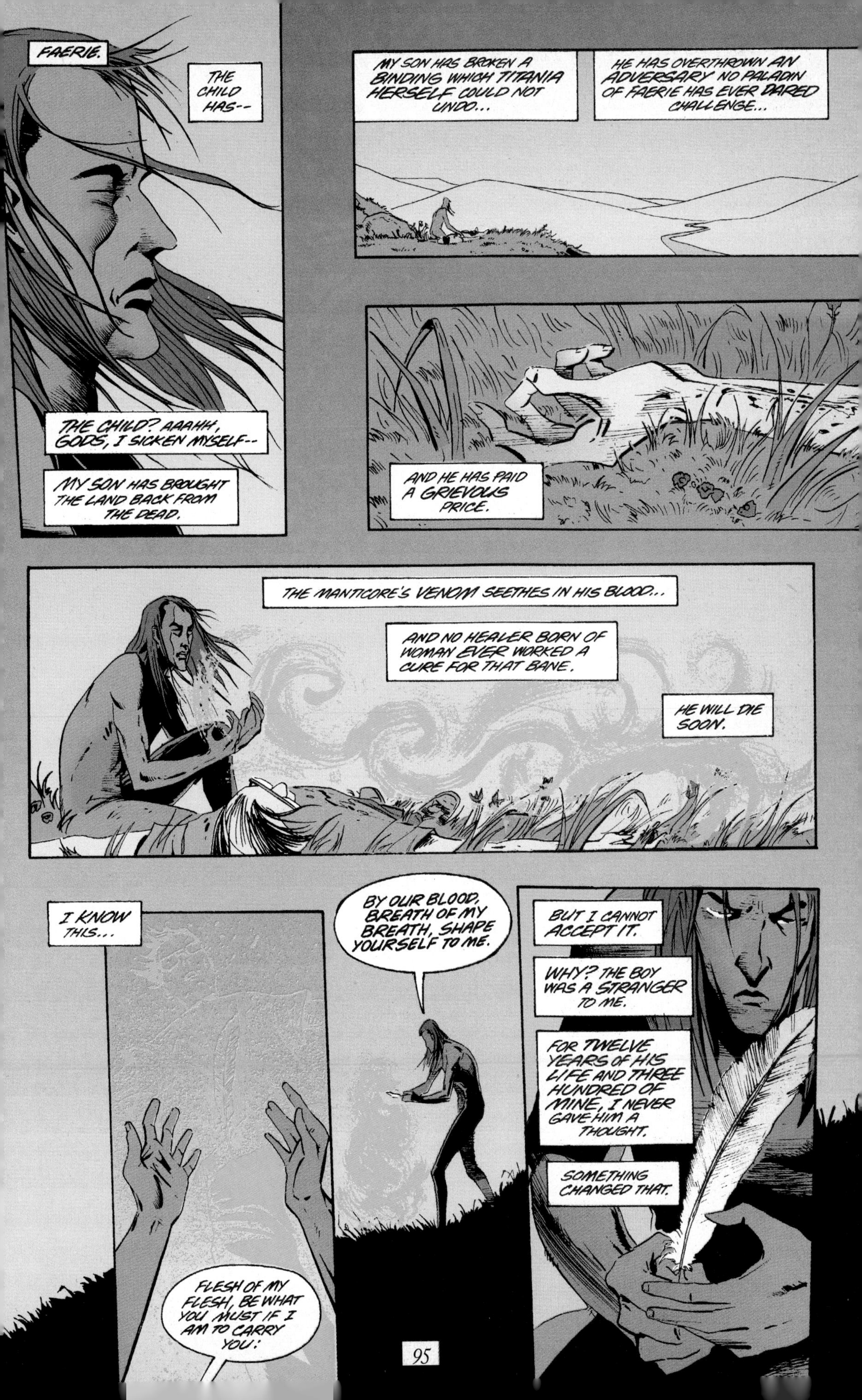
FAERIE.
THE CHILD HAS--
THE CHILD? AAAHH, GODS, I SICKEN MYSELF--
MY SON HAS BROUGHT THE LAND BACK FROM THE DEAD.
MY SON HAS BROKEN A BINDING WHICH TITANIA HERSELF COULD NOT UNDO...
HE HAS OVERTHROWN AN ADVERSARY NO PALADIN OF FAERIE HAS EVER DARED CHALLENGE...
AND HE HAS PAID A GRIEVOUS PRICE.
THE MANTICORE'S VENOM SEETHES IN HIS BLOOD...
AND NO HEALER BORN OF WOMAN EVER WORKED A CURE FOR THAT BANE.
HE WILL DIE SOON.
I KNOW THIS...
BY OUR BLOOD, BREATH OF MY BREATH, SHAPE YOURSELF TO ME.
FLESH OF MY FLESH, BE WHAT YOU MUST IF I AM TO CARRY YOU:
BUT I CANNOT ACCEPT IT.
WHY? THE BOY WAS A STRANGER TO ME.
FOR TWELVE YEARS OF HIS LIFE AND THREE HUNDRED OF MINE, I NEVER GAVE HIM A THOUGHT.
SOMETHING CHANGED THAT.

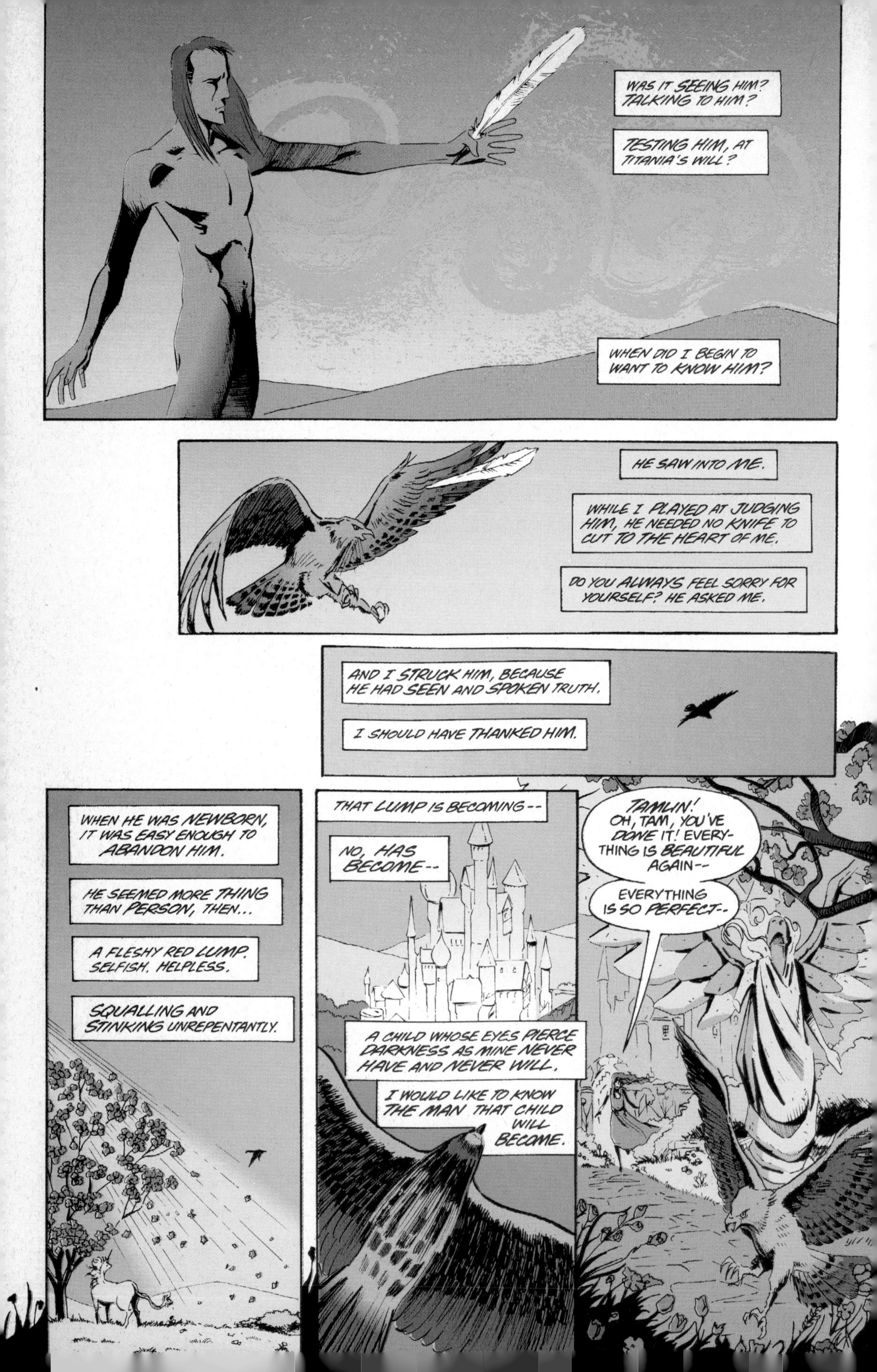
WAS IT SEEING HIM? TALKING TO HIM?
TESTING HIM, AT TITANIA'S WILL?
WHEN DID I BEGIN TO WANT TO KNOW HIM?
HE SAW INTO ME.
WHILE I PLAYED AT JUDGING HIM, HE NEEDED NO KNIFE TO CUT TO THE HEART OF ME.
DO YOU ALWAYS FEEL SORRY FOR YOURSELF? HE ASKED ME.
AND I STRUCK HIM, BECAUSE HE HAD SEEN AND SPOKEN TRUTH.
I SHOULD HAVE THANKED HIM.
WHEN HE WAS NEWBORN, IT WAS EASY ENOUGH TO ABANDON HIM.
HE SEEMED MORE THING THAN PERSON, THEN...
A FLESHY RED LUMP. SELFISH. HELPLESS.
SQUALLING AND STINKING UNREPENTANTLY.
THAT LUMP IS BECOMING--
NO, HAS BECOME--
A CHILD WHOSE EYES PIERCE DARKNESS AS MINE NEVER HAVE AND NEVER WILL.
I WOULD LIKE TO KNOW THE MAN THAT CHILD WILL BECOME.
TAMLIN! OH, TAM, YOU'VE DONE IT! EVERYTHING IS BEAUTIFUL AGAIN--
EVERYTHING IS SO PERFECT--

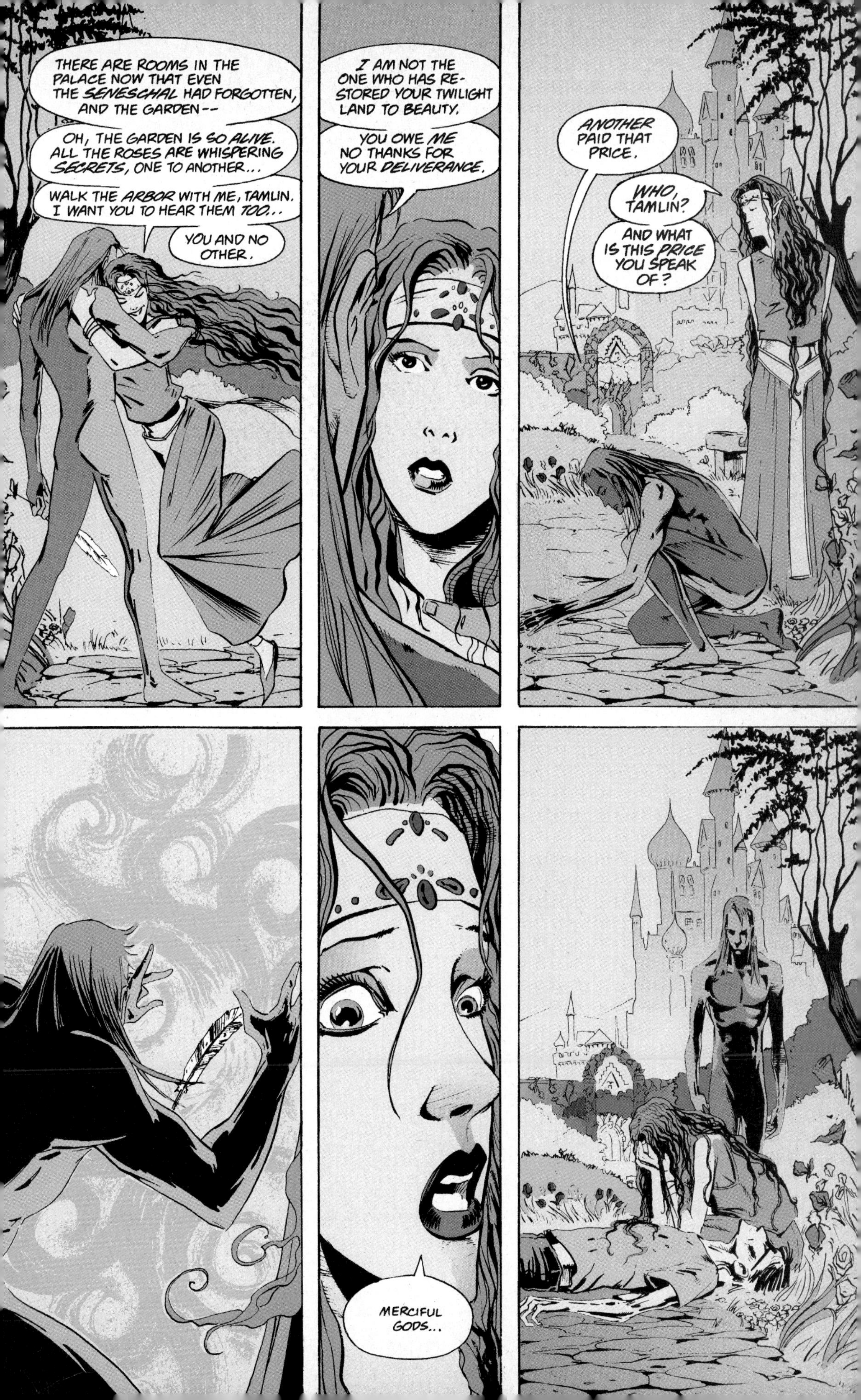
THERE ARE ROOMS IN THE PALACE NOW THAT EVEN THE SENESCHAL HAD FORGOTTEN, AND THE GARDEN--
OH, THE GARDEN IS SO ALIVE. ALL THE ROSES ARE WHISPERING SECRETS, ONE TO ANOTHER...
WALK THE ARBOR WITH ME, TAMLIN. I WANT YOU TO HEAR THEM TOO...
YOU AND NO OTHER.
I AM NOT THE ONE WHO HAS RESTORED YOUR TWILIGHT LAND TO BEAUTY.
YOU OWE ME NO THANKS FOR YOUR DELIVERANCE.
ANOTHER PAID THAT PRICE.
WHO, TAMLIN?
AND WHAT IS THIS PRICE YOU SPEAK OF?
MERCIFUL GODS...

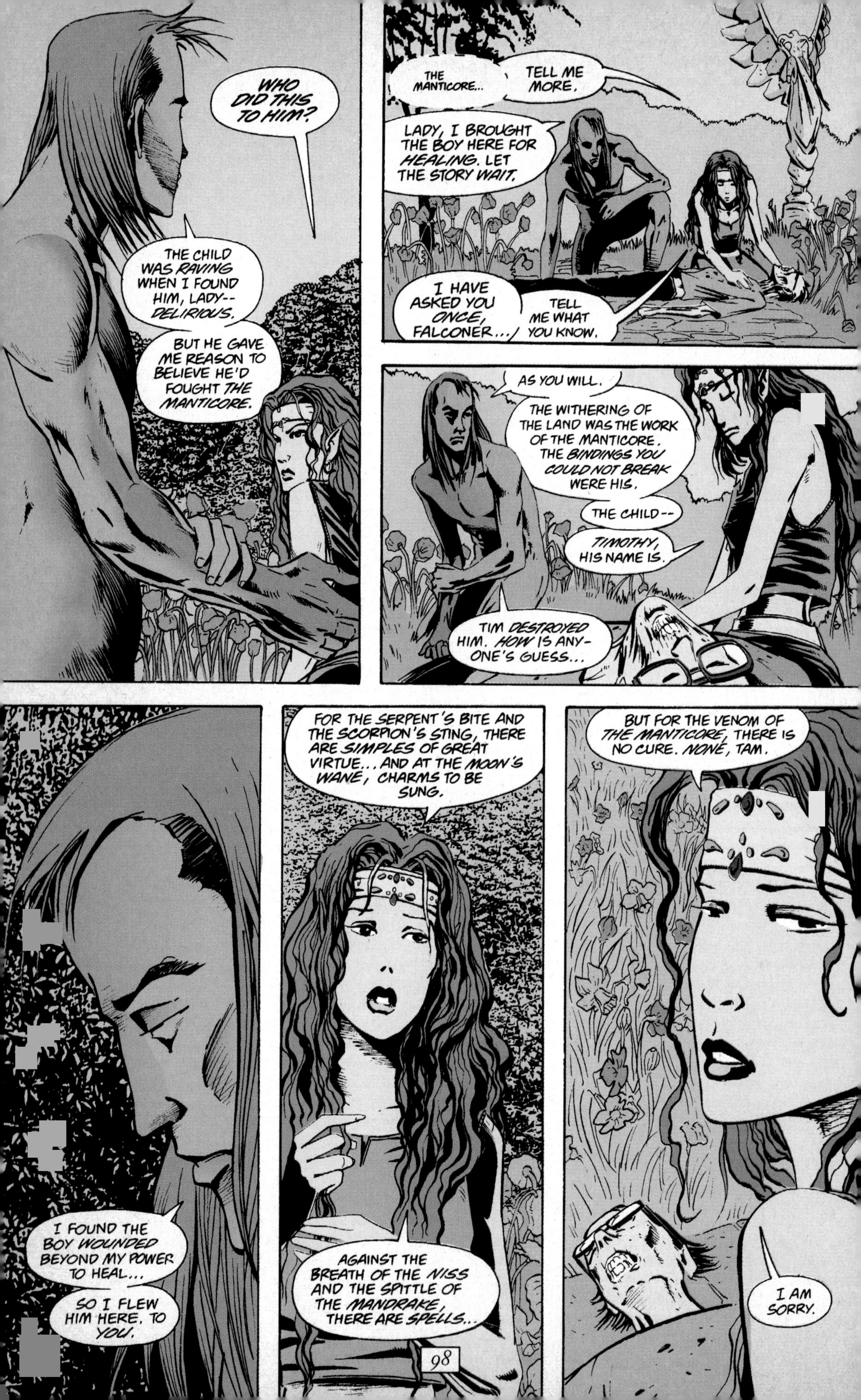
WHO DID THIS TO HIM?
THE CHILD WAS RAVING WHEN I FOUND HIM, LADY-- DELIRIOUS.
BUT HE GAVE ME REASON TO BELIEVE HE'D FOUGHT THE MANTICORE.
THE MANTICORE...
TELL ME MORE.
LADY, I BROUGHT THE BOY HERE FOR HEALING. LET THE STORY WAIT.
I HAVE ASKED YOU ONCE, FALCONER...
TELL ME WHAT YOU KNOW.
AS YOU WILL.
THE WITHERING OF THE LAND WAS THE WORK OF THE MANTICORE. THE BINDINGS YOU COULD NOT BREAK WERE HIS.
THE CHILD--
TIMOTHY, HIS NAME IS.
TIM DESTROYED HIM. HOW IS ANYONE'S GUESS...
I FOUND THE BOY WOUNDED BEYOND MY POWER TO HEAL...
SO I FLEW HIM HERE. TO YOU.
FOR THE SERPENT'S BITE AND THE SCORPION'S STING, THERE ARE SIMPLES OF GREAT VIRTUE... AND AT THE MOON'S WANE, CHARMS TO BE SUNG.
AGAINST THE BREATH OF THE NISS AND THE SPITTLE OF THE MANDRAKE, THERE ARE SPELLS...
BUT FOR THE VENOM OF THE MANTICORE, THERE IS NO CURE. NONE, TAM.
I AM SORRY.

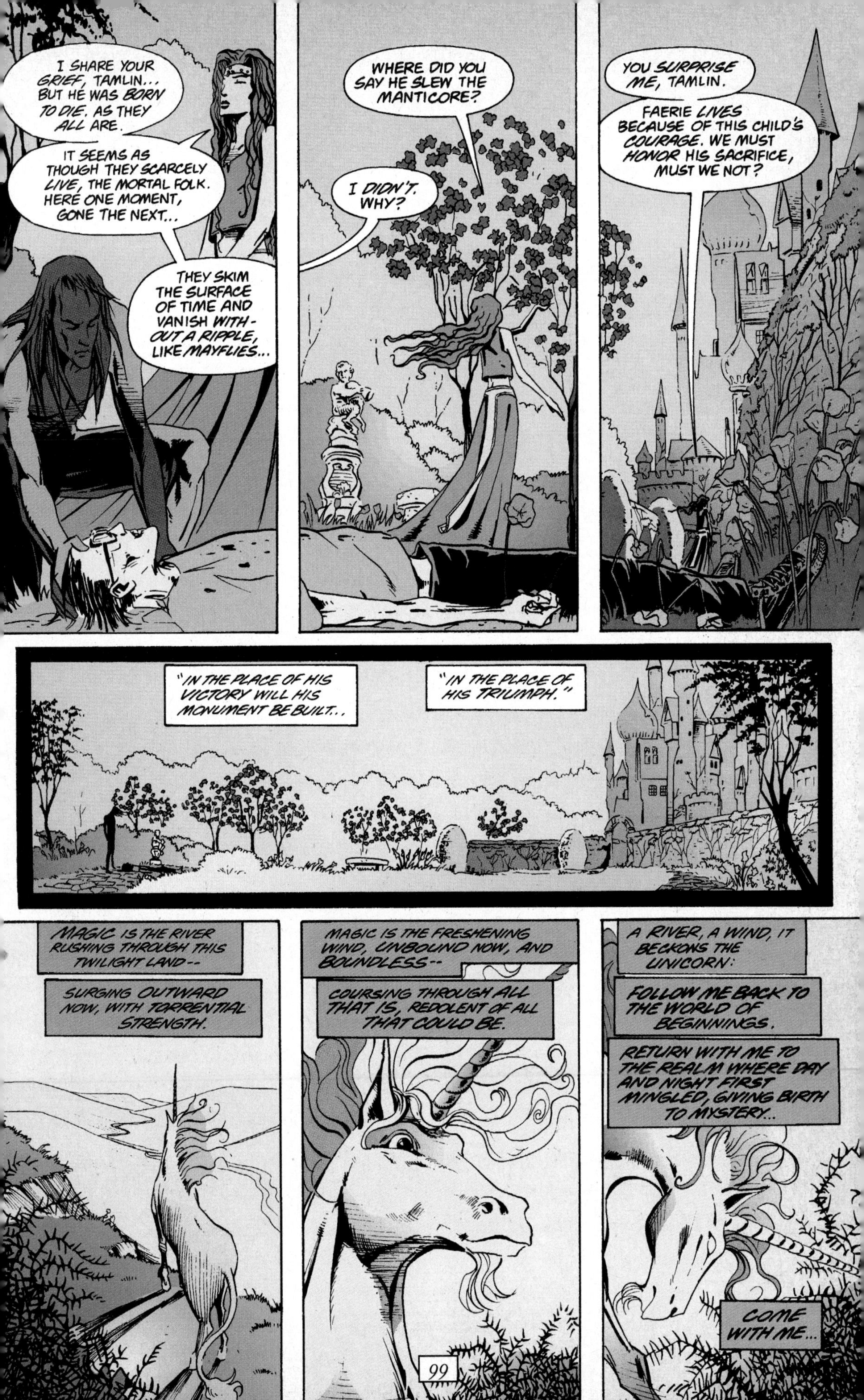

I SHARE YOUR GRIEF, TAMLIN... BUT HE WAS BORN TO DIE. AS THEY ALL ARE.
IT SEEMS AS THOUGH THEY SCARCELY LIVE, THE MORTAL FOLK. HERE ONE MOMENT, GONE THE NEXT...
THEY SKIM THE SURFACE OF TIME AND VANISH WITH-OUT A RIPPLE, LIKE MAYFLIES...
WHERE DID YOU SAY HE SLEW THE MANTICORE?
I DIDN'T. WHY?
YOU SURPRISE ME, TAMLIN.
FAERIE LIVES BECAUSE OF THIS CHILD'S COURAGE. WE MUST HONOR HIS SACRIFICE, MUST WE NOT?
"IN THE PLACE OF HIS VICTORY WILL HIS MONUMENT BE BUILT...
"IN THE PLACE OF HIS TRIUMPH."
MAGIC IS THE RIVER RUSHING THROUGH THIS TWILIGHT LAND--
SURGING OUTWARD NOW, WITH TORRENTIAL STRENGTH.
MAGIC IS THE FRESHENING WIND, UNBOUND NOW, AND BOUNDLESS--
COURSING THROUGH ALL THAT IS, REDOLENT OF ALL THAT COULD BE.
A RIVER, A WIND, IT BECKONS THE UNICORN:
FOLLOW ME BACK TO THE WORLD OF BEGINNINGS.
RETURN WITH ME TO THE REALM WHERE DAY AND NIGHT FIRST MINGLED, GIVING BIRTH TO MYSTERY...
COME WITH ME...

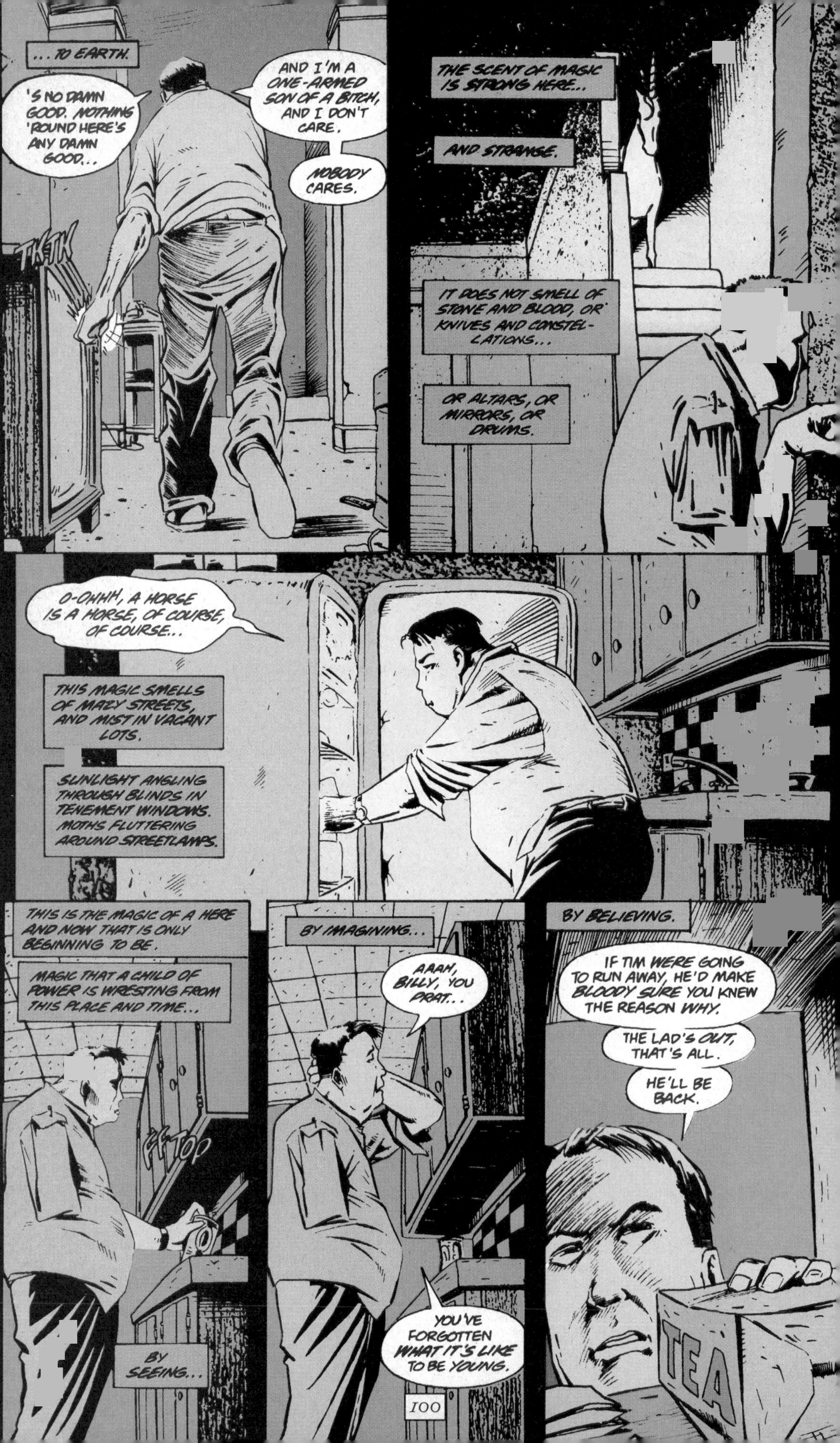
...TO EARTH.
'S NO DAMN GOOD. NOTHING 'ROUND HERE'S ANY DAMN GOOD...
AND I'M A ONE-ARMED SON OF A BITCH, AND I DON'T CARE.
NOBODY CARES.
TKTK
THE SCENT OF MAGIC IS STRONG HERE...
AND STRANGE.
IT DOES NOT SMELL OF STONE AND BLOOD, OR KNIVES AND CONSTEL-LATIONS...
OR ALTARS, OR MIRRORS, OR DRUMS.
O-OHHH, A HORSE IS A HORSE, OF COURSE, OF COURSE...
THIS MAGIC SMELLS OF MAZY STREETS, AND MIST IN VACANT LOTS.
SUNLIGHT ANGLING THROUGH BLINDS IN TENEMENT WINDOWS. MOTHS FLUTTERING AROUND STREETLAMPS.
THIS IS THE MAGIC OF A HERE AND NOW THAT IS ONLY BEGINNING TO BE.
MAGIC THAT A CHILD OF POWER IS WRESTING FROM THIS PLACE AND TIME...
BY SEEING...
BY IMAGINING...
AAAH, BILLY, YOU PRAT...
YOU'VE FORGOTTEN WHAT IT'S LIKE TO BE YOUNG.
BY BELIEVING.
IF TIM WERE GOING TO RUN AWAY, HE'D MAKE BLOODY SURE YOU KNEW THE REASON WHY.
THE LAD'S OUT, THAT'S ALL.
HE'LL BE BACK.
TEA

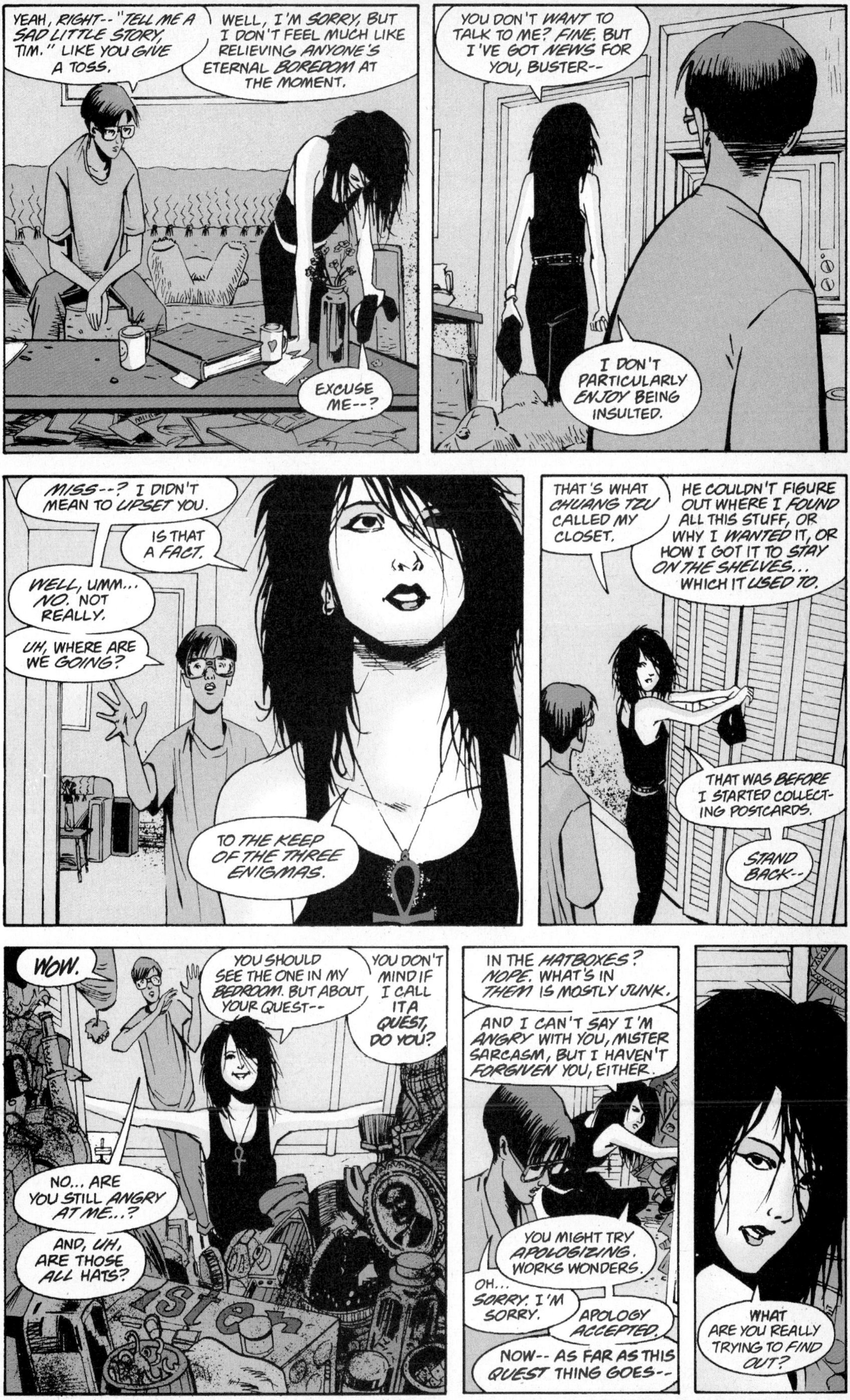

YEAH, RIGHT-- "TELL ME A SAD LITTLE STORY, TIM." LIKE YOU GIVE A TOSS.
WELL, I'M SORRY, BUT I DON'T FEEL MUCH LIKE RELIEVING ANYONE'S ETERNAL BOREDOM AT THE MOMENT.
EXCUSE ME--?
YOU DON'T WANT TO TALK TO ME? FINE. BUT I'VE GOT NEWS FOR YOU, BUSTER--
I DON'T PARTICULARLY ENJOY BEING INSULTED.
MISS--? I DIDN'T MEAN TO UPSET YOU.
IS THAT A FACT.
WELL, UMM... NO. NOT REALLY.
UH, WHERE ARE WE GOING?
TO THE KEEP OF THE THREE ENIGMAS.
THAT'S WHAT CHUANG TZU CALLED MY CLOSET.
HE COULDN'T FIGURE OUT WHERE I FOUND ALL THIS STUFF, OR WHY I WANTED IT, OR HOW I GOT IT TO STAY ON THE SHELVES... WHICH IT USED TO.
THAT WAS BEFORE I STARTED COLLECTING POSTCARDS.
STAND BACK--
WOW.
YOU SHOULD SEE THE ONE IN MY BEDROOM. BUT ABOUT YOUR QUEST--
YOU DON'T MIND IF I CALL IT A QUEST, DO YOU?
NO... ARE YOU STILL ANGRY AT ME...?
AND, UH, ARE THOSE ALL HATS?
IN THE HATBOXES? NOPE. WHAT'S IN THEM IS MOSTLY JUNK.
AND I CAN'T SAY I'M ANGRY WITH YOU, MISTER SARCASM, BUT I HAVEN'T FORGIVEN YOU, EITHER.
YOU MIGHT TRY APOLOGIZING. WORKS WONDERS.
OH... SORRY. I'M SORRY.
APOLOGY ACCEPTED.
NOW-- AS FAR AS THIS QUEST THING GOES--
WHAT ARE YOU REALLY TRYING TO FIND OUT?

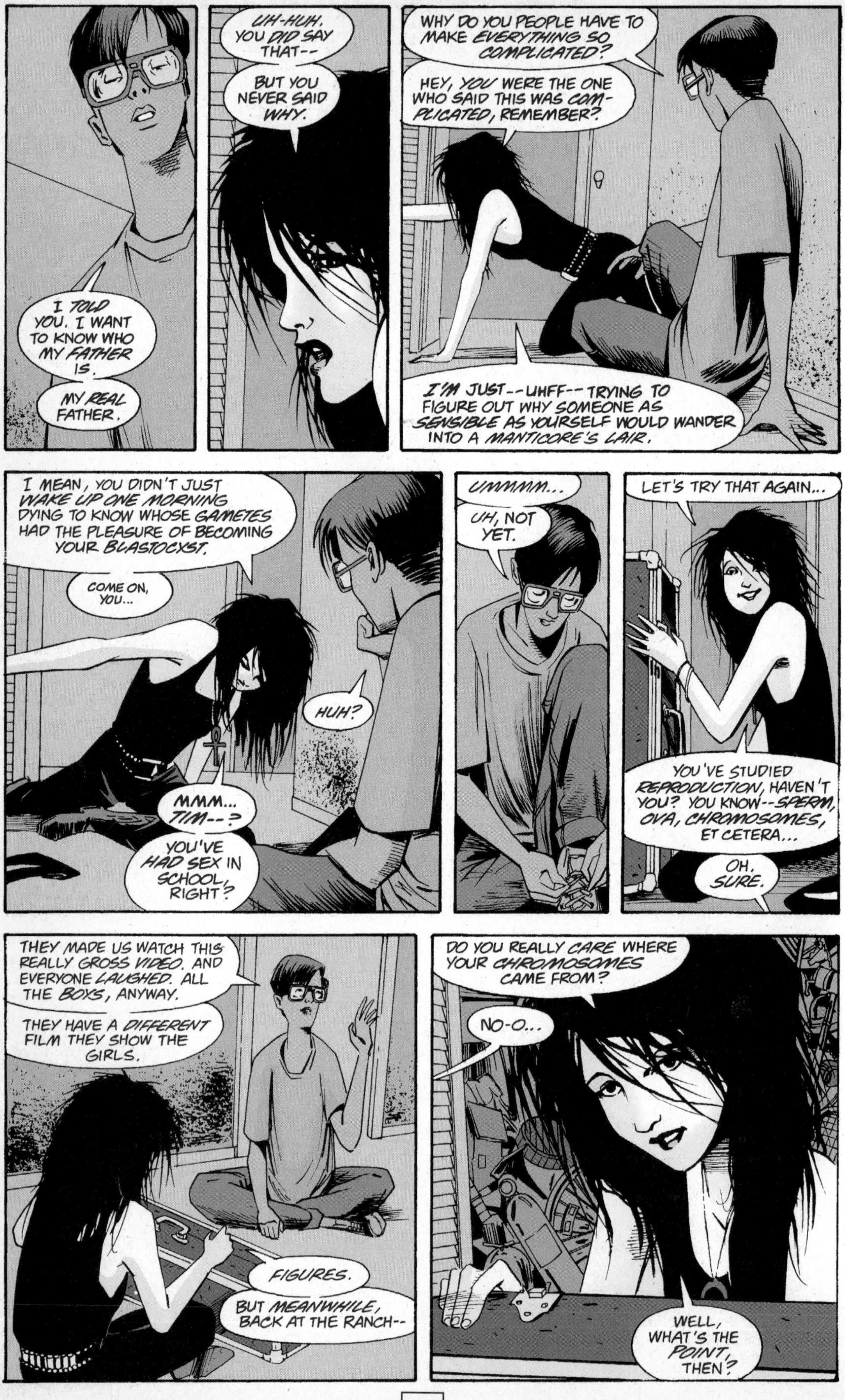
I TOLD YOU. I WANT TO KNOW WHO MY FATHER IS.
MY REAL FATHER.
UH-HUH. YOU DID SAY THAT--
BUT YOU NEVER SAID WHY.
WHY DO YOU PEOPLE HAVE TO MAKE EVERYTHING SO COMPLICATED?
HEY, YOU WERE THE ONE WHO SAID THIS WAS COMPLICATED, REMEMBER?
I'M JUST--UHFF--TRYING TO FIGURE OUT WHY SOMEONE AS SENSIBLE AS YOURSELF WOULD WANDER INTO A MANTICORE'S LAIR.
I MEAN, YOU DIDN'T JUST WAKE UP ONE MORNING DYING TO KNOW WHOSE GAMETES HAD THE PLEASURE OF BECOMING YOUR BLASTOCYST.
COME ON, YOU...
HUH?
MMM... TIM--?
YOU'VE HAD SEX IN SCHOOL, RIGHT?
UMMMM...
UH, NOT YET.
LET'S TRY THAT AGAIN...
YOU'VE STUDIED REPRODUCTION, HAVEN'T YOU? YOU KNOW--SPERM, OVA, CHROMOSOMES, ET CETERA...
OH. SURE.
THEY MADE US WATCH THIS REALLY GROSS VIDEO, AND EVERYONE LAUGHED. ALL THE BOYS, ANYWAY.
THEY HAVE A DIFFERENT FILM THEY SHOW THE GIRLS.
FIGURES.
BUT MEANWHILE, BACK AT THE RANCH--
DO YOU REALLY CARE WHERE YOUR CHROMOSOMES CAME FROM?
NO-O...
WELL, WHAT'S THE POINT, THEN?

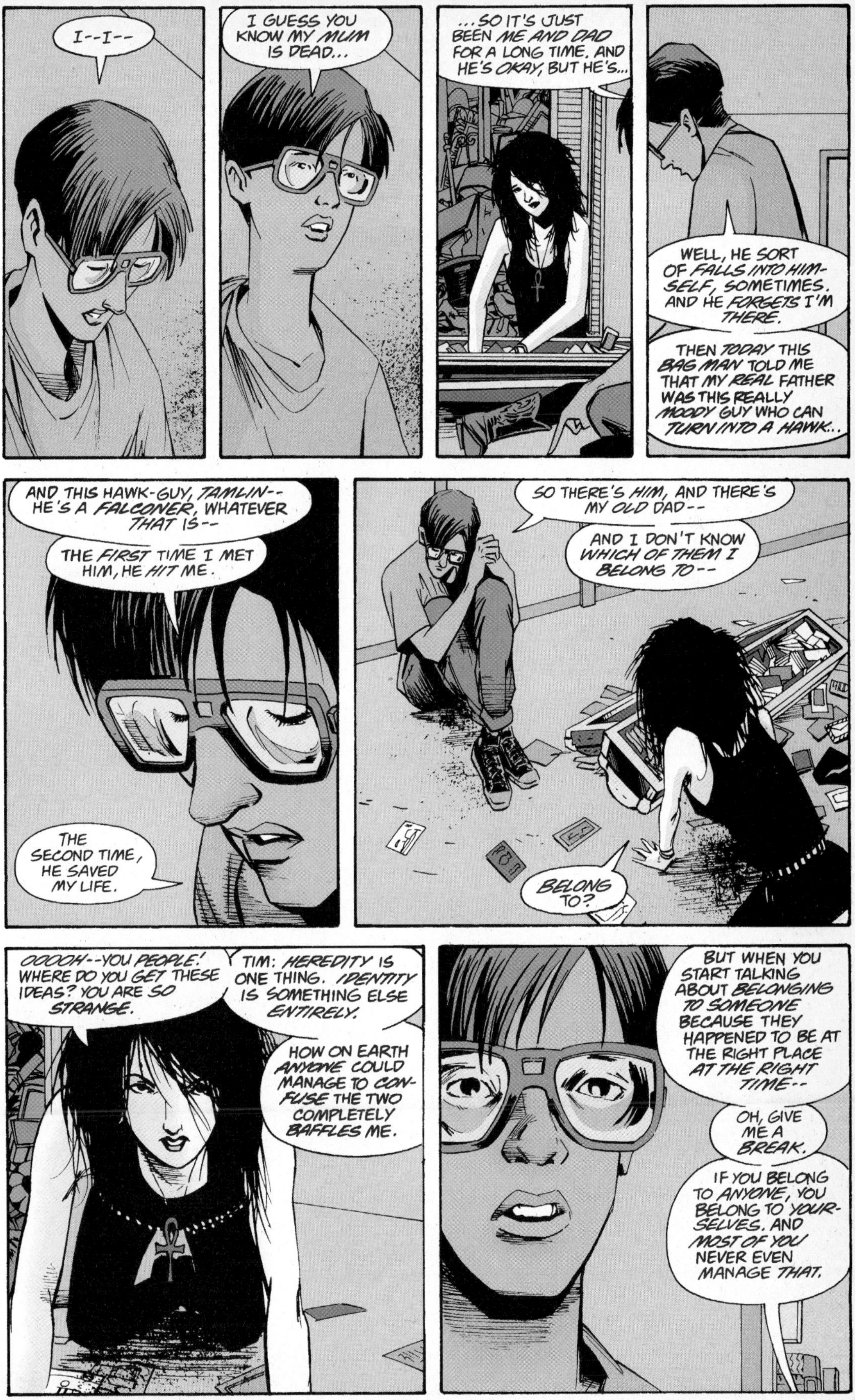
I--I--
I GUESS YOU KNOW MY MUM IS DEAD...
...SO IT'S JUST BEEN ME AND DAD FOR A LONG TIME. AND HE'S OKAY, BUT HE'S...
WELL, HE SORT OF FALLS INTO HIMSELF, SOMETIMES. AND HE FORGETS I'M THERE.
THEN TODAY THIS BAG MAN TOLD ME THAT MY REAL FATHER WAS THIS REALLY MOODY GUY WHO CAN TURN INTO A HAWK...
AND THIS HAWK-GUY, TAMLIN-- HE'S A FALCONER, WHATEVER THAT IS--
THE FIRST TIME I MET HIM, HE HIT ME.
THE SECOND TIME, HE SAVED MY LIFE.
SO THERE'S HIM, AND THERE'S MY OLD DAD--
AND I DON'T KNOW WHICH OF THEM I BELONG TO--
BELONG TO?
OOOOH--YOU PEOPLE! WHERE DO YOU GET THESE IDEAS? YOU ARE SO STRANGE.
TIM: HEREDITY IS ONE THING. IDENTITY IS SOMETHING ELSE ENTIRELY.
HOW ON EARTH ANYONE COULD MANAGE TO CONFUSE THE TWO COMPLETELY BAFFLES ME.
BUT WHEN YOU START TALKING ABOUT BELONGING TO SOMEONE BECAUSE THEY HAPPENED TO BE AT THE RIGHT PLACE AT THE RIGHT TIME--
OH, GIVE ME A BREAK.
IF YOU BELONG TO ANYONE, YOU BELONG TO YOURSELVES. AND MOST OF YOU NEVER EVEN MANAGE THAT.

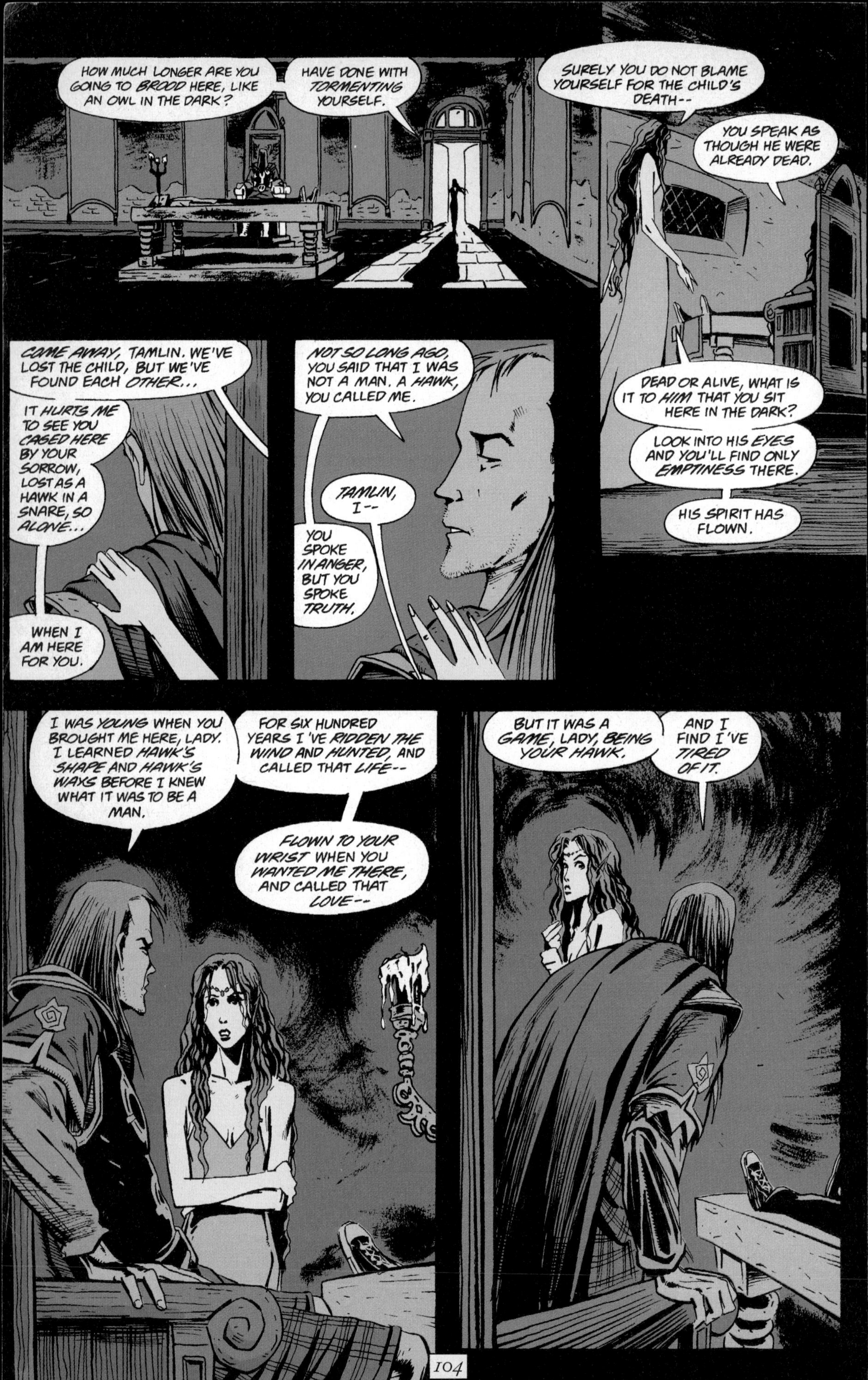
HOW MUCH LONGER ARE YOU GOING TO BROOD HERE, LIKE AN OWL IN THE DARK?
HAVE DONE WITH TORMENTING YOURSELF.
SURELY YOU DO NOT BLAME YOURSELF FOR THE CHILD'S DEATH--
YOU SPEAK AS THOUGH HE WERE ALREADY DEAD.
DEAD OR ALIVE, WHAT IS IT TO HIM THAT YOU SIT HERE IN THE DARK?
LOOK INTO HIS EYES AND YOU'LL FIND ONLY EMPTINESS THERE.
HIS SPIRIT HAS FLOWN.
CAME AWAY, TAMLIN. WE'VE LOST THE CHILD, BUT WE'VE FOUND EACH OTHER...
IT HURTS ME TO SEE YOU CAGED HERE BY YOUR SORROW, LOST AS A HAWK IN A SNARE, SO ALONE...
WHEN I AM HERE FOR YOU.
NOT SO LONG AGO, YOU SAID THAT I WAS NOT A MAN. A HAWK, YOU CALLED ME.
TAMLIN, I--
YOU SPOKE IN ANGER, BUT YOU SPOKE TRUTH.
I WAS YOUNG WHEN YOU BROUGHT ME HERE, LADY. I LEARNED HAWK'S SHAPE AND HAWK'S WAYS BEFORE I KNEW WHAT IT WAS TO BE A MAN.
FOR SIX HUNDRED YEARS I'VE RIDDEN THE WIND AND HUNTED, AND CALLED THAT LIFE--
FLOWN TO YOUR WRIST WHEN YOU WANTED ME THERE, AND CALLED THAT LOVE--
BUT IT WAS A GAME, LADY, BEING YOUR HAWK.
AND I FIND I'VE TIRED OF IT.

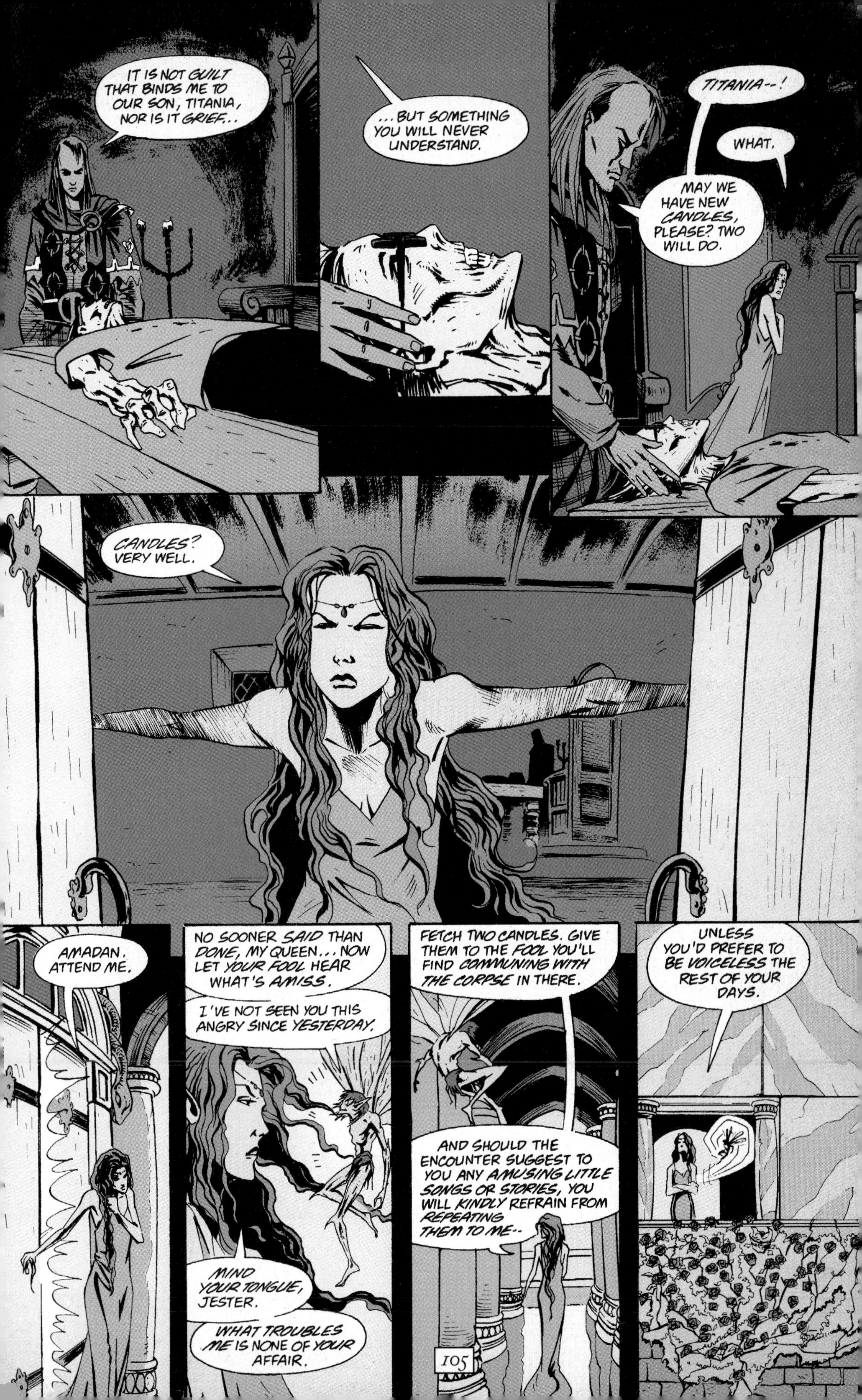

IT IS NOT GUILT THAT BINDS ME TO OUR SON, TITANIA, NOR IS IT GRIEF...
...BUT SOMETHING YOU WILL NEVER UNDERSTAND.
TITANIA--!
WHAT.
MAY WE HAVE NEW CANDLES, PLEASE? TWO WILL DO.
CANDLES? VERY WELL.
AMADAN. ATTEND ME.
NO SOONER SAID THAN DONE, MY QUEEN... NOW LET YOUR FOOL HEAR WHAT'S AMISS.
I'VE NOT SEEN YOU THIS ANGRY SINCE YESTERDAY.
MIND YOUR TONGUE, JESTER.
WHAT TROUBLES ME IS NONE OF YOUR AFFAIR.
FETCH TWO CANDLES. GIVE THEM TO THE FOOL YOU'LL FIND COMMUNING WITH THE CORPSE IN THERE.
AND SHOULD THE ENCOUNTER SUGGEST TO YOU ANY AMUSING LITTLE SONGS OR STORIES, YOU WILL KINDLY REFRAIN FROM REPEATING THEM TO ME--
UNLESS YOU'D PREFER TO BE VOICELESS THE REST OF YOUR DAYS.

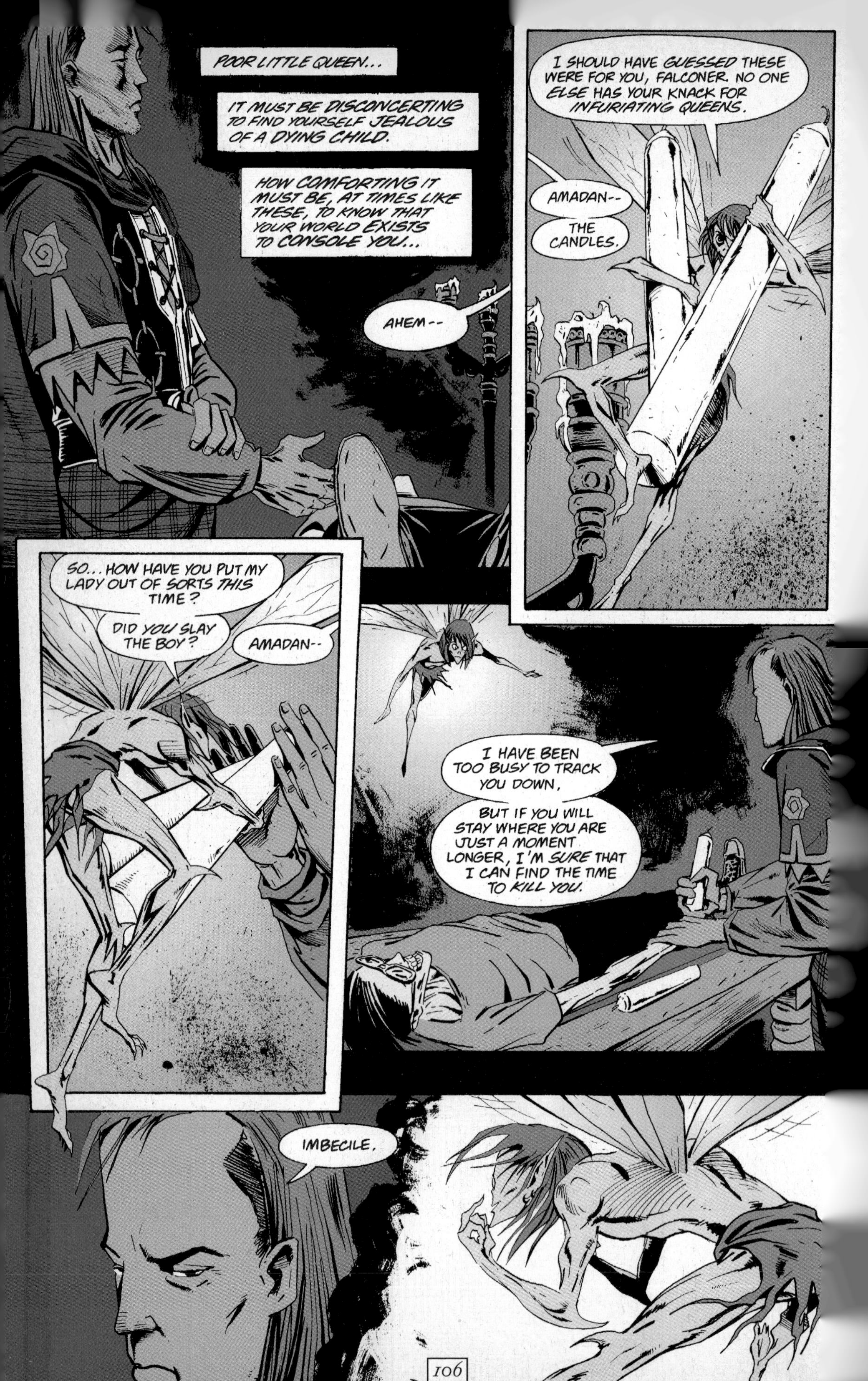
POOR LITTLE QUEEN...
IT MUST BE DISCONCERTING TO FIND YOURSELF JEALOUS OF A DYING CHILD.
HOW COMFORTING IT MUST BE, AT TIMES LIKE THESE, TO KNOW THAT YOUR WORLD EXISTS TO CONSOLE YOU...
AHEM--
I SHOULD HAVE GUESSED THESE WERE FOR YOU, FALCONER. NO ONE ELSE HAS YOUR KNACK FOR INFURIATING QUEENS.
AMADAN--
THE CANDLES.
SO... HOW HAVE YOU PUT MY LADY OUT OF SORTS THIS TIME?
DID YOU SLAY THE BOY?
AMADAN--
I HAVE BEEN TOO BUSY TO TRACK YOU DOWN,
BUT IF YOU WILL STAY WHERE YOU ARE JUST A MOMENT LONGER, I'M SURE THAT I CAN FIND THE TIME TO KILL YOU.
IMBECILE.

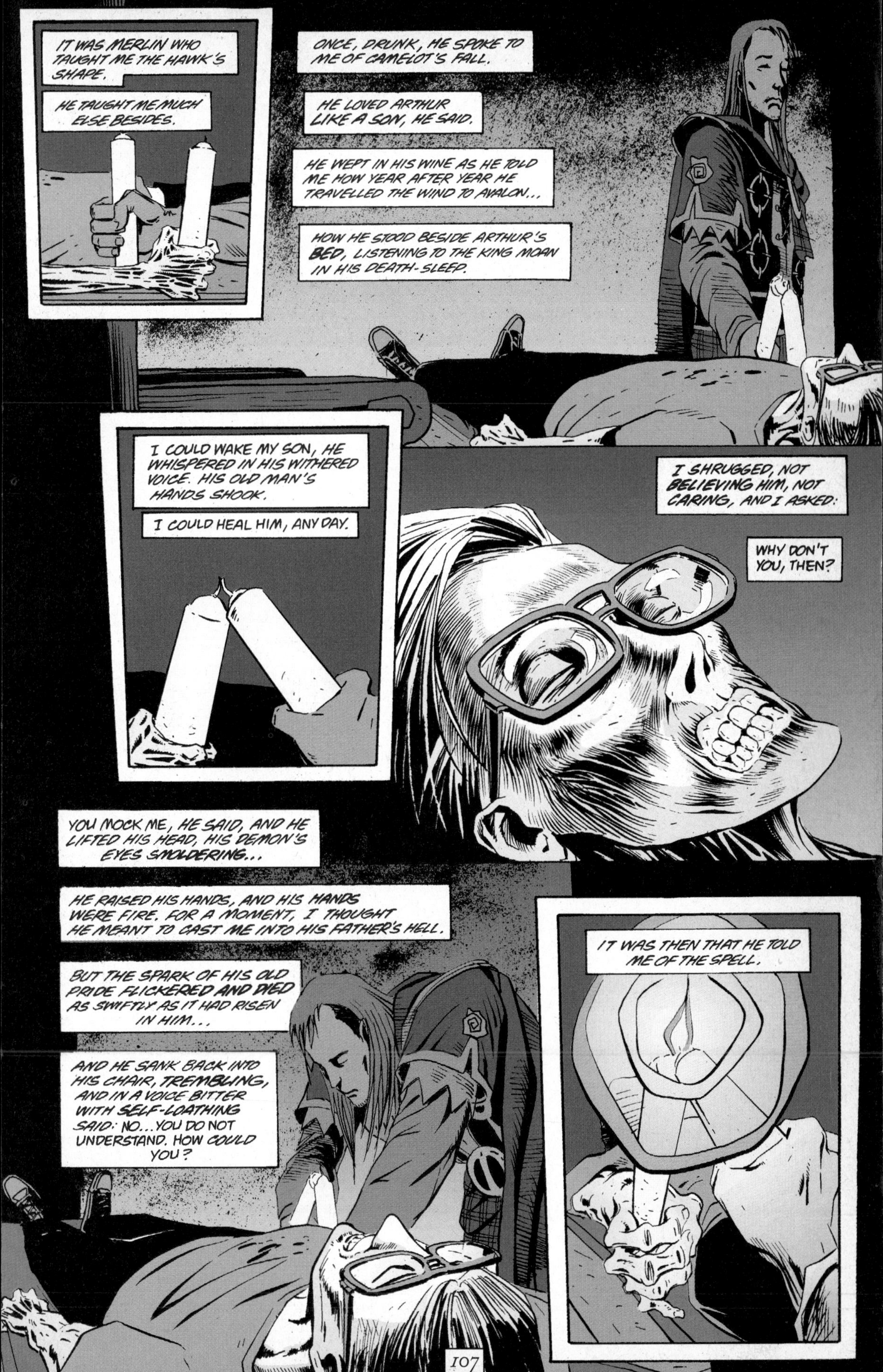

IT WAS MERLIN WHO TAUGHT ME THE HAWK'S SHAPE.
HE TAUGHT ME MUCH ELSE BESIDES.
ONCE, DRUNK, HE SPOKE TO ME OF CAMELOT'S FALL.
HE LOVED ARTHUR LIKE A SON, HE SAID.
HE WEPT IN HIS WINE AS HE TOLD ME HOW YEAR AFTER YEAR HE TRAVELLED THE WIND TO AVALON...
HOW HE STOOD BESIDE ARTHUR'S BED, LISTENING TO THE KING MOAN IN HIS DEATH-SLEEP.
I COULD WAKE MY SON, HE WHISPERED IN HIS WITHERED VOICE. HIS OLD MAN'S HANDS SHOOK.
I COULD HEAL HIM, ANY DAY.
I SHRUGGED, NOT BELIEVING HIM, NOT CARING, AND I ASKED:
WHY DON'T YOU, THEN?
YOU MOCK ME, HE SAID, AND HE LIFTED HIS HEAD, HIS DEMON'S EYES SMOLDERING...
HE RAISED HIS HANDS, AND HIS HANDS WERE FIRE. FOR A MOMENT, I THOUGHT HE MEANT TO CAST ME INTO HIS FATHER'S HELL.
BUT THE SPARK OF HIS OLD PRIDE FLICKERED AND DIED AS SWIFTLY AS IT HAD RISEN IN HIM...
AND HE SANK BACK INTO HIS CHAIR, TREMBLING, AND IN A VOICE BITTER WITH SELF-LOATHING SAID: NO... YOU DO NOT UNDERSTAND. HOW COULD YOU?
IT WAS THEN THAT HE TOLD ME OF THE SPELL.

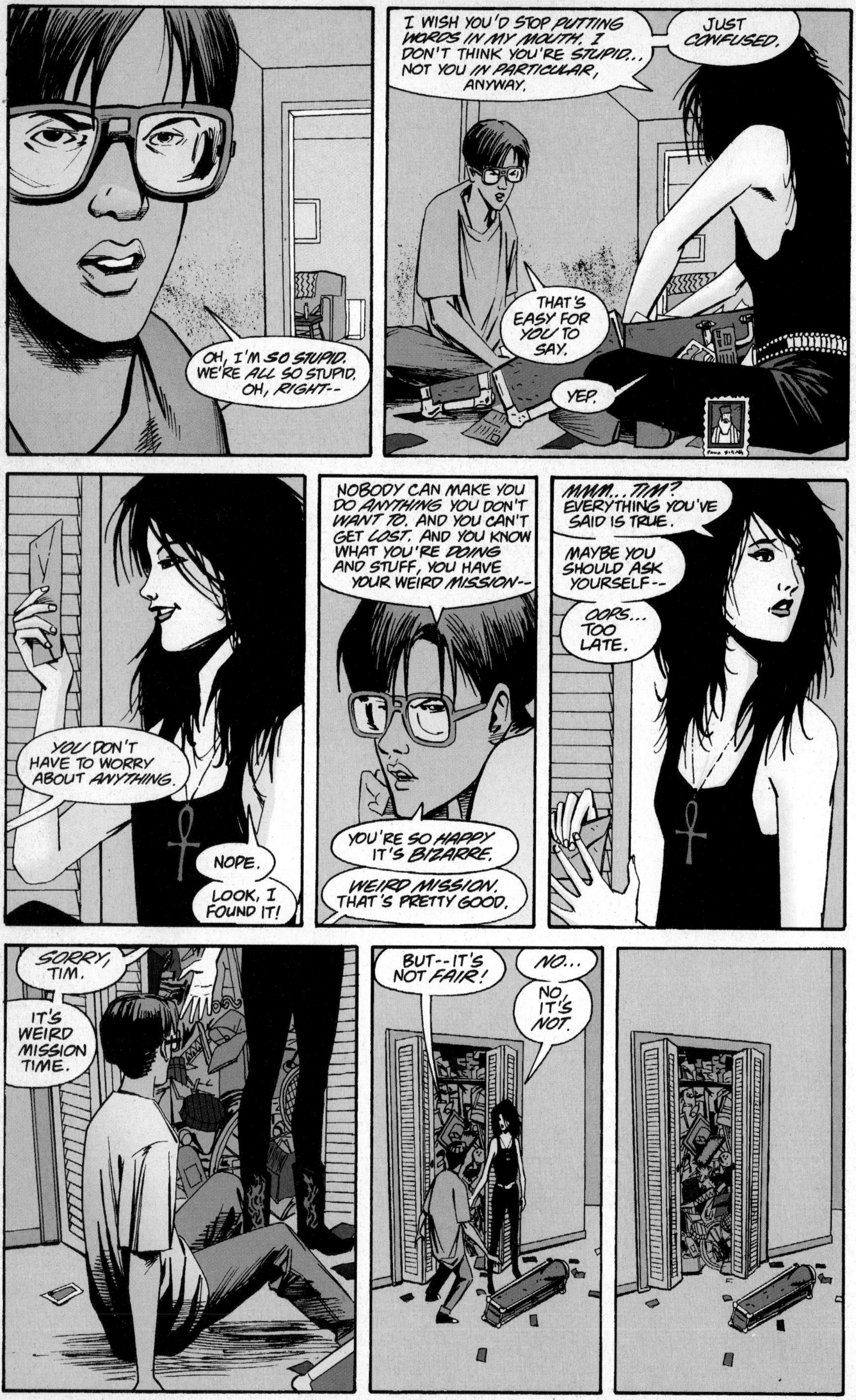
OH, I'M SO STUPID. WE'RE ALL SO STUPID. OH, RIGHT--
I WISH YOU'D STOP PUTTING WORDS IN MY MOUTH. I DON'T THINK YOU'RE STUPID... NOT YOU IN PARTICULAR, ANYWAY.
JUST CONFUSED.
THAT'S EASY FOR YOU TO SAY.
YEP.
YOU DON'T HAVE TO WORRY ABOUT ANYTHING.
NOPE.
LOOK, I FOUND IT!
NOBODY CAN MAKE YOU DO ANYTHING YOU DON'T WANT TO. AND YOU CAN'T GET LOST. AND YOU KNOW WHAT YOU'RE DOING AND STUFF, YOU HAVE YOUR WEIRD MISSION--
YOU'RE SO HAPPY IT'S BIZARRE.
WEIRD MISSION. THAT'S PRETTY GOOD.
MMM... TIM? EVERYTHING YOU'VE SAID IS TRUE.
MAYBE YOU SHOULD ASK YOURSELF--
OOPS... TOO LATE.
SORRY, TIM.
IT'S WEIRD MISSION TIME.
BUT--IT'S NOT FAIR!
NO...
NO, IT'S NOT.

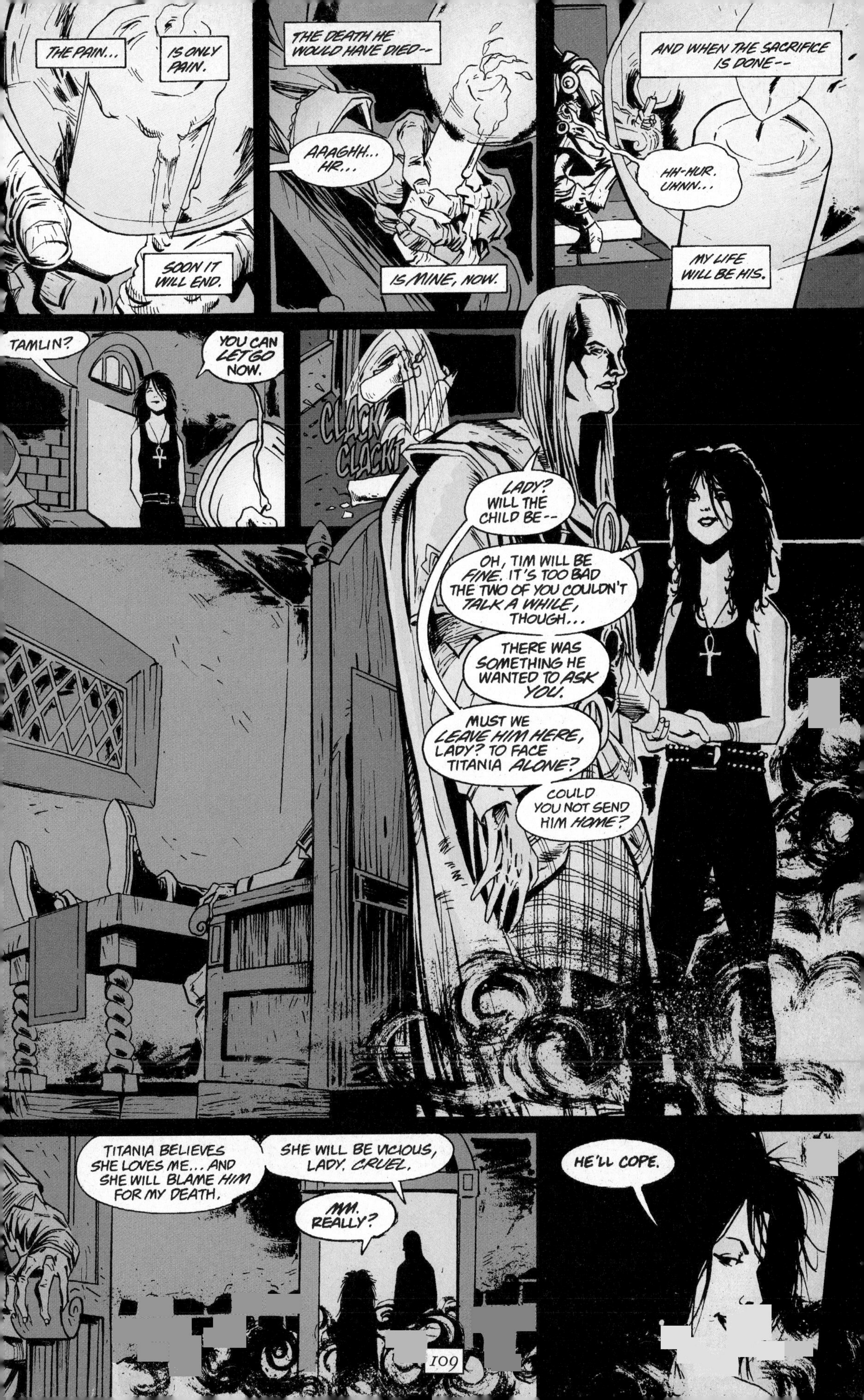
THE PAIN...
IS ONLY PAIN.
SOON IT WILL END.
THE DEATH HE WOULD HAVE DIED--
AAAGHH... HR...
IS MINE, NOW.
AND WHEN THE SACRIFICE IS DONE--
HH-HUR. UHNN...
MY LIFE WILL BE HIS.
TAMLIN?
YOU CAN LET GO NOW.
CLACK CLACK!
LADY? WILL THE CHILD BE--
OH, TIM WILL BE FINE. IT'S TOO BAD THE TWO OF YOU COULDN'T TALK A WHILE, THOUGH...
THERE WAS SOMETHING HE WANTED TO ASK YOU.
MUST WE LEAVE HIM HERE, LADY? TO FACE TITANIA ALONE?
COULD YOU NOT SEND HIM HOME?
TITANIA BELIEVES SHE LOVES ME... AND SHE WILL BLAME HIM FOR MY DEATH.
SHE WILL BE VICIOUS, LADY. CRUEL.
MM. REALLY?
HE'LL COPE.

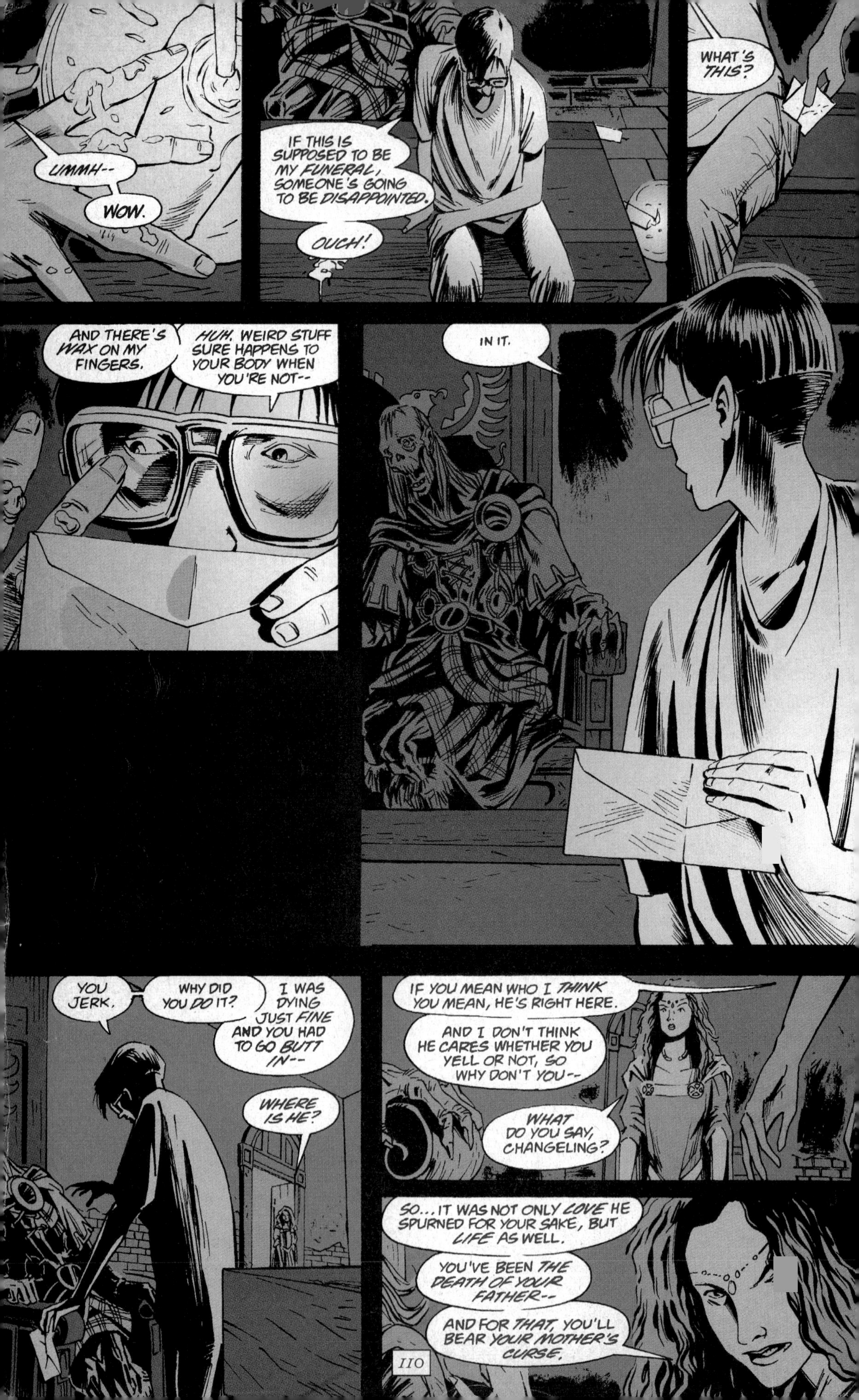
UMMH--
WOW.
IF THIS IS SUPPOSED TO BE MY FUNERAL, SOMEONE'S GOING TO BE DISAPPOINTED.
OUCH!
WHAT'S THIS?
AND THERE'S WAX ON MY FINGERS.
HUH. WEIRD STUFF SURE HAPPENS TO YOUR BODY WHEN YOU'RE NOT--
IN IT.
YOU JERK.
WHY DID YOU DO IT?
I WAS DYING JUST FINE AND YOU HAD TO GO BUTT IN--
WHERE IS HE?
IF YOU MEAN WHO I THINK YOU MEAN, HE'S RIGHT HERE.
AND I DON'T THINK HE CARES WHETHER YOU YELL OR NOT, SO WHY DON'T YOU--
WHAT DO YOU SAY, CHANGELING?
SO... IT WAS NOT ONLY LOVE HE SPURNED FOR YOUR SAKE, BUT LIFE AS WELL.
YOU'VE BEEN THE DEATH OF YOUR FATHER--
AND FOR THAT, YOU'LL BEAR YOUR MOTHER'S CURSE.

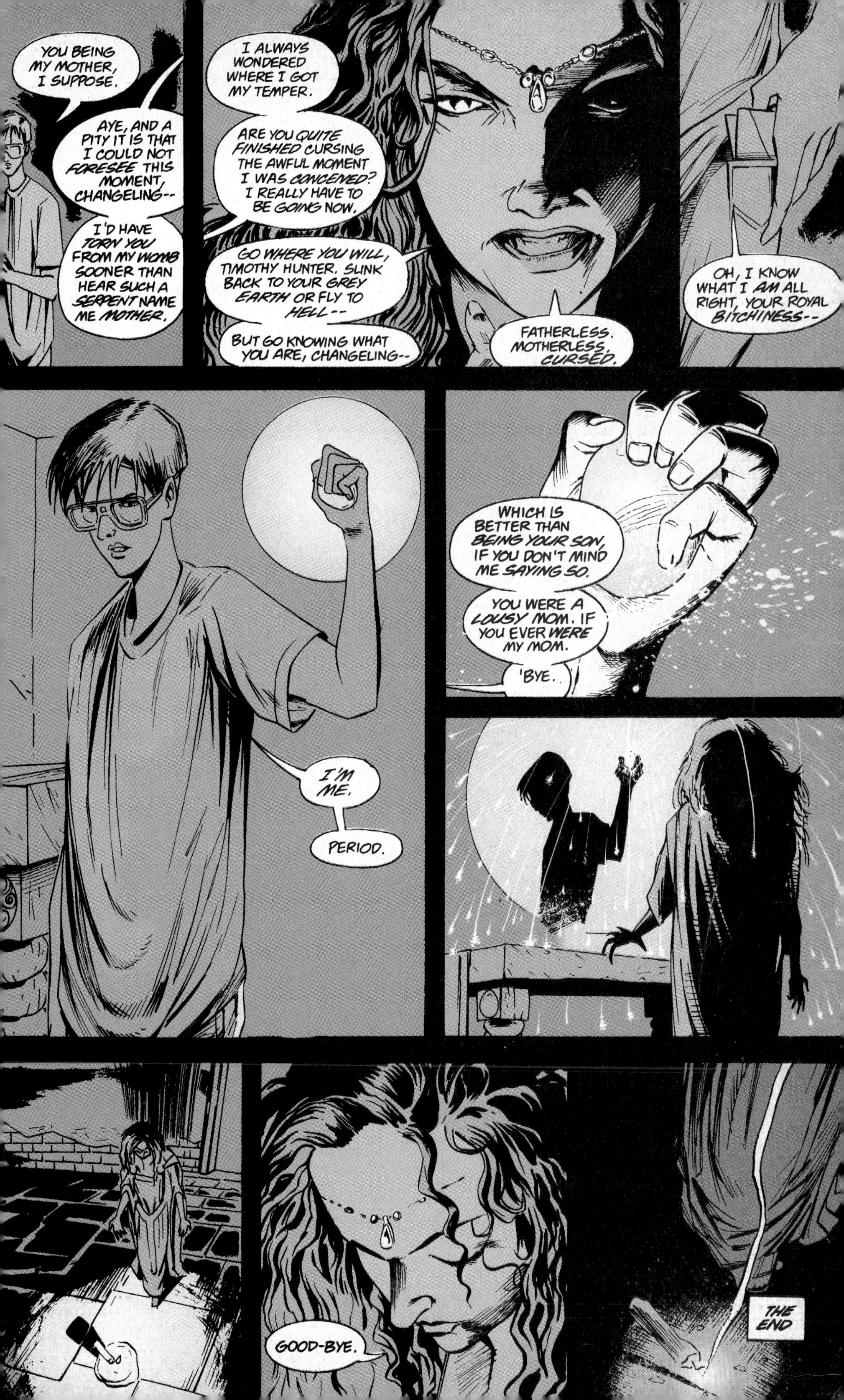
YOU BEING MY MOTHER, I SUPPOSE.
AYE, AND A PITY IT IS THAT I COULD NOT FORESEE THIS MOMENT, CHANGELING--
I'D HAVE TORN YOU FROM MY WOMB SOONER THAN HEAR SUCH A SERPENT NAME ME MOTHER.
I ALWAYS WONDERED WHERE I GOT MY TEMPER.
ARE YOU QUITE FINISHED CURSING THE AWFUL MOMENT I WAS CONCEIVED? I REALLY HAVE TO BE GOING NOW.
GO WHERE YOU WILL, TIMOTHY HUNTER. SLINK BACK TO YOUR GREY EARTH OR FLY TO HELL--
BUT GO KNOWING WHAT YOU ARE, CHANGELING--
FATHERLESS. MOTHERLESS. CURSED.
OH, I KNOW WHAT I AM ALL RIGHT, YOUR ROYAL BITCHINESS--
I'M ME.
PERIOD.
WHICH IS BETTER THAN BEING YOUR SON, IF YOU DON'T MIND ME SAYING SO.
YOU WERE A LOUSY MOM. IF YOU EVER WERE MY MOM.
'BYE.
GOOD-BYE.
THE END

LOOK FOR THESE OTHER VERTIGO BOOKS:

GRAPHIC NOVELS

DHAMPIRE: STILLBORN
Nancy A. Collins/Paul Lee

DOG MOON
Robert Hunter/Tim Truman

MENZ INSANA
Christopher Fowler/John Bolton

MERCY
J. M. DeMatteis/Paul Johnson

MR. PUNCH
Neil Gaiman/Dave McKean

THE MYSTERY PLAY
Grant Morrison/Jon J Muth

TELL ME, DARK
Karl Wagner/Kent Williams

**VERTIGO VÉRITÉ: SEVEN MILES
A SECOND**
David Wojnarowicz/James Romberger

VERTIGO VOICES: THE EATERS
Peter Milligan/Dean Ormston

COLLECTIONS

ANIMAL MAN
Grant Morrison/Chas Truog/
Tom Grummett/Doug Hazlewood

BLACK ORCHID
Neil Gaiman/Dave McKean

THE BOOKS OF MAGIC
Neil Gaiman/John Bolton/Scott Hampton/
Charles Vess/Paul Johnson

THE BOOKS OF MAGIC: BINDINGS
John Ney Rieber/Gary Amaro/Peter Gross

THE BOOKS OF MAGIC: SUMMONINGS
John Ney Rieber/Peter Gross/Peter Snejbjerg/
Gary Amaro/Dick Giordano

THE BOOKS OF MAGIC: RECKONINGS
John Ney Rieber/Peter Snejbjerg/
Peter Gross/John Ridgway

BREATHTAKER
Mark Wheatley/Marc Hempel

DEATH: THE HIGH COST OF LIVING
Neil Gaiman/Chris Bachalo/
Mark Buckingham

DEATH: THE TIME OF YOUR LIFE
Neil Gaiman/Chris Bachalo/
Mark Buckingham/Mark Pennington

**DOOM PATROL: CRAWLING FROM
THE WRECKAGE**
Grant Morrison/Richard Case/various

ENIGMA
Peter Milligan/Duncan Fegredo

HELLBLAZER: ORIGINAL SINS
Jamie Delano/John Ridgway/various

HELLBLAZER: DANGEROUS HABITS
Garth Ennis/William Simpson/various

HELLBLAZER: FEAR AND LOATHING
Garth Ennis/Steve Dillon

HOUSE OF SECRETS: FOUNDATION
Steven T. Seagle/Teddy Kristiansen

**THE INVISIBLES:
SAY YOU WANT A REVOLUTION**
Grant Morrison/Steve Yeowell/
Jill Thompson/Dennis Cramer

JONAH HEX: TWO-GUN MOJO
Joe R. Lansdale/Tim Truman/
Sam Glanzman

PREACHER: GONE TO TEXAS
Garth Ennis/Steve Dillon

**PREACHER:
UNTIL THE END OF THE WORLD**
Garth Ennis/Steve Dillon

PREACHER: PROUD AMERICANS
Garth Ennis/Steve Dillon

SAGA OF THE SWAMP THING
Alan Moore/Steve Bissette/
John Totleben

THE SYSTEM
Peter Kuper

TERMINAL CITY
Dean Motter/Michael Lark

TRUE FAITH
Garth Ennis/Warren Pleece

V FOR VENDETTA
Alan Moore/David Lloyd

VAMPS
Elaine Lee/William Simpson

WITCHCRAFT
James Robinson/Peter Snejbjerg/
Michael Zulli/Steve Yeowell/
Teddy Kristiansen

THE SANDMAN LIBRARY

**THE SANDMAN:
PRELUDES & NOCTURNES**
Neil Gaiman/Sam Kieth/
Mike Dringenberg/Malcolm Jones III

THE SANDMAN: THE DOLL'S HOUSE
Neil Gaiman/Mike
Dringenberg/Malcolm Jones III/
Chris Bachalo/Michael Zulli/
Steve Parkhouse

THE SANDMAN: DREAM COUNTRY
Neil Gaiman/Kelley Jones/
Charles Vess/Colleen Doran/
Malcolm Jones III

THE SANDMAN: SEASON OF MISTS
Neil Gaiman/Kelley Jones/
Mike Dringenberg/
Malcolm Jones III/various

THE SANDMAN: A GAME OF YOU
Neil Gaiman/Shawn McManus/various

**THE SANDMAN:
FABLES AND REFLECTIONS**
Neil Gaiman/various artists

THE SANDMAN: BRIEF LIVES
Neil Gaiman/Jill Thompson/Vince Locke

THE SANDMAN: WORLDS' END
Neil Gaiman/various artists

THE SANDMAN: THE KINDLY ONES
Neil Gaiman/Marc Hempel/
Richard Case/various

THE SANDMAN: THE WAKE
Neil Gaiman/Michael Zulli/
Jon J Muth/Charles Vess

**DUST COVERS-THE COLLECTED
SANDMAN COVERS 1989-1997**
Dave McKean/Neil Gaiman

OTHER COLLECTIONS OF
INTEREST

CAMELOT 3000
Mike W. Barr/Brian Bolland

RONIN
Frank Miller

WATCHMEN
Alan Moore/Dave Gibbons

For the nearest comics shop carrying collected editions and monthly titles from DC Comics, call 1-888-COMIC BOOK.

98020

ALL VERTIGO BACKLIST BOOKS ARE SUGGESTED FOR MATURE READERS